D1551544

Origins of
Great Ancient Civilizations

Kenneth W. Harl, Ph.D.

THE
GREAT
COURSES®

PUBLISHED BY:

THE GREAT COURSES
Corporate Headquarters
4840 Westfields Boulevard, Suite 500
Chantilly, Virginia 20151-2299
Phone: 1-800-832-2412
Fax: 703-378-3819
www.thegreatcourses.com

Kenneth W. Harl, Ph.D.

Professor of Classical and Byzantine History, Tulane University

Kenneth W. Harl is Professor of Classical and Byzantine History at Tulane University in New Orleans, where he has been teaching since 1978. He earned his Bachelor's degree from Trinity College and went on to earn his Master's and Ph.D. from Yale University.

Dr. Harl specializes in the Mediterranean civilizations of Greece, Rome, and Byzantium and in the ancient Near East. He has published numerous articles and is the author of *Civic Coins and Civic Politics of the Roman East, A.D. 180–275* and *Coinage in the Roman Economy, 300 B.C. to 700 A.D.* He is a scholar on ancient coins and the archaeology of Asia Minor (modern Turkey). He has served on the Editorial Board of the *American Journal of Archaeology* and is currently on the Editorial Board of the *American Journal of Numismatics*.

Professor Harl's skill and dedication as an instructor are attested by his many teaching awards. He has earned Tulane's annual Student Award in Excellence nine times. He is also the recipient of Baylor University's nationwide Robert Foster Cherry Award for Great Teachers.

Table of Contents

Origins of Great Ancient Civilizations

Professor Biography i

Course Scope 1

Lecture One   Cradles of Civilization 3

Lecture Two   First Cities of Sumer 18

Lecture Three   Mesopotamian Kings and Scribes 32

Lecture Four   Hammurabi's Babylon 47

Lecture Five   Egypt in the Pyramid Age 62

Lecture Six   The Middle Kingdom 76

Lecture Seven   Imperial Egypt 91

Lecture Eight   New Peoples of the Bronze Age 106

Lecture Nine   The Collapse of the Bronze Age 121

Lecture Ten   From Hebrews to Jews 136

Lecture Eleven   Imperial Assyria 152

Lecture Twelve   The Persian Empire 168

Maps 184

Timeline 190

Glossary 197

Biographical Notes 206

Bibliography 212

Origins of Great Ancient Civilizations

Scope:

The early civilizations of the Near East during the Bronze Age (3500–1000 B.C.) and Early Iron Age (1100–500 B.C.) have been the preserve of archaeologists and linguists. Before the late 19th century, these civilizations were unknown, save for brief, often inaccurate biblical references. To modern readers, these civilizations are remote and forbidding, in contrast to Classical Greece and Rome. Yet each year, discoveries and scholarly publications have revealed the fundamental contributions of the ancient Near East to later Western civilization. Therefore, this course presents the main achievements and contributions of these early civilizations from Sumer to Achaemenid Persia.

The first six lectures deal with the emergence of urban-based, literate civilizations in the Early and Middle Bronze Ages (c. 3500–1550 B.C.). Three such civilizations appeared in the river valleys of the Tigris–Euphrates, Nile, and Indus. All three owed much to earlier Neolithic villages, yet each represented a significant break in previous patterns of life. The Sumerians and Egyptians are known through their writings, whereas the glyphs used in the Indus valley are as yet undeciphered.

The next three lectures deal with the achievements and collapse of the Late Bronze Age (1550–1000 B.C.). In this period, civilization had expanded by trade and imperial wars far beyond the river valleys of Egypt and lower Mesopotamia (Iraq). The pharaohs of Dynasty XVIII and XIX forged a great empire in the Levant, but they succeeded because other peoples—Canaanites, Hurrians, and Hittites—had long adapted Mesopotamian civilization. Great bureaucratic states emerged, foremost the Egyptian and Hittite Empires, as well as the kingdoms of Assyria and Babylonia. The Aegean world, future home to Classical Hellenic civilization, was also part of this wider political and cultural order, although the order collapsed in the two centuries following 1200 B.C.—a period often compared to the Dark Ages following the collapse of imperial Rome.

The last three lectures deal with the achievements of the empires and states of the Early Iron Age. Assyrians, Babylonians, and Persians, in turn, built more effective imperial orders and reinterpreted Near Eastern cultural traditions. Phoenicians and Aramaeans revived trade, on sea and land, respectively, and promoted alphabetic writing, while the Hebrews defined the religious and ethical future of Western civilization. The reign of Darius

I (521–486 B.C.), Great King of Persia, represented the climax to 35 centuries of Near Eastern history, for he ruled the most successful empire to date, stretching from the shores of the Aegean Sea to the Indus Valley. Yet Darius I also marked a turning point, when he and his empire were drawn into a conflict with distant Greeks, who had evolved along quite different lines since the end of the Late Bronze Age.

Lecture One
Cradles of Civilization

Scope: In circa 3500–3000 B.C., the earliest civilizations in the river valleys of the Tigris–Euphrates, Nile, and Indus emerged from Neolithic villages, which in turn, rested on achievements in domesticating plants and animals and improving material culture over the previous eight centuries. The flood plains of the three rivers allowed for intensive cultivation of grains necessary to sustain cities. Greater organization was required to build canals and irrigation systems to regulate the rivers. In the Fertile Crescent, ancestors of the Sumerians concentrated in lower Mesopotamia (Iraq), where they built early cities by the time of the Uruk Period (c. 3500–3100 B.C.). Long-distance trade sustained economic growth and spread urban-based civilization and literacy. Egypt witnessed a similar shift from Neolithic village to literate civilization, but the ease of communication offered by the Nile resulted in regional states rather than cities, which coalesced into the two kingdoms of Lower and Upper Egypt. In 3100 B.C., King Narmer of Upper Egypt conquered the southern region and forged the world's first kingdom. In the Indus valley, probably the land known as Meluhha in Sumerian texts, archaeology has revealed a similar urban-based civilization centered at the sites of Mohenjo-Daro and Harappa, but details of these cities are obscure given the absence of literary records.

Outline

I.   This course focuses primarily on the origins, evolution, and achievements of the great ancient civilizations located between the Nile and the Indus Rivers, that is, the region known today as the Middle East.

   A.   How are these civilizations, so remote in the minds of most people, important to us today? The answer is that they act as the cultural basis for many of the civilizations that emerged later on the Eurasian landmass and have come to dictate the destinies of many in our world.

B. Mesopotamia (Greek: "land between the rivers") is the ancient name for Iraq and is the earliest known civilization. This civilization, perhaps more than any other, established the foundations for future civilizations.

C. The civilizations we shall examine invite comparisons to other early civilizations, such as those in China and India, the Megolithic civilizations of Western Europe, and the civilizations of the Americas.

D. Finally, it is important to understand the origins of the great traditions that come out of the Near East (known to us as the Middle East), because they stand behind the traditions of Classical Greece.

II. We begin by looking at the cradles of these early civilizations—the three river systems of the Tigris–Euphrates, the Nile, and the Indus.

A. The Tigris–Euphrates river system rises in the mountain ranges of eastern Turkey and runs through Iraq, flowing into the Persian Gulf.

B. The Nile arises from sources in east Africa and, from the First Cataract (a set of falls and rapids), serves to divide Egypt in the north from what is now Sudan in the south.

C. The Indus river system was the cradle of later Indian civilization, but this civilization was only discovered in the 1920s and is still largely unknown to us.

III. The literate, urban civilizations that first emerged in Mesopotamia (southern Iraq), including Sumer, rested on achievements of people of the Neolithic Age ("New Stone Age") (c. 7000–5000 B.C.).

A. Archaeologists and anthropologists working in Israel and eastern Turkey have been able to detect the domestication of plants and animals between 11,000 and 6000 B.C. This is the first step in the development of settled communities.

B. By 6000 B.C., Neolithic villages emerged in the area that became known as the Fertile Crescent, that is, the region encompassing the modern countries of Iraq, Syria, Jordan, Israel, and Lebanon. These villages were also found deep in Asia Minor, or Anatolia.

C. Archaeologists have studied several impressive Neolithic villages, including the famous biblical site of Jericho that showed occupation stretching back to 6000 B.C. and Çatal Hüyük, located on the Konya plain in south central Turkey. Finds from this site have been exhibited at the Museum of Anatolian Civilizations in Ankara.

D. Note, however, that these Neolithic villages were not located in the river valleys. Instead, Jericho and Çatal Hüyük, along with Jarmo and Tell Halaf in northern Iraq, were all located in regions where the soil could be easily worked with relatively primitive hand tools. Thus, the available technology limited the size of these villages.

IV. The inevitable pressures of rising population, coupled with technological improvements, led to an important change, documented circa 4500 B.C.; this change was a shift of populations into the river valleys, particularly into lower Mesopotamia.

    A. The movement was brought on by several breakthroughs, including the creation of improved tools and plows and the domestication of oxen. By 3500 B.C., plows were pulled by two to eight oxen, as evidenced by an early pictogram of an ox plow.

    B. Populations moved into lower Iraq and began to clear the dense undergrowth of the delta. This period, known as the al-Ubaid Period (c. 4500–3500 B.C.), was marked by larger settlements, intensive agriculture, and increasing concentrations of population.

    C. The Tigris and Euphrates were not easy rivers to tame.

        1. Neolithic settlers in these regions had to drain the marshes and channel the river systems into irrigated fields, which required a good deal of experimentation and social organization.

        2. Further, both rivers are difficult to navigate; the Euphrates is slow and sluggish and has been known to change its course frequently, with disastrous results. The Tigris, in contrast, is swift and could not be navigated efficiently until the advent of steam power. Both rivers are subject to repeated, violent, and unpredictable flooding.

        3. Nonetheless, by 3500 B.C., the landscape of lower Iraq was beginning to acquire its current appearance, with regulated fields crossed by dikes, ditches, and canals.

D. Developments in technology and agriculture produced cities in Mesopotamia by 3500 B.C. The end of the al-Ubaid Period is dated to the time that Uruk, home of the legendary figure Gilgamesh, consolidated into a city, marking the start of what is known as the Uruk Period (c. 3500–3100 B.C.).

V. At the same time that true cities emerged in Mesopotamia (c. 3500–3100 B.C.), similar developments were taking place in the regions of two other river systems, the Nile and the Indus.

   A. Agriculture and urban-based civilization appeared slightly later in the Nile region than they had in Sumer.
   1. Until 6000–5000 B.C., farming in the Nile region was impossible. The Sahara Desert did not dry up and assume its current guise until about 5000 B.C.; with the drying of the desert, the Nile was pushed to its current course, and farming became possible.
   2. The Nile was, however, a much easier river system to tame than the Euphrates or the Tigris. The Nile is predictable, flooding at regular intervals and depositing thick, rich soil along its banks.
   3. Goats, cattle, wheat, and barley arrived in the Nile valley as Levantine imports sometime after 5000 B.C., resulting in the rapid emergence of Neolithic-style villages in Egypt.
   4. These villages did not evolve into the city pattern seen in Sumer. In Egypt, this is known as the Gerzean Period (c. 3500–3100 B.C.). What will drive Egyptian civilization is the unification of Egypt under Narmer in 3100 B.C.

   B. The Indus valley shows similar patterns to the Nile valley. True cities emerged in this region perhaps 900 or 1,000 years later than in Sumer, probably around 2600 B.C.
   1. Sites in this area have been excavated only since the 1920s. We shall probably never be able to read the available samples of writing, but we believe the Sumerians knew this land as Meluhha.
   2. We see many of the same features in the Indus valley that we saw in both Mesopotamia and Egypt, that is, a period of Neolithic villages, starting from about 6000 B.C., with the same basic crops and animals, followed by relocation of the populations into the river valleys by about 2600–2500 B.C.

3. We know of two major sites of the later Indus valley civilization, Mohenjo-Daro and Harappa, both in Pakistan today. Both were clearly complex cities resting on the same type of agriculture and canal and dike systems seen in Mesopotamia.
4. By 1700 B.C., these cities were abandoned. About 700 years later, new cities emerged, at which point, the axis of Indian civilization had shifted from the Indus to the Ganges.

VI. In the next lecture, we shall launch our study with Mesopotamia and Sumer, where the key to civilization was developed—writing.

Further Reading:

R. Adams, and H. R. Nissen, *The Uruk Countryside.*

J. M. Kenoyer, *Ancient Cities of the Indus Valley Civilization.*

H. W. F. Saggs, *Civilization before Greece and Rome.*

Questions to Consider:

1. What were the achievements of Neolithic villages that made possible the birth of civilization in the Tigris–Euphrates, Nile, and Indus valleys in circa 3500–2600 B.C.? Why did urban, literate civilization appear first in Sumer?
2. In what ways did developments in Egypt and the Indus valley parallel or differ from the pattern seen in Sumer during the Uruk Period?

Lecture One—Transcript
Cradles of Civilization

Hello, my name is Kenneth Harl and I teach Ancient Byzantine and Early Medieval at Tulane University in New Orleans. I shall be your lecturer for the next 12 lectures dealing with the origins, evolution, and achievements of the great ancient civilizations, which are today located between the rivers of, essentially, the Nile and the Indus. That is the region that traditionally has been known as the Near East, but in modern parlance is often known as the Middle East. We shall also touch upon some of the early civilizations in the Aegean world on Crete and in Greece, but they will be rather tangential to our main focus. Before we start lecturing on the origins of these great ancient civilizations, I think we should reflect for a moment on the importance of the civilizations to us. They are very remote in the minds of most people; that alone should be a reason why we should study them. But, they're also important because they act as the cultural basis for many of the civilizations that will emerge on the Eurasian landmass and will dictate the destinies of many of the people living today on the globe.

In the case of the civilization to Mesopotamia, the earliest we know of, Mesopotamia is the ancient name for Iraq. It means "the land between the rivers"; it's the Greek word for the region. That civilization, perhaps more than any other we shall look at, will really set the basis for what a civilization should be; that is, it should be urban-based, it should be literate, it should be based on intensive agriculture, and it also will depend very heavily on trade—not just local and regional markets, but long-distance trade. In many ways, we'll be astonished to learn that it is in the early cities of Sumer, the earliest of those civilizations in Mesopotamia, where many of the basics of organized life, or civilized life, first emerged between 3500 and 3100 B.C.

We will also look at Egypt, another very ancient civilization, and a civilization well known to people because of the fascination with Egyptian objects. This goes back, at least, to the Roman age, and there is a certifiable—not disease—but obsession known as Egyptomania, first afflicting late Roman republican senators and continuing through the Roman age right down to the modern age. Again, this course is in the nature of an introduction to the origins, evolution, and achievements of Egyptian civilizations and, therefore, the three lectures we devote to early Egypt act as really an entrée into other courses that offer far more detailed examination of Egyptian life, religion, and culture.

Also, these civilizations are perhaps known through those interested in Biblical history and in the great religious traditions of the west and, again, there will be a lecture dealing with the Hebrews. The Hebrews are really rather late to the whole cultural scene of this world. We'll start in the so-called Iron Age at the time of the divided kingdom. For those familiar with the terminology of the Old Testament, that is at the time of the kingdoms of Israel and Judah. We will look at the historical information we have on the Hebrews, the evolution of these kingdoms, and the basis upon which the great religious vision of the west—that is, the transcendent monotheistic God of Abraham, Yahweh as he's known in his Hebrew name—how that notion comes about among the Hebrews and how it is transmitted to later generations. That is perhaps one of the most important, if not the all-important achievement, certainly for western civilizations, coming out of these great traditions. Again, this will act as an entrée for those interested in studying the great religious traditions that issue forth from these early Hebrews.

We will end with the Persian Empire. The Persian Empire was established in the 6th century B.C. This is an empire that, in many ways, sums up the achievements of all the early civilizations. They are the first literate civilizations that go back to ancient Sumer in the period known as the Uruk period, from 3500 to 3100 B.C. The Persians will also incorporate Egypt and all of the other lands that have been influenced or contributed to these early civilizations. And, with the Persian Empire, with that great achievement—the most successful state, in many ways, until the Roman Empire, under King Darius who ruled from 521 to 486 B.C.—we shall end this course. That is an appropriate point to stop because King Darius is the great king of Persia, as he would be known in the contemporary records; he is the great king who wars with the Greeks and embarks on this very important new chapter in history—that is, the struggle between the Persian Empire and the Greek city-states and that opens up a whole new set of relationships and developments, at least in the Western tradition. So, that's a fitting point to stop.

Above all, I think these civilizations we shall examine will invite comparison to other early civilizations. Those interested in the civilizations of China, later of India, even the megalithic Stone Age civilizations of Western Europe and, above all, the civilizations of the Americas, will find many fruitful comparisons in the analysis we're going to offer. And, finally, I think it's all important for all of us to understand the origins of these great traditions that come out of the Near East, or as many would say today, the

Middle East. They do stand behind the traditions of classical Greece. The Greeks themselves acknowledged their great debt to these older civilizations. The Greeks were fascinated with early Egypt and as Plato has said in several occasions, the Greeks never invented anything on their own. They got it from the earlier peoples, although he adds the provisos that everything the Greeks took, they improved, dealing obviously with the Greek perspective. This is the aim of the course and, by the end of the course we'll be able to wrap up what we have learned about these great traditions and how they will influence subsequent developments.

With that said, I think it is best to look at the cradles of these early civilizations, and those are three river systems today—that is the Tigris and Euphrates River, which run through Iraq. These rivers rise in the great mountain ranges that are now Eastern Turkey—which in the ancient times, at least the classical times from the 5th century B.C., would have been known as Armenia, that great table land—and flow into the Persian Gulf. The other is the Nile, arising from its sources in East Africa, both at Lake Victoria, as well as the tributaries that come out of Abyssinia, and the Nile from what is known as the first cataract, that is a set of falls and rapids that divides Egypt off from Sudan today. Egypt is north of the first cataract; that area of the Nile will be the location of, again, another important early civilization. Finally, we will look at what we can learn from the Indus Valley civilization—that is, the Indus, which is, in many ways, the cradle of later Indian civilization. Unfortunately, that civilization only discovered in the 1920s is still largely unknown to us because we cannot read the writing and we have far more limited information. So, the Indus civilization will be really understood in context with Mesopotamia and Egyptian civilization. We have to use a lot of comparison to discern what the developments are.

Well, the literate urban civilizations that first emerge in southern Iraq—or Mesopotamia to use the ancient name—are in Sumer, and that would be the extreme southern sections of Iraq today. Regions that are well south of Baghdad and, in ancient times, the so-called region Shatt el-Arab—that is, the delta area of Iraq and the region of Kuwait were actually part of the Persian Gulf. The ancient coastline has advanced well over 200 miles into the Persian Gulf since the Middle Ages. These civilizations that emerged, urban civilizations and particularly the civilization of Sumer, really rested on achievements of people of the Neolithic Age—that is, the new Stone Age. That refers to a stage in human development when humans got extremely good in creating a stone tool kit, as anthropologists like to say.

They were expert in flaking of flint and obsidian to create tools and weapons, and between 11000 and 6000 B.C., archeologists and anthropologists—especially those working in Israel and what is now eastern Turkey—have been able to detect the domestication of plants and animals, which was the first essential step for the development of settled communities and, ultimately, the evolution of cities and a literate civilization. The best guess is, at this point, that eastern Turkey—these would be the areas of the upper Khabur River, the Euphrates, southeastern Turkey, today—in these areas, humans domesticated the pig, legumes, and nuts. In the Levantine regions—and the Levantine regions refer to the coastal areas of Syria, Lebanon, Israel, and the Jordan Valley, most of what is now Jordan—would not be involved in this; it's a mix of sort of a desert scrub area, but in these regions, humans domesticated first cattle, goats, and the two primary grains, barley and wheat.

Sometime early on—and it's still to be determined—between 8000 and 6000 B.C., these two zones of domesticated crops and animals came into contact and swapped the different items. By 6000 B.C., across the Near East in areas of the Levant and Mesopotamia—that is, Iraq and the coastal areas of the Levant, along the eastern Mediterranean and that whole zone—was usually known as the Fertile Crescent, stretching from the Persian Gulf to the Mediterranean Sea and would be essentially, today, the modern countries of Iraq, Syria, Jordan, Israel, and Lebanon.

In that Fertile Crescent and deep into what is known as Asia Minor or Anatolia—that is, Asiatic Turkey today—emerged Neolithic villages. These comprised settlements of hundreds of people, probably none of them ever really attained a thousand, but they were permanent dwellings with rather sophisticated architecture in stone, mud brick, or wood. The settling down of populations and the shift from hunting and food-gathering over to agriculture and stock-raising allowed the support of denser populations and specialists, people who could spend all of their time working on certain types of skills and manufactured goods because they could be sustained by the surplus of the agriculture and the animals that were being raised. In effect, you're beginning to move to complex societies.

That allowed for important inventions and breakthroughs and in these Neolithic villages, we have very early indications of work in ceramics and ceramics are important because the storage jars were necessary for storing grains and oils, dried fruits, and that offered rat-proof storage because as soon as you settled down, you've got rats all over the place and one can debate whether rats fall under the category of domesticated animals or not.

And, once ceramics were perfected and you were able to create the kind of kilns and conditions to do ceramics, metals were not far behind. First gold, silver, and copper, and by 3500 B.C., bronze is being smelted from copper and tin. There are several very impressive Neolithic villages that have been studied. Jericho, the famous Biblical site, shows continuous occupation stretching back at least to 6000 B.C., with ever increasing sophistication in the buildings and specialization in labor and in occupations, as well as the domestication of these plants and animals. These animals and plants have to be evolved over time into the type of nutritional creatures and crops that are represented today.

The other important settlement is on the Konya Plain in central Turkey, south central Turkey; today, that is Çatal Hüyük underneath Hasan Dag, the great volcanic mountain in Turkey. And, Hasan Dag is actually depicted on the paintings from Çatal Hüyük somewhere around 5200 B.C.; it looks like an eruption and Çatal Hüyük's finds have been brilliantly displayed and put into exhibit in the Ankara Museum of Anatolia Civilizations. Already, you can see that these Neolithic villages were really quite sophisticated. There is the so-called famous bull room, which was apparently a ritual chamber with the heads of sacrificial bulls, the skeletal remains. There are figurines of great mother goddess later represented as Cybele in the Greek tradition and so, in the Neolithic villages from 6000 to about 4500 B.C., you're dealing with very sophisticated societies.

However, it's important to stress that when one plots on the map where these villages are located, they are not located in the river valleys. They're located in the areas where the soils can be easily worked such as Jericho or at Çatal Hüyük, where all of this ash is being washed off the volcanic mountain. Another such settlement is Jarmo in northern Iraq, in the foothills of the Zagros Mountains or Tell Halaf in Northern Iraq. These were all regions where the relatively primitive tools—hand tools, essentially—all you're doing is scratching the surface of the earth to plants, to these grasses, but that humans could get at the soil relatively easily and so the technology and the conditions put a limit on the size of these villages. They would never really evolve into true cities in these regions. It is also important to stress that we do not have any evidence for agriculture going on in Egypt at this point, and Egyptian agriculture is actually rather late, arriving to the very end of this period sometime around 5000 or 4500 B.C., and we'll get to that in a moment. Well, the inevitable pressures of rising population, the demand for more lands and technological improvement, led to an important change documented sometime around 4500 B.C. Again, we are dealing with physical evidence; we are not dealing with any written records, we do not yet have writing, so we don't know the names of these people or the languages they spoke. Although, we're beginning to get some sort of sense of whom they may be because they are obviously the ancestors of the literate populations that we will be studying very soon.

In any case, there is a shift into the river valleys, particularly into lower Mesopotamia, Iraq, the historical land of Sumer. There were several important breakthroughs that allowed this; one was the creation of improved plows and tools, and the domestication of oxen to pull these plows and, by 3500 B.C., there are pretty impressive plows pulled by either two to eight oxen. One of the earliest pictograms—that is, pictures that lead to writing in Sumer—is of an ox plow. It's a very early device in Sumerian tradition. Improved tools—mostly made out of wood, some out of metal— and population moves into this area of lower Iraq, and begins to clear the dense undergrowth of the delta areas, these very, very rich areas, and starts putting in settlements and this period is marked by larger settlements, intensive agriculture, and an increasing concentration of population in southern Mesopotamia. We call it the al-Ubaid period, named after the Arabic name of a site in lower Iraq, where the first of these villages has been excavated. And, for the next thousand years to about 3500 B.C. in southern Mesopotamia, southern Iraq, we can see major technological changes that lead to, ultimately, the development of cities by 3500 B.C.

Now, there were a number of important preconditions to do this. The rivers of the Tigris and the Euphrates are not easy rivers to tame. Once people decided to move into this area—and this must have been the people living in these Neolithic villages on the rim of the river valleys who moved in and met whatever hunter and food gatherers and people living on fishing in these zones—they had to drain the marshes. They had to channel the river systems into irrigated fields. This took a long time, a lot of experimentation, and a lot of social organization. Furthermore, both rivers are difficult to navigate. The Euphrates is meandering; it's slow, it's sluggish, it's not really ideal for communications, it has a number of tributaries, and over the course of Mesopotamian history, it has been known to change its course quite frequently with disastrous results. And, certainly, by the historic period, from 3000 B.C. on, large sections of the Euphrates would have been embanked and the river would have actually been higher than the surrounding countryside, and teaching this course all the time in New Orleans, I'm able to make this analogy to the Mississippi River to all my Louisiana students and they understand immediately what's going on. In early Mesopotamia, man is trying to draw a division between earth and water, where nature makes no distinction. The Tigris, on the other hand, is a very swift river; it's difficult to navigate and, really, it's only with the advent of steam power that you really can move ships up the Tigris. So, the river systems in Mesopotamia will break up the landscape.

Their very unpredictable and uncertain nature is dependent on the fact that they are snow fed, that the snows of Armenia, when they melt, feed these rivers and so the rivers are subject to repeated, violent, unpredictable flooding, captured very, very much in early Mesopotamian mythology. That is, early stories of the flood, which later incorporated into the *Epic of Gilgamesh* the whole notion of taming the water, particularly Apsu, the sweet waters, as opposed to the bitter or the salt waters. The god of waters in Mesopotamian mythology is Enki or, as he's known in his Babylonian Akkadian name, Ea. He's benevolent to mankind, but he's always tricky. You never know where Enki's going to move and one always thinks that trying to direct water in those early irrigation ditches must have been very, very frustrating for these people and, clearly, the qualities of Enki are the qualities of water, especially water used in the irrigated fields. And so, Mesopotamian civilization came to depend very much on the regulation and exploitation of those river valleys and the great rivers of the Tigris and the Euphrates and, by 3500 B.C., already the landscape of lower Iraq is acquiring its current appearance of regulated fields. The marshes have been drained. It's crisscrossed with ditches and dikes and canals; it's a very well manicured and regulated area, where all the arable land that possibly can be irrigated and farmed is put under cultivation.

Well, these long developments in technology and agriculture produce cities by 3500 B.C. And, there has been some extraordinarily sophisticated and very, very good survey work, as it's called, that is looking at sites in lower Mesopotamia, particularly around the city of Uruk, the great city that is the home of the legendary figure, Gilgamesh. We can date the end of this so-called al-Ubaid period and the start of the Uruk period, named after the city of Uruk, when Uruk consolidates into a city. That means the agriculture is so sophisticated, the tools are so advanced, that population can move into a city, many of the smaller villages are abandoned, and essentially, most cities have farmland around them for maybe a radius of 15 or 20 miles and, then, the outlying villages are much farther out. But, the population starts consolidating in the cities and the first cities of Sumer; when we speak of these populations, this is 10,000, 15,000, 20,000 people. Uruk, by 2900 B.C., is in its area, half the size of Imperial Rome. Now, much of the enclosed area are gardens, fields; there's an enormous temple complex to Ianna, or Ishtar in her Babylonian name, that very, very tricky goddess who keeps trying to seduce Gilgamesh who's the patron divinity of the city. Nonetheless, this is a remarkable achievement. No Neolithic village ever approached the type of cities that begin to emerge in Sumer from 3500 B.C. on, and those cities will have to be sustained by not only agriculture, but by the development of trade and other types of activities, which will eventually lead to writing and literate civilization, which will be the subject of an upcoming lecture.

Well, the developments in Sumer are remarkable and between 3500 and 3100 B.C., true cities have emerged. At the same time, there were movements in this direction in the other two river valley systems. One of them is the Nile and the other is the Indus. The Nile is a bit later; contrary to what popular perceptions might be, agriculture and urban-based civilization in the Nile was slightly later than that of Sumer, by several centuries at least, and there were several reasons for this. First, until about 6000 to 5000 B.C., you couldn't farm in the Nile. The Sahara Desert only starts to dry up and assume its current guise by 5000 B.C. and in so doing, pushes the Nile to its current course, which is essentially a canyon flowing through a desert, and the Niger, the great river system of west Africa, into its current course and the tributaries and the secondary river systems all dry up and, slowly, the Sahara turns into that great desert barrier that it is today. Before that date, the Nile was a set of marshes; it was dense, it was overgrown with all sorts of vegetation, ideal for people living off fish and fowl, but certainly not suitable for farming and I guess the best description that one anthropologist has described to me is that the Nile, up until 5000 B.C. or slightly later, must have looked very much like the area of the Sudd that is the far south of the Sudan today, which is a very dense area, difficult to penetrate even by modern ship. So, it isn't until 5000 B.C. when the floor of the Nile Valley begins to assume its current guise.

Now, the Nile proves to be a much easier river system to tame than the Euphrates and the Tigris. It is very predictable; it floods at just the right time and when it floods, it brings in the thick silt from the Abyssinian highlands and deposits it on the Nile floor, so that there is this very, very rich soil, similar to what you have in Mesopotamia with the Euphrates and Tigris, but you could easily move up out of the flood zones, wait for the river to recede, move in, and plant. And, the Nile is, without doubt, regarded as probably the most fertile river in the ancient world. The most fertile land of the ancient world is the land of the black earth and when the

Nile is brought under intensive cultivation and regulated, it can yield three harvests a year. This is reported by Greek and Roman authors and, as I've often noted to my classes in Roman history, Egypt provided one-third of the grain supply for the Imperial city of Rome. From the viewpoint of the Imperial government, Egypt was all-essential; one could sink such worthless provinces as Britain into the North Atlantic and the Imperial government might actually be better off.

With that said, the irony is that the crops necessary to sustain organized complex life had to be brought in. That is, the goats, cattle, and the wheat and barley are Levantine products that arrived in the Nile sometime after 5000 B.C., when it was still comparatively easy to cross the Sinai and so that agriculture was brought in from somewhere else. Now, that resulted in the emergence, very rapidly, of Neolithic style villages up and down the Nile valley. These villages show a complicated and very sophisticated village culture, but we do not get to the evolution to the type of city pattern seen in Sumer at all. In 3500 B.C., as Uruk emerges as a city, as great walled cities are emerging in Sumer, you are still essentially in a village culture—a very sophisticated Neolithic village culture, this is often known as the Gerzean Period that stretches from 3500 to 3100 B.C. It is contemporary with the Uruk period in Sumer and, by all standards, it looks like souped up Neolithic villages, rather than true cities. What will change in Egypt and what will drive Egyptian civilization is an extraordinary event in 3100 B.C., when a man named Narmer in the Egyptian tradition, who rules in what was then known as upper Egypt—that is, in the southern regions—the upper part of the Nile valley will conquer and unify the 700 miles or so of Egyptian valley into a kingdom. And, overnight, comparatively speaking, Egypt leaps from Neolithic villages to the colossus of a kingdom and that comes just at the very end of this Gerzean Period. Then, Egyptian civilization develops at an extraordinary pace under a unified monarchy and attains the great achievements of the pyramid age.

Well, here are a few words on the last of the last of the river valley systems—that is, the Indus Valley and here, again, we see similar patterns. The Indus Valley moves to true cities perhaps 900 or 1000 years later than Sumer, and close to—let's say, Sumer achieves it in 3100 B.C.—it's about 2600 B.C. or 2500 B.C. that we begin to have cities in the Indus Valley. Here, we're really at a loss. These civilizations were excavated only in the 1920s on; actually, one of them was found because the locals were using the glazed fired bricks to lay down the British railway system in what is now Pakistan and they wondered, where are these bricks coming from? And, they're plundering these ancient cities to lay down the railroad beds. We don't know the names of these towns; we can't read their writing. We'll probably never read their writing, but we believe that it is known in Sumerian records as Meluhha, a land to the distant east linked to Sumer by trade. It shows a lot of the same features we saw in both Egypt and Mesopotamia. There is a period of Neolithic villages, certainly starting from 6000 B.C. on, with the same basic crops and animals. These emerge in the regions of Baluchistan in the hills and more easily worked soils and, by 2600 or 2500 B.C., the populations are starting to locate on the lower Indus valley and on its upper tributaries.

There are two major sites named after their modern names in Pakistan today. One of them is Mohenjo-Daro, the other is Harappa, and the city construction is quite impressive. They are clearly complicated cities resting on the same type of agriculture, canal, and dike system we see in Mesopotamia. They also are linked by trade with Mesopotamia and one of the commodities that the Sumerians and, later, the Akkadians report coming from this civilization is cotton. It seems that these people are among the earliest people to domesticate cotton and turn it into usable cloth. There's very good evidence of trade connections between this Indus Valley civilization and the cities of Sumer in the Persian Gulf. There are ports and sites that have been excavated along the way. We're not sure why this civilization declines, but by 1700 B.C., these cities will be abandoned and it isn't until nearly 700 years later that new cities emerge and, at that point, the axis of Indian civilization has shifted from the Indus to the Ganges and that shift is associated with the arrival of peoples known as the Indo-Aryans, who are the speakers of an Indo-European language that will give rise to Sanskrit and the languages of India. But, all we can tell is that by 1700 B.C., these urban civilizations have come to an end and are nearly forgotten in the Indian tradition, even though the material culture seems to be the basis for later Hindu civilization.

So at this point, by 3000 B.C., complex civilizations have emerged in Egypt and Sumer; within several centuries, one will emerge in the Indus Valley and we must return our focus to Mesopotamia and Sumer because it is in the first cities of Sumer that not only long-distance trade is developed, but the most important gift—the key to civilization—writing.

Lecture Two
First Cities of Sumer

Scope: Cuneiform tablets from 2800 B.C. on illuminate the economic, social, and religious life of the first Sumerian cities. The Sumerians are also revealed as the progenitors of the urban civilization of the ancient Near East based on writing and long-distance trade. Sumerian merchants and immigrants carried their writing, material culture, and aesthetics to Elam and Akkad, to northern Mesopotamia and the Levant, and even to the Egyptian Delta. Cuneiform ultimately inspired diverse writing systems across Eurasia. Sumerians spoke an agglutinative language (without any known relative), from which pictograms were readily adapted to represent either phonograms or ideograms. By 2600 B.C., cuneiform had been developed to express every grammatical nuance of spoken Sumerian and, thus, made possible government and literature. Furthermore, cuneiform was adapted to the unrelated languages Akkadian and Elamite. Writing had been invented to facilitate commerce and exchange within early Sumerian cities. Long-distance trade fed Sumer with laborers, building materials, and luxuries vital for urban life, and exports of Sumerian manufactured goods stimulated economic growth across the Near East.

Outline

I. In this lecture, we shall look at the first cities of Sumer, which emerged in southern Iraq, or Mesopotamia.

   A. In the last lecture, we discussed the intensive agriculture needed to support large populations in emerging cities. Here, we'll examine two other components necessary for urban civilized life: trade and writing.

   B. This lecture will cover three periods of early Mesopotamian history, the first of which is the Uruk Period (c. 3500–3100 B.C.). This period saw villages evolve into cities quite rapidly. Uruk itself was home to the legendary figure Gilgamesh; another well-known city was the biblical Ur, probably the largest city of Sumer in the Uruk Period.

C. The other two periods that we shall look at in this lecture are the Proto-Literate Period (c. 3100–2800 B.C.) and the Early Dynastic Period (c. 2800–2300 B.C.). The principal political organization during all this time was the city-state.

II. How did conditions in Sumer in the late Uruk Period lead to the development of long-distance trade and writing?

A. The cities of Sumer were of considerable size compared to previous concentrations of populations. The whole of Sumer, which was approximately the size of Connecticut, may have attained a population of 500,000 or more. The population of Uruk in the time of Gilgamesh (c. 2700–2650 B.C.) has been estimated at 20,000 residents.

B. There were at least 20 major city-states in Sumer and a number of lesser towns. Major city-states included Nippur in central Sumer, which was seen as the most sacred city of the land.

C. The Sumerians thought of themselves as a single people—they referred to themselves as the "black-haired people"—but they were loyal to the individual city-states and the divinities associated with cities.

D. The temple stood at the heart of each city. Some scholars have argued that the development of the conditions that led to the rise of cities was driven by the need to pay rents and dues owed to the great temples.

E. Sumerian cities lacked, however, materials that could be used for building; hardwoods, metal, and stone had to be imported, as did more exotic goods. Such goods could only be obtained by developing trade routes into western Iran or to the north, up the Tigris and Euphrates and into Syria and Asia Minor. Even in the Uruk Period, trade routes linked the cities of Sumer with these other areas.

F. The Sumerians were remarkable merchants, and some of them appeared in Egypt quite early. We have evidence of a Sumerian community in the western Delta of Egypt, and Sumerian settlements are also documented quite far up the Tigris, into Syria.

G. Merchant convoys demanded organization, which came from the temples. Each of the great temples in a Sumerian city-state was run by a group of priests, among whom was a figure known as an *en* ("overseer"). The *en* managed the economic and administrative side of the temple, as opposed to the ritual and religious side.

III. Long-distance trade and the concentration of surplus goods in Sumerian cities created the conditions for the invention of writing.

    A. A full-fledged writing system must be able to express every nuance of the spoken language. This level was probably not attained in Sumer until about 2800 B.C.

    B. Economic development drove the need to invent writing.

    C. Sumerian was well-suited for the transition from spoken to written language. It is an agglutinative language, meaning a "stuck-together" language. The grammar and syntax of Sumerian were indicated by adding prefixes and suffixes to root words.

    D. Since Sumerian was the first language to be committed to writing, it became the religious language of urban-based civilization in Mesopotamia and was adopted as a literary and religious language by later peoples who came to rule over the area.

    E. Writing was done with a stylus in wet clay. As a result, the shapes of the characters tended to be in the form of a wedge. When Sumerian writing was first discovered in the 19th century, it was called *cuneiform*, which means "wedge-shaped."

    F. In keeping inventories, scribes first recorded small icons, such as pictures of cattle, along with tally marks using the base-10 system.

        1. Sumerian was a largely monosyllabic language and was rich in homonyms and homophones. This structure enabled a pictogram to be used to represent a single sound (*phonogram*) or, later, a single object or idea (*ideogram*).

        2. This concept could be extended to allow a pictogram to represent an idea. In English, a pictogram for *Sun* might be extended to express the homonym *son*, then to an ideogram for *day*.

        3. We have a number of interesting examples of pictograms used to express sounds or groups of sounds that come from a rich record of tablets, starting from around 3300 B.C.

        4. By the end of the Uruk Period, there were at least 2,000 well-known symbols used by all Sumerian scribes to represent a basic group of pictograms, phonograms, and ideograms.

G. The written Sumerian language was also used by the Akkadians to the north and the Elamites to the east. Therefore scribes felt the need to differentiate the meanings of their symbols, and the result was the use of *determinatives*. These were additions and modifications to the symbols to indicate their parts of speech, that is, whether the pictogram indicated the noun *ti* or the verb *ti*.

H. Some scholars argue that the concept of writing was brought to Egypt by Sumerian merchants in the late Uruk Period. The indecipherable glyphs of the Indus valley that appear around 2500 B.C. seem also to be based on Sumerian script.

Further Reading:

Samuel Noah Kramer, *History Begins at Sumer.*

H. R. Nissen, *The Early History of the Ancient Near East, 9000–3000 B.C.* Translated by E. Lutzeier and K. Northcott.

Questions to Consider:

1. Why was long-distance trade so important for sustaining the cities of Sumer? What were the products exchanged? How was trade organized? How did this trade transform both the cities of Mesopotamia and their trading partners in Syria, Anatolia, and Iran?

2. Why did Sumerian temples emerge as the prime markets and centers of production in the Uruk Period? What were the social and economic consequences? How did this fact dictate the invention and use of writing?

Lecture Two—Transcript
First Cities of Sumer

In this lecture, I plan to deal with the first cities of Sumer and in the previous lecture I had discussed the emergence of those early cities in southern Iraq, or Mesopotamia, as well as the development of agriculture. You need, essentially, four components to have urban civilized life; you need the intensive agriculture that can support the big populations and you need cities, we've discussed those. Now, I want to bring in the other two components and those are trade and writing. In Sumer and in those early cities of Sumer, we see both of these factors in play. I'll be discussing, essentially, what historians divide up into three periods of early Mesopotamian history. The first is the Uruk period of which I spoke earlier that extends from 3500 to 3100 B.C. That is a period that sees villages evolve into cities quite rapidly. The most famous one is the city of Uruk, which was excavated and is the home of Gilgamesh in legend. The other important city that has been revealed to us in this period is Ur, well known to those familiar with biblical text. Ur was probably the largest city of Sumer and, at the time, was located on the shore, or just off the shore; now, it's about 200 miles inland because of the silting up of the river system.

We'll then also look at two other periods, which are often known as the Proto-Literate from 3100 to 2800 B.C., and the early dynastic periods from 2800 to 2300 B.C. And, just briefly to let you know of coming attractions, the periods we're discussing right now are periods in which the principle political organization is essentially a city-state. It's only in 2300 B.C. that we get the emergence of territorial empires with Sargon of Akkad; so in some ways, this period really does represent a continuous development because most developments are occurring within the context of city-states in which the temple, or the temples, of the principle divinity in that city are really the political, social, and economic foci of those cities.

Let's look at Sumer in that late Uruk period and these cities, and why the conditions in these cities led to the development of long-distance trade and writing, which are two factors that are closely related; the trade, actually, in many ways generates the need for writing. First, the cities of Sumer are of considerable size compared to any other kind of concentration of population previously. One estimate is that Uruk, in the time of Gilgamesh, maybe 2900 B.C., numbered at least 20,000 residents and this is unprecedented. Sumer, in size, was probably equivalent to the size of the modern state of Connecticut. Its population may have attained as much as 500,000—in the time of Gilgamesh, 2900 B.C., maybe more—and without a doubt, is the most densely populated region on the globe at the time. There were at least 20 major city-states in Sumer and a number of lesser states and satellite towns; these included the city of Nippur in central Sumer, which is seen by the Sumerians as the most sacred city of their land and where the kingship was initially lowered from heaven by the gods. It is seen as the middle of the world. Ur and Uruk are important towns. In eastern Sumer is the city of Lagash, which we'll be discussing in an upcoming lecture, because we have particularly good records from that town and the people known as the Sumerians thought of themselves as a single people; usually, they referred to themselves as the black-haired people, but loyalties were really centered on the individual city-states and on the divinities, the tutelary gods of each city.

The temple stood at the heart of the city; some scholars have argued that the whole development of intensive agriculture and the conditions that led to the rise of cities was driven to pay the rents and dues owed to the temples. There is some evidence for this, especially at the city of Eridu, an early Sumerian city where, from 4500–3000 B.C., we cannot only trace the development of agriculture, but even the development of the temple, which starts from a rather simple complex and becomes the enormous ziggurat, which are these mud brick pyramids, in effect, of levels and they are temples to the gods. Probably the best description of a ziggurat comes from Genesis in which they're described. It's remembered in the Tower of Babel, the story of the Tower of Babel, they are gateways to heaven. They're a way of getting close to communicating with the gods. At Eridu, you have actually a continuous cult to a fish god, probably an early version of Ninurta or Ningirsu in later Sumerian mythology. The temples generated an enormous amount of business. They covered vast parts of the city; in fact, the great temples in a Sumerian city should be thought of as a city within a city. Gilgamesh, in the epic, especially known in its later Babylonian version written down in the time of Hammurabi or later, in the Epic of Gilgamesh and even in the Sumerian text, he is credited with turning one-third of the city over to Ianna or Ishtar—the goddess who was always trying to marry Gilgamesh and he keeps putting her off—and her father, An or Anu, the lord of the heaven. And so, within the temples were vast storage complexes of grain and various goods, and an enormous number of scribes had to emerge to keep inventory over this. There were also specialized occupations carried on in the temple; these included potters, people working metal—in the Uruk period, bronze is smelted from copper and tin. The potter's wheel is invented so you can turn out sophisticated manufactured pottery and ceramics. Rugs, textiles, large numbers of later population in the temples are nothing more than textile workers. We get that when we have inventory or lists from the historic period. So, all of these temples were, in effect, the primary engines fueling economic growth within the city.

The problem with Sumer—and again, I can always make an appeal to this to my students in New Orleans—is when you live in a river valley system, you're essentially farming primeval muck. There aren't any rocks around, there aren't any metals—one reason why geology isn't all that big in Louisiana. There are no stones to study; and the same is true in Iraq. You had to bring in the hard woods, the stones, and the metals for building material. There was also a demand for exotic goods such as lapis lazuli, a very treasured turquoise stone that comes from Iran, particularly. All of these goods could only be obtained by developing trade routes, long-distance trade routes, into western Iran or north up the Tigris and Euphrates into Syria and Asia Minor—that is, modern Turkey. And, from the start, even in the Uruk period, trade routes linked the cities of Sumer with these other areas and as a result of this exchange and this increasing volume of trade, not only did manufactured goods go out from Sumer—that is, such items as bread and date wine, which all the peoples outside of Sumer really appreciate. They cannot produce bread and date wine. Also, rugs, textiles, well wrought furniture, weapons in bronze, jewelry, and ceramics in a variety that one cannot begin to imagine, all of these goods flow out to these outlying areas of Syria, Asia Minor, and Iran and that will stimulate developments within those Neolithic villages, so in time, those people will adopt the urban-based civilization in Sumer that produced these goods.

In return, the Sumerians keep bringing in population in the form of slaves and immigrants, replenishing the population that would die in the river valley system because fever and disease is so common in those areas; they brought in the raw materials that allowed them to build those finished goods. So, the cities in Sumer, from the start, were sustained by long-distance trade. And Mesopotamian civilization, which is involved in Sumer, spreads out across the Near East and the Sumerians are remarkable merchants; some of them appear in Egypt quite early at the site of Buto. In the western delta, there's evidence of a Sumerian community there, which may have been quite important in precipitating certain developments in early Egypt under the pharaohs of the First Dynasty. They are obviously now documented very far up the Euphrates. The excavation of the city of Ebla—in Syria today, in what is now eastern Syria, near the Euphrates—

done by Italians about 25 years ago, has revealed that urban-based literate civilization emerged in Syria centuries earlier than anyone had imagined, compliments of Sumerian merchants who moved up there, settled there, and taught the higher arts of civilization. This has been documented, in many ways, by very clever anthropological and archeological studies.

These merchants were not independent operators who moved up there—far from it. The merchants had armed retinues; they had trains of mules. The primary animal of burden in the ancient Near East is the mule, and horses were originally domesticated to breed with donkeys for mules. There are no horse-drawn carts, there's no riding of horses; it's all mules and walking. And, the camel will not be domesticated until the Iron Age, after 900 or 800 B.C. So, you're dealing with mule trains and human labor, moving these goods or riverboats and, eventually, seaborne commerce. Therefore, that meant organization and the temples took the lead. Each of the great temples in a Sumerian city-state was run by a group of priests; among those priests was a figure usually known as the cuneiform text, as an *en* or overseer. He managed the economic and administrative side of the temple in the city, as opposed to, say, the ritual and religious side.

Many would see in the en, which essentially means overseer, the origins of the eventual kings of the Sumerian city-states. Furthermore, the merchants were organized into private partnerships, directed by the temple and the priestly families that dominated the temples—later known in Akkadian text as the *karum*—and so these are big, really large-scale, trading concessions, not peddlers and small-time merchants backed by the investments of the temple in the city-state. So, this long-distance trade is of immediate concern to everyone in the city and later on, when we get territorial empires built by great kings such as Sargon of Akkad, Ur-nammu, and Hammurabi, who is known to most for his law code, they all were very keen on this trade and waged campaigns to secure trade routes—open up trade routes—because the labor, the slaves and immigrants, and all the raw materials were essential to sustaining urban life in Mesopotamia. And, that is a fact of life in Mesopotamian civilization. Those cities can only exist by a very complicated system of long-distance trade.

Those trade connections and the concentration of great surpluses in the Sumerian cities created the conditions for the invention of writing. Now, there's a great deal of debate over the origins of writing and whether writing really changes human memory; this gets into biological and anthropological studies. But, at least in Sumer, we have before us the evidence that shows us almost every stage of moving from what are essentially pictures—or as scholars like to call them, pictograms—into full-fledged writings. Full-fledged writing, by my definition, means that you're able to reproduce on a two-dimensional form, whether it be mud, brick, or clay, which is the principle building material of Mesopotamia. That is, you essentially use the mud and you turn it into tablets for writing or bricks for building, and if you fire it in a kiln, the stuff is virtually indestructible. It's almost like stone. Or, whether you write it on papyrus or you write it on vellum, that writing system will be able to express every nuance of the spoken language, including verbs, including tense, and including mood; by reading the text, one knows exactly what was said by the author of that text. To attain that level in writing—that is probably only attained in Sumer about 2800 B.C.—that is at the end of what scholars like to dub the Proto-Literate period, but the Sumerians do achieve it. That achievement is remarkable because all subsequent writing systems in Eurasia, in my opinion, ultimately go back to this writing system created in the cities of Sumer.

There are several reasons driving this need for writing. One was the economic development; you had to have some kind of inventory. You've got to keep control over these records, given the scale of trade and the number of items coming into the temples. Second, the Sumerian language, as well, was well suited for this jump from speaking to a written language and that is because Sumerian is an agglutinative language. What do we mean by that? That means a stick-together language; it comes from the Latin "to glue" or "to stick" and Sumerian operates on the same principles—it's not the same language, but—the same principles of Turkic languages or Finno-Ugarian languages, represented in Europe by the Finnish and Hungarian. The grammar and syntax of a language is indicated by the adding of prefixes and suffixes to the root word so that the word is changed by these endings and the internal basic word does not change. This is different from inflected languages represented by the two great language families in western Eurasia. That is, the Indo-European languages represented by most of the languages of Europe—Iran and India, today—or what used to be called the Hamito-Semitic, or sometimes now called, the Afro-Asiatic languages. Those are the Hamitic and Semitic languages spoken largely over North Africa and the Near East today—such languages as Arabic and Hebrew, or the Hamitic languages, such as Berber or ancient Egyptian. Sumerian belongs to neither language group.

In fact, Sumerian doesn't belong to any language group we know. This raises the obvious question—how do we read it in the first place? Here, again, we were lucky in that Sumerian, being the first language to be committed to writing, became the religious language of the urban-based civilization of Mesopotamia so later peoples, who came to rule over this area or came under the influence of the Sumerians, adopted Sumerian as a literary and religious language and, therefore, they had to learn it. And therefore, they had to create dictionaries and bilingual inscriptions and texts and vocabularies in order to learn this unfamiliar language and it is through those types of documents that the structure of Sumerian was finally determined. The language is still being studied and is not completely understood; there are breakthroughs and improvements on Sumerian grammar that are still occurring, but we can read it now with a great deal of confidence. Certainly, the literate Sumerians, starting from 2500 B.C. on, were pretty clear on what it says.

The writing material was wet clay and, as a result of writing in wet clay with a stylus, you tend to shape your characters in the form of a wedge and so the writing, when it was first discovered in the 19th century, was called cuneiform from the Latin word *cuneus* wedge—wedge-shaped writing. Cuneiform refers to the writing system, not the language that's being expressed. Cuneiform, as a writing system, will be used by many different peoples, including non-Sumerian speakers. It will be used in Semitic languages, such as Akkadian, the language of Ebla—that town in northern Syria—Indo-European languages, such as Hittite, and otherwise unrelated languages, such as Hurrian or Urartian, which are languages that occur later in this course. You have basic writing materials, you have the impetus to creating writing, and it seems that the way the development occurred was that scribes who were assigned to keeping records in the temple accounts did that by using, essentially, little tokens. These would take the form of little animals, very often reproduced in art history textbooks; they could be cattle or they could be sheep, as well as tally marks that were base-ten system, so that four of those with one cattle represented four cattle.

And we do have a number of these tally marks, tokens, and figurines that survive in the early years of the Uruk period, around 3500 B.C., and they're made out of clay and fired, and it was a way of keeping an account of livestock and grain. Very quickly, the scribes learned for ease—many of the breakthroughs in writing are really propelled by laziness and the need for convenience—they took these three-dimensional objects and turned them into two-dimensional images and they, in effect, inscribed them on wet clay and then fired the clay and there, presto, you didn't need the objects; you had, simply, a clay tablet with a two-dimensional representation of the numerals along with the picture or pictogram.

Here's where the nature of the Sumerian language kicks in. Sumerian was a language with large numbers of monosyllabic words and since it was based on an agglutinative principle, very often, monosyllabic words were strung together to create more complex words, or prefixes and suffixes were put on those basic words to express mood or tense for a verb, or number or gender for a noun or adjective. As a result of that, very quickly, the Sumerians could take what was a pictogram and apply it to a sound because in the Sumerian language, which by definition was language rich in what we would call, homonyms and homophones—that is words that sound the same, written the same, but have different meanings, or words that sound the same, but are written slightly differently. The example in English would be the word well, which could be a noun or adverb—that would be a homonym. A homophone would be a word that sounds alike and is spelled differently, such as the word sun for the sun in the sky, or son, the male human. So, Sumerian had large numbers of these possible combinations and, therefore, very early on, it was easy for Sumerian scribes, writing around 3400 B.C., to make the conclusion that they have word called *ti*, which represents a "bow," as in a bow and arrow—that word could be extended to cover the homophone, that is the same word *ti* when used as a verb, which means "to live" and, therefore, what was originally a picture, could then be applied to use as sound because it's a monosyllabic word in both cases. Once again, the English example would be sun and son; what you do is you take a picture of the sun and you use it to represent the human. They could also then take that concept and extend it a bit further. We can take the concept as a picture sun and extend it to denote an idea, or an ideogram as philologists would say, and that would be, say, day or even sunlight. So, you see where the original power of those pictograms—those, in effect, pictures—could be applied to express more complicated concepts.

Very quickly in the record, these scribes began to devise a whole bunch of pictograms, which they started applying in various ways to express sounds or groups of sounds and, therefore, take an important step toward writing. There's a number of interesting examples that come from the tablets and, fortunately, we have a very rich record of tablets and we know that a number of symbols that they attempted to use back in 3300 B.C. eventually were discarded along the way and the system got simplified down to about 700 symbols from several thousand.

For instance, there was a pictogram for the word head, or *sag* in Sumerian; you could combine that with the word that apparently represented food, which looks like a kind of bowl that one would use to eat their grain or porridge—*ninda*, in Sumerian—and so you combine the bowl with the head and, presto, you have the verb "to eat." You can simplify that sign into what was, essentially, an ideogram, and apply that to represent the verb "to eat." You can do that by combining the head, *sag*, with the verb *na*, which is water—or the pictogram *na*, which is water—"to drink." So, there are several different ways these symbols could be grouped up into more complex words and the result was that by, say, 3100 B.C., by the end of the Uruk period, there are at least some 2000 well known, well established symbols used by all Sumerian scribes in all cities to represent a basic group of phonograms and pictograms and ideograms. Now, is this true writing? No, not quite yet, but it's getting close. There were limits to this system because you couldn't express complicated sentences, subordinate clauses, tense and mood; you were still at a fairly basic level.

Now, one of the ways that the language got extended was the fact that, very quickly, not only Sumerians were using it, but two other peoples—the Akkadians to the north, just immediately to the north, of the Sumerians, who adopted very early the same urban based civilization you see in Sumer; they also picked up writing. They spoke a Semitic language, which had nothing to do with Sumerian and so they were starting to apply these symbols created for the monosyllabic, agglutinative language of Sumerian to their inflected Semitic tongue. To the east, were a group of people known as the Elamites; they would be today dwelling in what is known as Khuzestan and Iran, the section of Iran that is actually inhabited by largely Arab speakers. And, Elam and the Elamites were, again, in close contact with the Sumerians by trade, they had adopted urban civilization, and their important cities at Susa and Anshan, connected by trade, they too, start using cuneiform. The fact that two non-Sumerian languages started using this script put pressure on the scribes to start differentiating what these symbols meant. What they came up with is something known as determinatives. That is, additions and modifications on the symbols that would indicate whether that word "ti" was the noun, the pictogram the bow, or ti the verb, to live. Once they got to that point where they started modifying the basic symbols to show the grammatical function of that symbol, the word that that symbol represented, then you're on the way to writing. It's not far behind where you can modify those symbols in such a way that you can write complete sentences and, somewhere between 2800 and 2600 B.C., the Sumerians achieve it.

It's also assisted by several other developments. One was that when the symbols were first made in the pictograms, they tended to be a cursive script because you're drawing heads and cattle and very sinuous objects. When you move to clay tablets and you start incising them, the medium used for writing dictates the form of the character and, again, laziness kicks in. What was once a head of a cow or a bowl becomes, essentially, a triangle and so there was a tendency, very early on, to turn these symbols into fairly abstract wedges, a set of wedges, and very quickly the original pictograms lose their picture quality. This is assisted by the fact that the Akkadians and Elamites who used the written system, they didn't even know what the picture originally was; they very often got the original cuneiform abstract symbols and that's what they learned and that's what they applied.

In addition, the earliest Sumerian texts are written vertically, from top to bottom, and they are in columns that are divided off. Someone figured out, around 3300–3200 B.C., that it was easier to write from left to right and that it reduced the chances of you marring the writing—you know, moving your hand over it and wiping out what you wrote, which is dangerous in columns. If you're moving this way, you could knock out half of the line you just very meticulously recorded; it's better to go from left to right and to write horizontally. Now, given the conservatism of most of these scribes, they're a little annoyed at this, that as a result of writing from left to right in the early stages, that the picture quality was lost, and so what they did is they took those original pictograms and very early on wrote them at a 90 degree angle from where they had been written when they moved to the horizontal writing, so that if you simply rotated a text in early pictograms written from left to right by 90 degrees, it lined up in neat columns and looked just like the way it used to be when Granddad wrote from top to bottom. And, by kicking the basic symbols over at a 90 degree angle, and by increasingly making them stylized because of the writing material the picture was rapidly lost, the writing system becomes quite abstract; it is quickly simplified, determinatives, other types of ways of indicating grammar are developed, and then the script is handed over to people such as the Akkadians and Elamites who have no knowledge of its origins and they take that written script and adapt it further.

That is a breakthrough of the first order. It is argued—and we'll return to this issue with early Egypt—that the concept of writing, not the symbols, but the concept of writing, was brought to Egypt by Sumerian merchants in the late Uruk period. It's a controversial issue still being debated, and I've changed my opinion several times on the matter; at the moment, I'm inclined to agree that there's some sort of Sumerian connection.

The indecipherable glyphs of the Indus Valley, which begin to appear around 2500 B.C., seem also to be based on Sumerian script. The Sumerian script becomes the basis of various syllabaries—that is, simplified writing systems in which syllables are expressed. These are in evidence as early as around 1900 B.C. in Northern Syria at the sites of Ugarit, particularly, and those syllabaries stand behind the writing systems of what are known as linear a and linear b in the Aegean world. That is, the early scripts of Crete and Greece and, eventually, these writing systems in the Levant get simplified in the early Iron Age, somewhere between 1000 and 900 B.C., into an alphabet representing consonants—simply consonants, not vowels. That is done by the Phoenicians and that alphabet is adopted by the Greeks and the Greeks add vowels and, essentially, what is used in the west today is a slightly Roman modification of that Greek alphabet with vowels that goes back to the Phoenician continental script that goes back to the syllabaries that go back to the cuneiform script in the Sumerian cities. So, ultimately, the writing structure can be traced back to the first cities of Sumer.

That makes the difference. With literacy, the rules are changed and if anthropologists and archaeologists still debate at what point in human history did speech become a form of communication so that the older generation could tell the younger generation all of its achievements, that's its abilities in hunting or making of tools or implements, that has broke the barrier of time, so that each generation could start with the knowledge of the previous generation. This occurred sometime in the distant human past; writing increases that power many times more. In fact, writing is still with us despite computer chips, and technology, and Internet; it is still the same rules that the Sumerian scribes created back in the Uruk period. He who can write well runs the civilization and everyone else does the grunt work.

Lecture Three
Mesopotamian Kings and Scribes

Scope: The Sumerians, although united in language and culture, were
divided politically. City-states clashed over border lands and trade
routes and battled Akkadians to the north and Elamites to the east.
In this era of warring states (c. 3000–2350 B.C.), *ensi* (dynasts)
drilled armies and employed scribes. Those *ensi* who imposed their
hegemony over rivals assumed the honorific *lugal*, "great man."
Lugals and *ensi* cloaked themselves in religious symbols, as seen
in the royal burials at Ur of about 2900–2800 B.C. Wars made the
kingship but also undermined dynasties, as seen in the costly clash
of Lagash under the family of Eannatum against Umma. In 2340
B.C., Sargon, king of the Akkadians, conquered Sumer and forged
the first territorial empire embracing Mesopotamia. His grandson,
Naram-sin, carried Akkadian arms into Anatolia. Akkadian
emperors had insufficient royal servants to rule their wide-flung
empire and faced the hostility of Sumerian cities. The Akkadian
Empire fragmented in 2200 B.C., but Ur-nammu, king of Ur,
constructed his own territorial empire a century later. Ur-nammu
issued a law code and sponsored vast building programs; his son,
Shulgi, developed royal administration. This Neo-Sumerian
Empire, too, fragmented by 2000 B.C., but two centuries later, an
Amorite prince of Babylon, Hammurabi (r. 1792–1750 B.C.),
forged the third Mesopotamian Empire.

Outline

I.   In the course of the development of city-states in Sumer, between about
3500 and 3000 B.C., all the arable and marginal land was taken;
eventually, the borders of the city-states began to run up against each
other. The result was border wars and battles over important trade
routes.

   A. Cuneiform tablets from around 2900–2800 B.C. inform us of the
political situation in Sumer, revealing long and bitter memories of
border wars among the city-states.

B. A number of city-states were in existence, including Ur, probably the largest city in Sumer; Larsa; and Eridu—all on the southern shores of the Persian Gulf.

C. Central Sumer also had a number of cities, including Uruk and Nippur, along with Lagash and Umma, rivals that vied for control of trade routes into the east.

D. To the north were Barsippa and Kish, probably representing the limits of Sumerian civilization. Kish was regarded as a seat of power in Sumer, and any ruler who could impose his control that far north essentially controlled the land of Sumer.

E. Both tablets and archaeology indicate that the political world of Sumer was larger than just the Sumerian city-states.

    1. Excavations in northern Syria, for example, have revealed the city of Ebla, which had adopted the full urban, literate civilization of Sumer by 2600 B.C.

    2. On the middle Euphrates was the city of Mari, and immediately to the north of the Sumerian city-states, between the valleys of the Tigris and Euphrates, were the Akkadians. These were a Semitic-speaking people who had adopted the urban institutions of Sumer and practiced similar religious rituals.

    3. To the east was the area of Elam, in what is now southwestern Iran. Its primary cities were Anshan and Susa. Elamites were regarded as the most dangerous of Sumer's immediate neighbors.

    4. To the far north, on the upper Tigris, the future land of Assyria had also adopted urban-based civilization in Ashur and Nineveh.

II. Scholars are mostly in the dark about the political organization of these city-states, although a number of theories have been proposed.

A. In general, the sources seem to indicate that the city-states were theocracies, run by a group of powerful families that controlled the cults. At least one member of the group held the title *en* ("overseer").

B. From about 2900 B.C., as the city-states began to clash, the need arose to organize soldiers and scribes. At about this time, we begin to encounter in the records men who could claim the early dynastic title *ensi* or *ensi-gar*. An *ensi* who could impose his hegemony over neighboring *ensi* could claim the title *lugal*, "great man."

C. Aspiring kings emerged quickly in early wars among city-states because they had the ability to mobilize soldiers and resources. We have indications of this situation in artwork.

D. *Ensi* could also draw on scribes to cloak themselves with symbols of legitimacy. This was born out by the excavations of Ur conducted in the 1920s–1930s by Sir Leonard Woolley. Grave goods from about 2600 B.C. indicate that these early *lugals* of Ur, often called the First Dynasty of Ur, were seen as figures close to the gods.

III. We also have some excellent documentation from Girsu, a satellite town of Lagash, recording the battles between Lagash and the rival city of Umma.

A. The first indication we have of the ancient struggle between these two cities comes from the reign of Eannatum (c. 2450 B.C.). Annals record fighting for the border zone between Eannatum and the *ensi* of Umma. As the victor, Eannatum exacted from Umma acknowledgment as a *lugal*, but there was no effort to annex Umma to build a larger state.

B. Such battles probably raged over the landscape of Sumer, resulting in only minor political changes. None of the city-states had the vision or the institutions required to create a wider political order.

C. Thus, Eannatum's grandson or nephew, Entemena (c. 2400 B.C.), repeated the whole process a generation later. Entemena was then followed by his son, Urukagina (c. 2350 B.C.), who had the same problems with Umma. Records indicate that Urukagina had to institute various reforms to restore order in his city-state. He, in turn, was overthrown by his rival in Umma, Lugalzagesi (r. c. 2340–2316 B.C.).

D. Lugalzagesi fell to Sargon of Akkad (r. 2334–2279 B.C.), the former cup-bearer of the king of Kish, who had assassinated his master.

IV. Sargon the Great seized power in Kish, recruited an army of Akkadians, and conquered the cities of Sumer. Once he had Sumer under control, he waged campaigns from the Persian Gulf to the Mediterranean.

    A. Sargon amassed an empire stretching well over 1,000 miles. His grandson, Naram-sin (r. 2254–2218 B.C.), waged wars even farther afield, penetrating into what is now central Turkey, Iran, and Syria.

    B. These kings of the Akkadian Empire marked a departure in Mesopotamian history. Beginning with Sargon, a great territorial empire was forged, and the two pillars of Near Eastern monarchies, a royal army and a royal professional bureaucracy, were put in place.

V. The Akkadian Empire lasted for only about a century.

    A. The Akkadians never won over the loyalty of the Sumerians, and by about 2200 B.C., the empire became fragmented. The coup de grace was delivered by Iranian tribesmen known as Gutians, who entered and sacked Agade, the capital of Akkad.

    B. Nonetheless, the Akkadians had proved what could be done, and by about 2100 B.C., a Sumerian ruler, Ur-nammu (r. 2112–2095 B.C.), the *lugal* of Ur, re-created the imperial state.

    C. Ur-nammu and his son, Shulgi (r. 2094–2047 B.C.), carried out additional reforms in the evolution of an effective Near Eastern monarchy.

        1. Ur-nammu issued the first comprehensive law code, intended for use in Sumer, Akkad, and Elam.

        2. Shulgi was responsible for developing the beautiful chancery script of cuneiform tablets and perfecting Sumerian cuneiform into a precise legal and administrative language.

        3. Shulgi also sponsored a literary revival; during his reign, many of the ancient Sumerian myths and traditions were recorded.

    D. This empire, sometimes known as the Third Dynasty of Ur, or the Neo-Sumerian Empire, itself lasted only about a century before it fragmented. By 2006 B.C., the Elamites had invaded and sacked Ur, carrying off the city's sacred gods.

E. Just as the Akkadians had, the Sumerians faced the problem of border control. Royal authority could be exercised only in the core southern regions of the empire. In the middle and upper areas of Mesopotamia, the outlying areas of Syria, or the border lands along Iran, royal authority depended on making alliances with local rulers.

F. The Amorites (or Amurru) were West Semitic speakers living in what is now eastern Syria and along the middle Euphrates. Between 2000–1800 B.C., they migrated into Mesopotamia as tribal communities and seized power in a number of cities.

   1. The Amorites established regional kingdoms and adopted Akkadian as their administrative language.

   2. This migration of Semitic speakers had a major linguistic and ethnic impact in southern Mesopotamia. By 1800 B.C., Sumerian was lost as a spoken language, and the Sumerians were assimilated into a larger Semitic-speaking population; however, Sumerian institutions and culture held on.

   3. One of these Amorite princes, Hammurabi (r. 1792–1750 B.C.), emerged as the leading figure in southern Mesopotamia and built a great empire centered at Babylon. With him, the institutions that had been developed over the last seven centuries reached perfection.

Further Reading:

Henri Frankfort et al., eds., *The Intellectual Adventure of Ancient Man: An Essay on Speculative Thought in the Ancient Near East.* Rev. ed.

H. W. F. Saggs, *The Greatness That Was Babylon.*

Questions to Consider:

1. How did inter-city and frontier wars transform the government and society of Sumerian cities in 2800–2400 B.C.? What accounted for the success of *ensi* in founding dynasties? How powerful were the *ensi* and *lugals* of Sumer? How important were religious symbols in sanctifying royal rule?

2. How did the Akkadian emperors Sargon and Naram-sin change the political and cultural destinies of Mesopotamia? What were the crucial institutions they forged? What accounted for the collapse of the Akkadian Empire?

Lecture Three—Transcript
Mesopotamian Kings and Scribes

In this lecture, I plan to look at the creation of wider political institutions in ancient Mesopotamia and, essentially, we shall be looking at three classes of people—kings, scribes, and soldiers—the three groups that are essential in building, first, the regional kingdoms and, finally, the territorial empires of what we call the early and middle Bronze Age. Now, in the previous lecture, I stressed the economic and social underpinnings of early Mesopotamian civilization and we particularly concentrated on Sumer—that is in the extreme southern portions of Iraq or Mesopotamia. In this lecture, we're going to have to widen our view because we'll be discussing other people who fall heirs to the civilization of Sumer and use those institutions to build the greater territorial states. The first of these will be the conqueror Sargon of Akkad, who was not a Sumerian at all.

To start the story off, we should go back into that earlier period, that so-called Uruk period around 3500 B.C., when the first cities began to appear around the great temples, the temples of the tutelary divinities of each city-state. As I noted, Sumer is a land divided up by marshes, by the river systems and their tributaries. It becomes crisscrossed with dikes and canals and by 3000 B.C. has assumed very much the appearance of the landscape that you would see today, with settled farms, carefully manicured fields, and various orchards and fruit trees; dates become a major commodity in Sumer. What happened in the course of the development of these city-states between roughly 3500 and 3000 B.C. is all the marginal and arable land was used up by the city-state. Eventually, these city-states ran into each other—that is, their borders started to march next to the borders of the neighbors and what happened is you had border wars and also battles over important trade routes, and I have to stress that both are causes of these early wars.

As I noted in the last lecture, Sumerian and Mesopotamian civilization, in general, was based on two major natural resources—mud and reeds. The major building material were mud bricks; they could be fired in kilns, so they'd be as hard as stone, but also the reeds that were used for building material, for the stylus in writing cuneiform had many purposes. Most of the other raw materials necessary for civilization had to be imported; that included metals, that included hardwood, such as cedar from Lebanon, stone, precious objects, all of that depended on trade routes, and by 3000 B.C., these city-states are now clashing with each other over the control of trade routes, as well as the marginal lands, which could be brought under cultivation.

Now, when the earliest cuneiform tablets become available and inform us of the political situation in Sumer—and this is usually around 2900 to 2800 B.C., in what we often call the early dynastic period, and this period will run down, essentially, to shortly before 2300 B.C., when Sargon of Akkad creates the first territorial state—we encounter a world that is already divided up into city-states and many of these city-states have very long and bitter memories over border wars. There are a number of city-states in Sumer, on the southern shore; foremost, was the city of Ur, probably the largest city in all of Sumer, and Larsa and Eridu, very early sites. They are now about 200 miles inland because of the silting up of the Tigris and the Euphrates. In the time of the early dynastic period—and really through the whole of what we call the Bronze Age down to roughly 1100 B.C.—the Tigris and Euphrates flowed separately into the Persian Gulf. They were also linked to the cities of Meluhha—that is, the Indus Valley civilization through trade, and Ur and Eridu were regarded as two very sacred cities and very ancient foundations.

In central Sumer, there were a number of cities including Uruk, the home of the legendary Gilgamesh, as he's known in his Akkadian name. His name in Sumerian is really Bilgames; the initial B goes into G from Sumerian to Akkadian. The city of Nippur, which was regarded as the center of the world and sacred to the god An, or Anu, who is the lord of the heavens. Also, there were Lagash and Umma, cities that are towards the Tigris that have a long-term animosity and particularly vied for control of the routes into the lands into the east in Elam. Then, to the north, probably representing the limit of Sumerian civilization, were the cities of Barsippa and Kish. Kish was regarded as a very early power in Sumer and anyone who could control Kish, any ruler who could control that far north, essentially controlled the land of Sumer; that is from Ur to Kish, essentially represented the extent of Sumerian-speaking city-states.

But, already the tablets indicate and increasing amounts of archeology indicate that the political world of Sumer was larger than just the Sumerian city-states. Some remarkable excavations going on in Syria have revealed the city of Ebla—which I mentioned in a previous lecture—that had adopted the full urban literate civilization of Sumer, certainly by 2600 B.C., that was in northern Syria. On the middle Euphrates is the city of Mari and then immediately to the north of the Sumerian city-states, between the valleys of the Tigris and Euphrates at their narrowest points where the rivers come together very closely before they fan out to find their separate course to the Persian Gulf, were the Akkadians, a Semitic-speaking group of people who had adopted the urban institutions of Sumer, worshipped their own gods, who were associated to the gods of Sumer, but very much used Sumerian religious rituals; they built ziggurats and they performed the same kind of civic festivals that are recorded in the Sumerian cities.

While the Akkadians were considered not the same as Sumerians, they were at least regarded as civilized and there's enough indication that by 2900 B.C., there had been a lot of intermixture, especially in the northern areas around Kish. We know of Sumerians with Akkadian names and Akkadians with Sumerian names. The association is very old; how far back it goes, we do not know. And, the Akkadians are speaking a Semitic language, which of course is unintelligible to the Sumerians, but they always revered the Sumerians and they later retained Sumerian as their religious language.

Immediately to the east was the area of Elam and Elam is, as I mentioned earlier, southwestern Iran today and the cities of Anshan and Susa were their primary cities. They, too, had the cuneiform-based civilization, but the Elamites were always regarded as kind of really on the margin of civilization. They're seen as the most dangerous of the immediate neighbors. And, the Elamites have this nasty reputation of intervening in Sumerian affairs and usually sacking major Sumerian cities and carrying off their cult statues. Finally, to the far north and the upper Tigris, it's already been revealed that the future land of Assyria had come to adopt that urban-based civilization. Those would be the cities of Ashur, which is really the ancient name of Assyria, as well as their primary god, Ashur, who's later identified with Marduk in the Babylonian tradition and Nineveh, especially what is known as level five of Nineveh. So, there is a wide network of city-states up and down the Tigris and Euphrates river system and extending into southwestern Iran and into northern Syria.

Well, all of these cities were linked by trade connections and, as I mentioned, from 2900-2800 B.C. on, these cities began to clash over borderlands and over trade routes. Now, we really are in the dark about how these earliest city-states were organized and there have been a number of theories proposed; most of them really have limited evidence—it's arguing back from other text, usually text from the Babylonian period from the time of Hammurabi, who ruled from 1792 to 1750 B.C., claiming that the way heaven is organized in the Babylonian pantheon, that that reflects political institutions of mortals. And so, in the *Enuma Elish*, the great Babylonian creation epic—which in its opening means "when on high," that's how it gets its name—that Marduk the supreme god had been invested with his powers by an assembly and so in earliest Sumerian city-states, you had some sort of council or assembly and they invested powers in a king. This has led rise to a number of theories, both by American scholars and, at one point, by Marxist scholars, but instead the sources seem to indicate that these city-states, from the very start, were essentially theocracies. They were run by a charmed group of powerful families that controlled the cults; at least one member, if not several members of that charmed set of families held the title *en* or overseer and, from the start, there was always a tendency to have a very tightly knit hierarchical government—and that makes sense. The mobilization of the vast amounts of labor necessary to conduct intensive agriculture, to put up the remarkable structures of the ziggurats and the great ziggurat at Ur, for instance, constructed much later in the Third Dynasty. It measures something like 400 feet square and it's about 75 feet high and it has millions and millions of these mud bricks from kilns. So, this is an enormous amount of power that has to be concentrated in the hands of either a dynast or a small group of oligarchs or aristocrats who could mobilize and make those demands.

So, our best guess is that the city-states started out being ruled by an elite group of families and that very quickly, starting from about 2900 B.C. on, it became clear, as the city-states started to clash over trade routes and over marginal lands, that someone had to organize these cities, and that meant organizing soldiers and also organizing scribes who could keep records of taxes and other commodities necessary to maintain the instruments of government and to maintain the army.

So, we begin to encounter in the records men who could claim the title *ensi*, or sometimes *ensi-gar*, a term that later comes to designate governor, but seems to be an early dynastic title used in these cities of Sumer. If an *ensi* of any particular city, such as the legendary Gilgamesh of Uruk, was able to beat up a bunch of other ensis, such as Agga of Kish, then the *ensi* might eventually take the title lugal, which originally meant nothing more than big man, top honcho in Sumer and eventually came to mean the title king. These early wars among the various city-states demonstrate that the kings or the aspiring kings emerge very quickly into these monarchical positions because they had the ability to mobilize soldiers and the resources to support those soldiers.

We have several indications of this; they come from artwork. One of them is a work known as *The Standard of Ur*, which is a lapis lazuli stone decorated in shell. It comes from Ur and it shows the scenes of peace and war, so it depicts early Sumerian soldiers. There's another relief known as *The Stelae of Vultures*, which is erected by Eannatum who is the *ensi* of Lagash and eastern Sumer that dates from about 2450 B.C. Both of these depictions show highly disciplined phalanx—that is, heavily armed infantrymen with large shields and spears carrying either leather or metal helmets. Already, chariots are appearing on the battlefield; these are carts that are drawn by mules or donkeys, not by horses, and they're really rather clumsy affairs and probably only a few of them were ever put on the battlefield for the nobility. But clearly, we're looking at city-states that are developing professional soldiers, men who could fight in close shock action. That required drill, that required training, and it required leadership. Those *ensi* who could provide that leadership could then establish the position as kings, transmit their power to their families.

Those same *ensi* could also draw upon the scribes—that is, the professional class of literate clerks—to keep records and to also cloak themselves with various symbols of legitimacy. These were primarily religious symbols. This has been borne out by the excavations of Ur conducted by Sir Leonard Woolley in the 1920s and 30s, and the objects are on display in the British Museum and they're really quite fantastic. These include objects that have come out of 16 different graves from Ur, roughly about 2600 B.C., and three of the graves are two royal figures and then one that appears to be a queen; all of them were attended with various servants and soldiers and ladies at court who were sacrificed. The largest number is 78; the smallest number for Queen Pu-abi is, I think, 15 attendants. All indications are that these early lugals of Ur, usually called the First Dynasty of Ur, roughly contemporary with the legendary Gilgamesh, were seen as, if not gods, certainly as figures close to the gods and the favorites of the gods. So, religious symbols, the ability to mobilize soldiers, and the use of the clerks meant city-states saw very quickly the emergence of these mini monarchies.

We have some excellent documentation of how these wars were fought and these come from the city of Lagash, or actually they technically come from Girsu, which was a satellite town of Lagash that was excavated by the French earlier in the 20th century. We have a number of records that record the battles between Lagash and the rival city of Umma, which is less than 20 miles away. The first indication that we have of this ancient struggle comes from the rein of a man named Eannatum, who lived perhaps in 2450 B.C., and he is hailed as the beloved of the god Ningirsu, later known as Ninurta in the Babylonian tradition, and we have some evidence of what actually went on in that war. We have some annals of Eannatum of Lagash. We're told:

> The *ensi* of Umma, [that is the opposing city] at the demand of the god, raided and devoured the irrigated land, the field beloved by Ningirsu [he is the god of Lagash] and he [that is the Umman *ensi*] ripped out the stelae and entered the plain of Lagash [fighting obviously for that vital border zone].

Then, we're told of a battle in which Eannatum mobilized the forces of his city:

> …and by the word of Enlil [lord of the winds] he hurdled the net upon them and heaped up piles of bodies on the plain… [This is an image that comes out of mythology; Marduk uses a net in the *Enuma Elish* to snare the monster Timod]. The survivors turn to Eannatum, they prostrated themselves for life, and they wept.

What Eannatum exacts from Umma is acknowledgment of Eannatum as a lugal, a great man. Sometimes, the city divinities might be taken from Umma to Lagash in which case you strip your opposing city of its supernatural defenders. You probably slaughter a generation of men of your opposing city, but that's about it. There's no effort to annex Umma, to build a wider state, and probably for centuries, these types of battles had raged over the landscape of Sumer with really minor political changes. None of the city-states yet had the institutions and the vision to create a wider political order.

So what happened after Eannatum is either his grandson or his nephew, Entemena—the relationship is a little uncertain—repeated the whole process a generation later. He was followed by his son, Urukagina, who had the same problem with Umma. By the third generation in this record of Urukagina, we know that there were difficulties in the city-state and Urukagina had to pass various types of reforms to restore order. He, in turn, was overthrown by his rival in Umma, who achieved the same type of victory; his name was Lugalzagesi. And, then, Lugalzagesi, who assumed the title of lugal and ruled as a prominent Sumerian figure, fell in turn to a figure known as Sargon of Akkad. Now, at this point, this was a major departure. Sargon of Akkad was not a Sumerian and, furthermore, Sargon of Akkad—and his name in Akkadian means "righteous king" and that's a name that's typical of kings looking for legitimacy—his mom was a flute player, which is the lowest class of concubine, or prostitute, in the Near East and he was an illegitimate son. This always reminds one of William the Conqueror of Normandy, that he's originally William the Bastard and becomes William the Conqueror. Sargon has that same problem; it's all part of a PR effort to clean up his legitimacy. He started off as the cupbearer of the King of Kish and did in his master, the King of Kish, and seized power in Kish and recruited an army of Akkadians—these are the Semitic peoples living to the north of Sumer. Then, he conquered the cities of Sumer; Umma, Lagash, Ur, Nippur—all of them—by mobilizing the greater forces of Akkad, which as far as we can tell, were really not divided along the same powerful city-state loyalties, but had a larger ethnic sense.

Sargon tells us of how he tears down all the walls of the Sumerian cities and, then, once he has Sumer under control, he waged campaigns from the lower sea to the upper sea and washed his weapons ceremoniously in each of these seas. We believe these to be the Persian Gulf and the eastern Mediterranean. We're told that he took various titles to reflect his new position. He called himself the King of Kish, the Ensi of Enlil, Lord of the Winds, the Appointed of Anu, the Lord of the Heavens, and King of Sumer and Akkad. For the first time, a ruler uses the regional designation of Sumer and Akkad. He handed down to his successors a brilliant legacy, an empire stretching from the eastern shores of the Mediterranean to the Persian gulf, stretching well over 1,000 miles and his grandson Naram-sin—which means the beloved of Sin, or the moon god—waged wars even further afield, penetrating into central Turkey today, campaigning into Iran to secure those trade routes, and bringing to heel the cities of Syria. He uses, as his titles, King of Sumer and Akkad; he starts with that as his title. It's already now a recognized regional title. King of Kings, King of the Four Corners of the Universe, Lord of the Universe, and God, or more likely *dinger*, is an ideogram in Akkadian that means, "he who will be deified to join the gods," close to the Latin notion of *deius*, a deified one.

Now, these kings of the Akkadian Empire really marked a new departure in Mesopotamian history. For one, they were effective because Sargon had the means to raise a royal army and in his conquest, he taxed the cities of Sumer to maintain that army. He boasts in his annals that he kept an army of 5,400 men who ate before him daily and I always think one of the reasons he has to conquer the Near East is just simply to feed his army. He also created a royal bureaucracy using those scribes on a scale never done before in a city-state and these scribes begin to record information in Akkadian, not in Sumerian, to make sure that taxation is collected within the cities of Sumer and that taxation is used to support royal institutions. Unlike the Sumerian city-states in those rivalries I described earlier, Sargon appoints the Akkadians—he calls them, in his annals, the sons of the Akkadians—as *ensi* over the cities Sumer, Elam, and Akkad. That is, he appoints royal officials and the term *ensi* comes to designate the term governors, in our sense of the word, who are removable by the king, subject to the king, and this is the beginning of a royal administration, complete with cuneiform documents and an army to back it up. Both Sargon and Naram-sin undertake massive rebuilding projects throughout Sumer and Akkad. At Ur, for instance, the great ziggurat is rebuilt and that ziggurat complex is at least 15 percent of the city. And so, for the first time, a great territorial empire has been forged and those two important pillars of Near Eastern monarchies are created for the first time—that is, a royal army and royal professional bureaucracy.

The Akkadian empire lasts for only about a century; it's brought down for several reasons. The coup de grace is delivered by Iranian tribesmen known as Gutians, who were on the frontiers of the empire, who enter and sack Agade, which is the capital of Akkad—which incidentally, has still to be recovered; it has not yet been located. Part of the problem was that the Akkadians never won over the loyalty of the Sumerians and the Sumerian cities resented living under these great Akkadian emperors. So, by 2200–2150 B.C., the Akkadian Empire does not so much collapse as fragment.

Nonetheless, they prove what could be done and very quickly, in about 2100 B.C., a Sumerian ruler, Ur-nammu the *lugal* of Ur, the greatest city of Sumer, recreates the Akkadian state. He, with Sumerian forces, marches up the great rivers. We're not sure if he penetrates to the Mediterranean, but he comes pretty close to resurrecting that great territorial empire of Sargon. He and his son, Shulgi, carry out more important reforms in the evolution of an ever more effective Near Eastern monarchy. One of them is the issuing of a law code and a law code that was apparently intended to be used for at least the southern core areas of the empire—that is, Sumer, Akkad, and Elam, which together constituted the most densely urbanized section of the Near East and by some reckoning, might well have as many as 1,000,000 people living there among some 25 great cities.

That is a major step of linking royal authority with this great law code. Now, that is a tradition that undoubtedly goes back into the Sumerian city-states; Urukagina passed various reforms when his city Lagash was socially disrupted by its wars with Umma. This was the first time we have a law code. It only survives in fragments; we have the prologue and we have about 43 clauses of it and it is the predecessor of the later law code of Hammurabi.

Shulgi in particular is responsible for developing the beautiful chancery script, as we would call it, of cuneiform tablets, and really perfecting Sumerian cuneiform into a very concise legal and administrative language. These characters could be inscribed on very small tablets and you have to understand, the tablet is a heavy item to send if you're sending out correspondence to direct your empire, and they're usually sealed in a clay envelope and sent off, and so weight is an all-important consideration in this. Shulgi makes sure that the scribes now have a standardized language so the king can send directives to his governors that are absolutely clear with what he wants and this is a major achievement. Shulgi is also responsible for sponsoring a major literary revival and it is in his reign that many of the ancient Sumerian myths and traditions are now written down and this is very late in Sumerian history. This is somewhere around 2075 B.C., close to eight or nine centuries after the appearance of literacy in some of those Sumerian cities.

Even so, the Sumerian empire, which is sometimes known as the Third Dynasty of Ur, or the Neo-Sumerian Empire, this empire too was destined to fragment. It only lasted for about a century; by 2006, the Elamites had invaded and sacked the city of Ur, carrying off the sacred gods of Ur. That would be Nanna or, as he's known in Babylonian, Sin, the god of the moon. This was a disgrace; it disorganized the capital city, but the Sumerians, just as Akkadians, faced the same problem of border controls, and in both empires you have to think of the core regions where the urban basis is located as where administration really could be effected. This is the wealthiest area, the most easily taxed, and when you get up to the middle and upper areas of Mesopotamia or the outlying regions in Syria or the border lands along Iran, their royal authority was far more limited, it depended very much on making alliances with local rulers. Sometimes, you had demonstrations in force. Naram-sin is believed to have been the third Akkadian Emperor to have sacked the city of Ebla and brought to a close its prosperity in northern Syria, probably as an example to other local rulers to stay in line. So, there was always a problem of border control and what happens is these border people are often armed and enrolled as allies and mercenaries and eventually go into business for themselves, and we suspect this happened both with the Akkadian and the Sumerian empire. This is a story that repeats itself later in the Near East and later throughout history where the border zones gain a monopoly on armed force and come in to the center and seize power for themselves.

That seems to have been the case with Neo-Sumerian Empire and, particularly, people living in what is now eastern Syria and the middle Euphrates known as the Amurru, or the Amorites, as they're rendered in the Old Testament, and that's sort of an unfortunate rendition. The term Amurru in Sumerian and Akkadian simply designated the west. These were West Semitic speakers; they spoke a language related to, but not identical to Akkadian. Between 2000 and 1800 B.C., they migrated into lower Mesopotamia, often as tribal regiments. They were tribal communities, many of them had fought in Sumerian armies, and they seized power in a number of the cities—including the cities of Isin and Larsa and Lower Mesopotamia, the city of Eshunna, in the middle Tigris, Mari on the middle Euphrates—and established regional kingdoms. They adopted Akkadian as their administrative language, since it was closely related to their vernacular. That migration of Semitic speakers had a major linguistic and ethnic impact in southern Mesopotamia.

By 1800 B.C., Sumerian is lost as a spoken language. The Sumerians are finally assimilated into a larger Semitic-speaking population, using various forms of Akkadian. However, Sumerian institutions and culture lasted; the newcomers adopted the Akkadian language and the urban literate-based civilizations that were evolved by Sumer—and one of these Amorite or Amurru princes, a man named Hammurabi, sixth of a generation of war lords, who had moved into the lower Euphrates and established, originally, what was nothing more than a tent city in a place called Babylon, emerged as the leading figure in southern Mesopotamia. He came to the throne in 1792 B.C. and spent 40 years bringing these various regional states to heel and wrote the final chapter of the great territorial empires of the early and middle Bronze Age and built the great Babylonian empire centered at Babylon. With Hammurabi, a new chapter is opened because in Hammurabi's Babylon, the institutions that had been evolved over the last seven centuries come to perfection. Hammurabi and his successors also rule over a brilliant renaissance in letters, in Akkadian literature and arts, and Babylon becomes the cultural center of Mesopotamia for the rest of antiquity, really down to the early middle ages, until it will finally be replaced by Muslim Baghdad.

Lecture Four
Hammurabi's Babylon

Scope: Hammurabi (r. 1792–1750 B.C.) ruled over the most successful bureaucratic state of early Mesopotamia. The vigilant ruler is revealed in his correspondence with his governors at Mari, on the middle Euphrates, as well as in his law code, in vernacular Akkadian, which has survived intact. To be sure, Hammurabi followed Sumerian tradition and his code was a compilation of customary laws, yet royal judges were expected to apply the laws throughout the empire, and Hammurabi linked the throne with the administration of justice. Simultaneously, Hammurabi and his successors patronized arts, letters, and scholarship. Akkadian was transformed into a literary language. Sumerian myths and legends were reworked into literary epics, including the Enuma Elish, the creation epic; a long epic on the flood featuring Atrahasis as the Babylonian Noah; and a version of the Epic of Gilgamesh. Babylonian scholars also achieved impressive breakthroughs in mathematics and astronomy. Babylon remained the cultural center of the Near East down to the Roman age, but Hammurabi's heirs failed to keep pace with innovations in warfare. In about 1595 B.C., King Mursiliš and the Hittite chariots surprised and sacked Babylon. By 1540 B.C., Kassites seized Babylon and ruled as a warrior caste down to 1157 B.C. Kassite Babylon was a lesser regional kingdom, but the city of Babylon remained the cosmopolitan cultural center, and Akkadian was the language of diplomacy, culture, and scholarship in the Late Bronze Age.

Outline

I. This lecture concludes our survey of Mesopotamian civilization in the Bronze Age, focusing on the career of Hammurabi (r. 1792–1750 B.C.).

    A. We began by looking at the emergence of cities in Sumer (c. 3500 B.C.), and we are tracing the evolution of this civilization through the Sumerians, Akkadians, and Babylonians; later on in the course, we'll bring in the Assyrians, who carried this civilization down to about 1200–1000 B.C. and the collapse of the Bronze Age.

B. Hammurabi's Babylon falls in the period of the Middle Bronze Age and is seen, in many ways, as the pinnacle of Mesopotamian civilization.

II. Recall that Hammurabi spent the 40 years of his reign bringing other regional states under his control.

A. In some ways, Hammurabi inherited a number of advantages from his predecessors, both the Neo-Sumerian kings and the Akkadian emperors. For example, a service aristocracy was already in place, as were the traditions of an effective army and military discipline.

B. Hammurabi profited from the fact that the course of the Euphrates shifted during the period of the Amorite migration (2000–1800 B.C.). This change of course favored Babylon, which emerged as the critical city on the lower Euphrates and the nexus of important trade routes.

C. The ruler was also a skilled diplomat, who managed to isolate his opponents and conquer them individually. By 1770–1760 B.C., he ruled a territorial empire that stretched from the Persian Gulf almost to the Mediterranean.

D. Hammurabi displayed relentless and meticulous attention to detail. This quality has been revealed to us from records in a library in the city of Mari on the middle Euphrates.

E. Hammurabi trained a superb royal army, as well as a militia or reserve force. These forces were comprised of heavy infantry, backed up with bowmen or javelin-men. We have no evidence, however, that these armies were equipped with the light chariots that came to dominate warfare in the Late Bronze Age. Indeed, some scholars hold that Hammurabi's state was toppled by the Kassites circa 1540 B.C. in part because the Babylonians failed to keep pace with military technology.

III. We know much about Hammurabi's state through two remarkable sets of documents, the first of which is his law code.

A. Hammurabi's code survives almost intact and consists of 282 laws. In examining these laws, we can get some sense of the sophistication of Babylonian civilization.

B. The code rests on earlier legal precedents, including the law code issued by the Neo-Sumerian emperor Ur-nammu and one issued nearly a century later by an Amorite ruler named Lipith-Ishtar (r. 1934–1924 B.C.).

C. Hammurabi's code was issued in Akkadian, the vernacular language, while all previous codes had been issued in Sumerian.

D. Hammurabi's code is not comparable to Justinian's, but it does list customary Babylonian laws by categories. The laws include royal rulings on customary matters in both civil and criminal litigation, organized in such a way that judges could use the code to decide cases by analogy and to invent new laws.

E. The code links the monarchy with law and with justice coming from the gods. This feature is an ancient one in Mesopotamian civilization: The king is the shepherd of his people. This is in contrast to Egyptian civilization, in which the pharaoh is a living god.
   1. The law code of Hammurabi would be received by the other peoples of the Middle East, who would then create their own legal systems based on that code.
   2. The prologue to Hammurabi's law code makes a powerful statement about the intent of royal government, outlining how kings in the Near East came to see their position.

F. Most of the code involves civil law, not criminal law, which by itself indicates the code's sophistication.
   1. The rules of adoption, divorce, and inheritance were incredibly complicated, particularly those pertaining to women and their rights to administer property.
   2. The laws of contract were extensive, and many cases were adjudicated through compensation with silver bullion.

G. One principle at work in Babylonian criminal law was *lex talionis* ("the law of like punishment"); that is, any injury or death suffered by one family had to be repaid by the offending family with an equal loss.

IV. The other documents that came out of Hammurabi's reign and those of his successors are literary epics, recast from traditional poems and stories of the Sumerians.

A. The most famous of these is the Epic of Gilgamesh, but even before this, there was probably an independent epic of a flood going back very early in Mesopotamian literature. The Sumerian Noah was Ziusudra from the city of Shuruppak. He is befriended by the god Enki, who advises Ziusudra to build an ark.

B. This independent legend was crafted into a full literary epic probably about a generation after the death of Hammurabi. In this Akkadian epic, the Babylonian Noah is Atrahasis ("Surpassing in Wisdom"). This story assumes the form that we know from the later Epic of Gilgamesh.

C. The story of the flood became linked with the hero of Uruk, Gilgamesh, yet in the Babylonian version, it gains a legal and moral aspect that is not seen in the Sumerian tale.

   1. In the Sumerian legend, Gilgamesh is a wild hero of the early dynastic age. In the Babylonian epic, the story is about the responsibility of kingship. Gilgamesh is introduced as a king who does not operate as a shepherd of the people. As a result, the gods create an anti-hero, Enkidu, who is sent to test Gilgamesh.

   2. In the Sumerian epic, Enkidu was merely a servant of Gilgamesh, but in the Babylonian tradition, he is the equal of Gilgamesh. The two undergo various trials and perform great acts as heroes.

   3. In the process of performing their great deeds, Enkidu and Gilgamesh offend the goddess Ishtar. Eventually, the gods judge the two heroes and determine that Enkidu must die.

   4. Enkidu's death then becomes the motive for the second half of the epic, in which Gilgamesh searches for the meaning of life. His search brings him to the Noah figure from the Sumerian tradition, who is known in the Babylonian account as Utanapishtim ("I who found life"). Utanapishtim is the only human to attain immortality through his survival of the flood.

   5. Utanapishtim's retelling of the flood story is a brilliant literary technique, later used by Homer in the *Odyssey*. He tells Gilgamesh that there is no everlasting life for humans.

D. The Epic of Gilgamesh established Akkadian as the literary language of the Near East for centuries to come. Akkadian also served as the diplomatic language for the Middle East for the rest of the Bronze Age and well into the Iron Age.

V. In addition to the legal and literary achievements of Hammurabi's reign, we are now discovering a wide range of other Babylonian scholarship.

   A. Remarkable achievements were made in astronomy and mathematics; indeed, one tablet seems to reveal that the Babylonians knew the Pythagorean Theorem. Babylonian mathematics was premised on a base-60 system, which we still use in reckoning time.

   B. Hammurabi transformed Babylon into the cultural and intellectual center of the Near East. The traditions of administration, military organization, and royal power created by Hammurabi would last, essentially, down to the Ottoman sultanate of the 1920s.

   C. Yet Hammurabi's empire failed to endure. In 1595 B.C., the Hittites of Asia Minor, under King Mursiliš I, sacked Babylon. This weakened the city and enabled its capture by the Kassites, who ruled as a military elite down to about 1157. Even under the Kassite kings, however, the cultural, administrative, and legal institutions of Hammurabi endured.

Further Reading:

A. George, trans. *The Epic of Gilgamesh.*

J. B. Pritchard, *The Ancient Near East: An Anthology of Texts and Pictures.* Vol. I.

Questions to Consider:

1. How effectively was the Babylonian Empire administered? Why did Hammurabi's monarchy set the standard for successive later empires? Why was Hammurabi's law code so important to later generations?

2. How impressive were Babylonian achievements in literature and scholarship? How did these achievements influence later intellectual developments?

Lecture Four—Transcript
Hammurabi's Babylon

In this lecture, I plan to conclude the survey of Mesopotamian civilization in the Bronze Age, and we're going to center on the career and kingdom of Hammurabi, King of Babylon from 1792–1750 B.C. That's an appropriate point to stop this survey because Hammurabi's career and the kingdom he forges really established the cultural underpinnings for Mesopotamian civilization, thereafter. Now, just to review where we've been and where we're going—we started with the emergence of cities in Sumer, starting about 3500 B.C., and that is approximately at the time that bronze becomes widespread in use. We are looking at how the civilization evolves, first through the Sumerians, then the Akkadians and the Babylonians; later on in the course, we'll bring in the Assyrians who carry this civilization down to about 1200 or 1100 B.C., when the Bronze Age collapses and there is a great break in the historical record in the Near East between what is the Bronze Age, and the following, Iron Age. So, Hammurabi's Babylon is in what is known as the middle Bronze Age; it is seen, in many ways, as the pinnacle of Mesopotamian civilization.

Just to review a bit the reasons for Hammurabi's success and, then, what his contributions were, let's recall that he spent 40 years of his reign bringing other regional states under his control. In this sense, he inherited a lot of the advantages of his predecessor, both the neo-Sumerian kings and the Akkadian emperors. There was already something of, what we would call, a service aristocracy—that is, noble families accustomed to serving the crown, serving at court, taking positions as governors, ministers, and having a sense of loyalty to a king, rather than aspiring to be independent dynasts of a city-state. He also inherited the traditions of a very effective army and military discipline, going back into those early city-states and first depicted on the Stele of Vultures and the Standard of Ur. So, there were already these institutions in place. Hammurabi would, of course, build upon them and perfect them in many ways.

He also profited from the fact that the course of the Euphrates apparently shifted during that period of the so-called Amorite migration between 2000 and 1800 B.C. This was the period that saw the displacement of Sumerian by Akkadian as the sole language in southern Mesopotamia. This is a feature of Mesopotamia that will repeat itself—that is, the changing course of the rivers will often leave cities without their ports, and the change of course actually favored Babylon, which emerges as the critical city on the lower Euphrates and the nexus of a whole set of important trade routes. The cities that suffer are cities such as Ur in the far south, where they lose their ports, their access to the sea, and furthermore, the lower courses of the Tigris and Euphrates are silting up, creating a vast marshland that is very often referred to as the Sea Lands, an area where Babylonian tax collectors really venture at their risk. It's a region that became home to people living a type of life, in some ways comparable to the current Marsh Arabs, as they're known in southern Iraq today. So, there were these factors that played to Hammurabi's advantage.

But, Hammurabi was also a very, very skilled diplomat; he managed to isolate his opponents and knock them off individually, and by the year 1760–1770 B.C., he ruled a territorial empire that stretched from the Persian Gulf, almost to the Mediterranean. It may not have been of the same territorial extent of Sargon's empire, but it was certainly better run. That was because of Hammurabi's relentless and meticulous attention and detail. This has been revealed to us not only in his law code, but above all, from a library from the city of Mari on the middle Euphrates that was one of the regional kingdoms that Hammurabi had to knock off. We have letters not only of those regional kings in Mari, but also letters of the governors that Hammurabi appointed. The range of topics raised in these letters and the supervision from Hammurabi and his ministers in Babylon, is astonishing. This may have been true of the Akkadian and Sumerian Empires, we just don't know; we don't have this type of library to document it, so there may be precedence for it.

But what comes through in these administrative documents is a king that, I think, is about as relentless in finding out the details of administration as, say, Philip II of Spain, that classic king of the Spanish Empire who had to worry about every directive coming out of some remote province of Peru, and Hammurabi had that capacity to pay attention to detail. He innovated on the bureaucracy, he added to the writing offices, and he extended the competence of the royal courts and justices. He also had trained a superb army, including a royal army on immediate call, but also levies of soldiers who were drilled at regular intervals. We would call these a kind of militia or, even, some would compare it to a reserve system or a national guard and, again, this was an army that had traditions going back into those early city-states. They are disciplined, heavy infantry, backed up with bowmen and javelin men—that is, skirmishers. There is no evidence that his armies were equipped with the light chariots that come to characterize warfare in the late Bronze Age. One argument is that Hammurabi's state was toppled or actually conquered by an outside dynasty, the Kassites, in 1540 B.C., in part because the Babylonians failed to keep pace in this military technology that produced the so-called light chariot, which is a new weapon on the battlefield we'll discuss later on in this course. Even so, it is an impressive state.

We know it through two really remarkable sets of documents that have come down to us; one of them is his law code, which survives almost in tact, 282 laws. It was obviously carved in many multiple copies and set up throughout the Babylonian Empire. The copy we have comes from Elam; it was actually carried off as a war prize in the 1150s when the Elamites came in. You usually come in and queue every couple of hundred years and sack Mesopotamian cities and it was carried off and used as some kind of war trophy. And so, this 8-foot monument actually survives in tact with all the laws. There are several important features about these laws and I think, in examining the laws of Hammurabi, you can get some sort of sense of the sophistication of Babylonian civilization that now rested on a very ancient tradition that went back 17 centuries of urban literate life, in one way or another. For one, the law code does rest on earlier legal precedents. We know there was a law code issued in the Neo-Sumerian Empire by Ur-nammu. There was another one issued about 100 or 75 years later by a fellow named Lipith-Ishtar who was one of these strong men ruling in the period before the emergence of Hammurabi. That code was in Sumerian and survives in fragments. Both that code and the early Sumerian code show many features in common with Hammurabi's code; they just don't survive intact, although they have preambles rather similar to Hammurabi's.

What is important about Hammurabi's Code are two points; first, the code was issued in Akkadian. That is, in the vernacular language—it was not issued in Sumerian as all previous codes were. That was a major triumph— that is, perfecting the Akkadian language to handle such complicated legal issues, litigation, many of the terms have to be adapted from Sumerian and in many ways, Sumerian law had to be adjusted with what would have been customary Babylonian law. We'd have a better sense of this if more of the Sumerian codes had survived, but it's clear that Hammurabi's code was not some sort of mindless translation of Sumerian prototype. There was a lot of careful legal thinking that went into framing those laws. To be sure, the code is not comparable to, say, the *Corpus Juris Civilis* of the Emperor Justinian, that brilliant code that includes a whole section on jurisprudence. The code is far less ambitious for Hammurabi; it's a listing of the various customary laws. Nonetheless, the laws are carefully listed by categories and those laws are often royal rulings on customary matters, both in civil and criminal litigation.

They are organized in such a way that the royal judges can use this code to judge cases by analogy and to invent new law. In that sense, this is a major step forward that it has not only been translated in Akkadian, but it has been updated and put in a form so that this law could be applied to everyday situations. This is not an academic exercise and it is clearly a law code that Hammurabi intended to apply to his entire empire, to all of his subjects. That is a major achievement and it links the monarchy with law and with the justice from the gods, and this is a very ancient tradition going back in Mesopotamian civilization; it's a feature of Mesopotamian kingship and the kingships that come to characterize the Near East—that is, the great king is the shepherd of the people. This is an image that is used going back to early Sumerian text; it's then used by Hammurabi, it's used by the Assyrian kings, and the Neo-Babylonian kings, such as Nebuchadrezzar—all of them style themselves in this fashion.

That is a feature of Mesopotamian political and legal life that will be different from Egypt—which we will be turning to very soon—in which the Egyptian pharaoh is a god. Certainly, by Dynasty III, he is the living god Horus, and while Egypt does have laws, it's hardly a chaotic society. Nonetheless, the kind of legal thinking, the necessity for putting together law codes administered by a monarch, does not come until relatively late in Egypt. It really begins in the Middle Kingdom. It doesn't have that same tradition and you can understand why. I mean the god king pharaoh is law; he will utter with the powers of the god, Ptah, what is appropriate for his subjects. That is an important distinction to make between Mesopotamian civilization and Egyptian civilization, and it will be the law code of Hammurabi far more than any kind of traditions in Egypt that will be received by the other peoples of the Middle East who will then create their own legal systems based on that law code. That will include, for instance, the kings of the Hittites who come to rule in Asia Minor in the middle and late Bronze Age and are the great rivals to Imperial Egypt. It's found in the law codes of the people known as the Hurrians, people of unknown origin whose language is unrelated to any other language, who dwell in northern Mesopotamia—what is now eastern Syria. We suspect much of this legal tradition all fed into what we suspect may be the law codes of the Elamites; it's just that we can't read Elamite very well. So, the law code of Hammurabi has much wider implications than just for Mesopotamian civilization, but it becomes the basis for legal systems used throughout the Near East.

You can capture the sense of Hammurabi's responsibility in this code in the prologue. And, as I say, it's quite traditional in many ways, but it's worth reading—at least what Hammurabi liked to project to his subjects and what his mission was in carrying out this code, and it runs in this fashion:

> When the lofty Anu, King of the Annuaki [who are the gods of the high sky] and Enlil lord of the heavens and earth, he who determines the destiny of the land, committed the rule of all mankind to Marduk [Marduk is the national god of Babylon, who was really a latecomer into the Mesopotamian pantheon]. When they [that is, the gods,] pronounce the lofty name of Babylon, when they made it famous among the quarters of the word and in the midst established an everlasting kingdom, whose foundations were firm as heaven and earth. At the time, Anu and Enlil called me, Hammurabi [these are the two supreme gods in the Sumerian Akkadian tradition]. Lord of the heaven, the benign creator god seated on the distant heavens and Enlil who is the creative power of the winds, and the force that orders the universe called me, Hammurabi, the exalted prince the worshipper of the gods, to cause justice to prevail in the land, to destroy the wicked and the evil, to prevent the strong from oppressing the weak, to enlighten the land, and to further the welfare of the people. Hammurabi the governor, named by Enlil am I, who brought about plenty and abundance.

It is a very powerful statement of at least the intent of royal government; whether it fell short or not in the actual practice is a rather moot point. It is important that this is how kings in the Near East come to see their position.

The code itself, to mention briefly about it, is a remarkable document and shows some really sophisticated legal thinking. For one, the vast majority of it is, what we would call, civil law, not criminal law, and that alone is an index of the sophistication of the code. The code reveals several important aspects about the society. One is the incredibly complicated rules of divorce and inheritance, and especially rules of property, that women could administer and powers of inheritance—what would be called in English, common law, the rights of dower and curtsy. That is, the woman has an interest of the income of the husband's property after his death or in the event of a divorce. There are very strict laws on inheritance, and in adoption, you cannot disinherit adopted children. This is laid out in very sophisticated language. The laws of contract are extensive with lots of cases of adjudication by settlement, by compensation; silver is clearly in large supply because payments are often done in silver.

This would be bullion measured out in the classic weight system known as talents, mina, and shekels; a weight system that might be familiar to people reading the Old Testament where this system of accounting occurs. It doesn't represent coins; it represents a weight of bullion. Furthermore, there's a considerable amount of legislation regarding the property of slaves and, actually, how they are to be treated and from what we can discern from the codes and the economic documents, there a number of slaves in Babylon, many of them attached to the temple used for specialized crafts, such as weaving, textile ceramics, and the like; some are agriculturists. These slaves are obviously coming into Babylon through a well-established slave trade, as well as the wars of conquest.

On the criminal side of the law code, it's a little disconcerting to most moderns to read Babylonian criminal law. Some scholars have argued that the Babylonian criminal law is actually harsher than the earlier Sumerian law and this is really based on rather limited evidence. There are two principles working away in this criminal law and you have to understand why they operate this way. One would be what the Romans called the *lex talionis*—that is, the law of like punishment. That would be expressed by any kind of insult or injury that especially results in bodily harm or death to the member of a family. That had to be repaid by the offending family with an equal loss; so if some fellow knocked out the right eye of the member of another family, that fellow was destined to lose his right eye—not his left eye, his right eye. The code is very, very specific. If you take out both eyes, then you've exceeded the law and then we've got a blood feud.

The whole principle of the Babylonian code is to intervene and make sure that the families accept royal justice as the final mediation, and in the process of doing this, the penalties must be harsh to satisfy the aggrieved family. Furthermore, Babylonians do not have the luxury of maintaining a prison system; in fact, no ancient society does. Penalties tend to be harsh and corporal, part of it is to set an example. Part of it is simply a fact that you cannot afford to maintain large prisons of people; you don't have the surplus food to do so. So, the Babylonian code isn't particularly any harsher in this regard than many medieval laws or laws running really into early modern Europe. It's only with the remarkable agricultural revolution in the 18th century where this begins to change, in a country such as England. So, that side of the code might be a little off-putting. Even so, there are some aspects of Babylonian law, and an example comes to mind that is a little distressing on the criminal side. There is a tendency not to distinguish intent of an action from the actual action and many cases of negligence and trespass are treated, essentially, in the category of felonies. One of my favorite laws in the code is that if an architect builds a house out of one of these mud brick constructions, and the house collapses and kills a member of the family, then that architect is put into a house and the house is collapsed on him—that's applying the *lex talionis* to its logical conclusion.

There's another set of literature that comes out of Babylon from Hammurabi's reign and that of his successors and continues under the reign of these Kassite rulers, conquerors from Iran who move in sometime around 1540 B.C. and take over Babylon and rule down to 1157 B.C. The Kassites actually maintain Babylonian institutions and civilization; they impose themselves as, essentially, a political military lead. These are the recasting of the traditional poems and stories from the Sumerians into literary epics. The most famous of these is the *Epic of Gilgamesh*, but even before the *Epic of Gilgamesh*, there was probably an independent epic on the so-called flood story—a traditional story going back very early in Mesopotamian literature.

There's evidence of it in the Sumerian tradition, and the Sumerian Noah is a fellow called Ziusudra. There are reports of him; he comes from the city of Shuruppak in Sumer and he is befriended by the god Enki, or Ea in his Babylonian name. Enki preserves him from the destruction of the flood by advising this Sumerian Noah to build an ark. This is clearly the basis of the biblical stories associated with Noah. That independent legend, or series of stories, is crafted into a full literary epic probably about a generation after the death of Hammurabi. We don't know who the author is; it is an Akkadian epic in which the Babylonian's Noah's name is Atrahasis, which means surpassing all in wisdom. By the time the story gets to the Babylonians, it is associated with a certain amount of the moral worth of this Babylonian Noah; this is why he is preserved by the favor of the god Enki, his piety.

The story begins to assume the form that we know from the later *Epic of Gilgamesh*, which is preserved centuries later in an Assyrian copy written during the reign of Ashurbanipal II in the 7th century B.C. It's really the Babylonian poets writing in Akkadian who turn this distant Sumerian legend into the literary masterpiece, which then becomes part of the wider *Epic of Gilgamesh*. That is quite an achievement because, again, it was a matter of adapting the Akkadian language and its peculiar verse form to recast a story that went back to the Sumerians, an entirely different language structure with an entirely different metrical system, and it's an indication of the literary activity going on at the time of Hammurabi and his successors. That story of the flood becomes linked with a story associated with the hero of Uruk, Gilgamesh—Bilgames as he would be known in Sumerian. We have stories of Bilgames, the Sumerian version of the hero, going back very early in the tablets. Some of these were rewritten in the time of Shulgi, the second king of the Third Dynasty of Ur; they have now been translated and made available, and in very good modern Penguin Books translation. Again, it's the Babylonian poets who take this Sumerian tale and turn it into the epic that has come down to us through an Assyrian copy, but is again an Akkadian masterpiece.

It is a literary epic. It is not a set of oral traditions that are recited, but it was written as a single piece; it survives on twelve tablets from the library of Ashurbanipal II and in this revised version of the epic—and it has been considerably revised and we now can demonstrate that by looking at the Sumerian originals—the story assumes a whole new legal and moral side to it, which you don't get in the Sumerian tales. In the Sumerian tales, Gilgamesh is a wild and woolly hero of the early dynastic age of beating up King Agga of Kish, going off to the Land of the Cedars, where he encounters this creature known as Humbaba, or in Sumerian, Huwawa, who's really treacherously lured into giving up his powers and is murdered. He very much is a figure of some sort of distant heroic age. In the Babylonian epic—written for the type of sophisticated audience of Hammurabi's day—the story is about the responsibilities of kingship.

Gilgamesh is introduced as a king who does not operate as a shepherd of the people, who does not follow the rules or the prologue of Hammurabi, and as a result, the gods create an antihero in the form of Enkidu who is sent to test Gilgamesh, overthrow Gilgamesh if necessary. That figure in the Sumerian epic was known as just a servant of Gilgamesh, he was not an important figure, whereas in the Babylonian tradition, he becomes the equal of Gilgamesh, the best of friends; there is a match up between the two, they have a contest, and it's a standoff, and Enkidu and Gilgamesh become best buddies and then go through a series of tests and trials, which are again recast in a very different tone from what we have in the Sumerian originals. These are trials of going out to the great distant western lands, the so-called region of the Cedars, which would today be Lebanon. In those regions, the heroes perform great acts as individual heroes, instead of representing some early trade mission—the way it's described in the Sumerian account—and in the process of conducting these great deeds they offend the god Ishtar, in Sumerian, Ianna. She is thwarted on several occasions, Gilgamesh rejects a marriage proposal, and eventually, the gods judge the two heroes and judge that Enkidu must die for the offense to the goddess. He dies a long and wasting death.

That death becomes the motive for the second half of the literary epic and causes Gilgamesh to search for the meaning of life, or some kind of everlasting life, and that brings him to that figure out of the Sumerian tradition, that Noah-type figure who is known in the Babylonian account as Utanapishtim, I who found life. He is a figure who is the only mortal who ever attained immortality because he survived the flood. The journey to this distant region—Dilmum is what it's called in the epic—may actually historically represent the island of Bahrein. Gilgamesh arrives there, he meets Utanapishtim who tells him the story of the flood, and it's a brilliant literary technique of retelling the epic of the flood within the greater *Epic of Gilgamesh*. It's the kind of technique, for instance, you encounter in Homer, in which Odysseus reports his travels to King Alkinoos in the *Odyssey*. You're dealing with really a high class of writing here.

Gilgamesh is curious about why the hubris resulted in the arrogance of his friend Enkidu in his death and not Gilgamesh, and Utanapishtim tells him the truth—there is no afterlife. There is no everlasting life; when one dies, they go down to the world of the dead. The Babylonian conception of the underworld is not extremely inviting. Apparently, the dead put on these sort of feather-type costumes and they sit around and eat mud. It's not a thrilling idea, and he tells Gilgamesh this is just not in the cards, but if you do wish to find the gift of everlasting life, you can find it in this flower, which Gilgamesh picks and then inadvertently loses on his way back to Uruk to bring this gift to mankind. It's really a remarkable retelling, a moral epic, which is a retelling of all these heroic deeds of a distant Sumerian past, now recast in a literary form for a sophisticated audience.

It established Akkadian as the literary language of the Near East for centuries to come. It is the literary language for all serious production. It is the diplomatic language of the Middle East through the whole of the rest of the Bronze Age and well into the Iron Age. The Egyptian pharaohs of the New Kingdom conducted their administration and diplomacy in Akkadian, not in Egyptian. Furthermore, in addition to the legal achievements of Hammurabi's reign and these wonderful literary productions, there is a whole range of scholarship that is now coming down to us, which reveals the type of activity going on in Babylon. This includes some remarkable achievements in astronomy, the predicting of solar and lunar eclipses, a mathematics that, based on one tablet, seems to indicate that the Babylonians knew the Pythagorean Theorem. They also are able to take cubed and square roots and they base their system on a base 60 system that we still use today every time we look at a watch; that division of time into 60s goes back to an old Babylonian reckoning. They're also quite impressive in other areas of their geometry and some of this mathematical tradition was eventually transmitted to the Greek world and it's upon this mathematical system that the Greeks build their own achievements.

So, Hammurabi turns Babylon into a great city, a city of a huge population, which by the time of 600 B.C. was a city without parallel anywhere in the Near East; it's a tremendous population. At one point, it may even achieve a million residents by some people's reckoning. It is the cultural and intellectual center of the Near East and it will be seen that way by successive conquerors—first, the Kassites who come in and take over Babylon and later, the Assyrian Emperors and the Persian kings—the great king of Persia who saw Babylon, essentially, as his cultural center.

Furthermore, the traditions of administration, of military organization, the power of the king, and the policy of the king to administer justice—these are, essentially, the job description and the institutions of the great king of the Near East. Hammurabi, in effect, creates that job of great king, a job that will last right down, essentially, to the Ottoman Sultanate of the 1920s. Now, his empire failed to endure. In 1595 B.C., the Hittites of Asia Minor, under the King Mursiliš I sack Babylon, give an attack coming out of left field—or west field, as it were—probably simply because Mursiliš thought he was a great conqueror, something to do. That capture of the city weakened Babylon, so it was captured by the Kassites who ruled as a military elite; these were people from the Iranian highlands, probably starting around 1540 B.C., but under the Kassite kings, the cultural and administrative and legal institutions endured. Akkadian had already been established as the literary language of the Near East and so the Kassites, just as later conquerors, will be seduced by this Babylonian civilization and will perpetuate and enrich it, and this becomes the governing principle in Near Eastern civilization down to the time of Alexander the Great.

Lecture Five
Egypt in the Pyramid Age

Scope: In about 3100 B.C. Narmer (Menes), king of Upper Egypt, conquered the lower kingdom; henceforth, sacral kings, later known as *pharaohs*, ruled over Egypt. Narmer and his successors ruled from a great court at Memphis, where regional lords, or *nomarchs*, sought royal patronage and acted as the king's agents in *nomes* and villages. The first pharaohs mobilized labor and resources to construct palaces, sanctuaries, and funerary complexes around the *mastaba*, or royal mortuary. Royal demands and patronage drove the Egyptians to leap from Neolithic villages to urban civilization in the early Archaic Period (c. 3100–2700 B.C.). Scribes adapted pictograms into hieroglyphic writing to facilitate royal recordkeeping. The pharaohs of Dynasties III and IV, during the Old Kingdom (c. 2700–2181 B.C.), presided over a mature civilization. Without need of officials or soldiers, the god-kings at Memphis mobilized national resources to build pyramids. The pyramid epitomized the power of the pharaoh, but the *nomarchs* gained power by furnishing the labor and materiel for pyramid construction. The later pharaohs of Dynasties V and VI had to contend with regional aristocrats who controlled leading sanctuaries. Royal pyramids declined in quality and size as *nomarchs* withdrew from Memphis and established their own courts and funerary complexes in their native *nomes*. With the death of Pepi II in about 2185 B.C., the pharaohs of Memphis lost control over the Nile valley for the next 150 years.

Outline

I. This lecture looks at developments in Egypt in the Bronze Age, taking place at about the same time as those we have seen in Mesopotamian civilization.

   A. First, we shall explore Egypt in the Early Dynastic, or Archaic, Period and the Old Kingdom (c. 3100–2181 B.C.). Much of our information for this period comes from Manetho, writing in Greek circa 280 B.C., who established a sequence for the dynasties.

B. Later lectures will deal with the Middle Kingdom and the New Kingdom of the Late Bronze Age.

II. We shall begin with some of the basic features of early Egyptian civilization.

A. Conditions in the Nile valley were different from those in Mesopotamia. Crops and animals, such as cattle, sheep, barley, and wheat, were brought into the Nile valley from the Near East between 5000–4500 B.C., when movement across the Sinai was much easier.

B. As noted earlier, the Nile did not assume its current course until after the drying up of the Sahara, which took place between 8000–4500 B.C. Before the Nile acquired its current form, farming and habitation in the Nile valley were limited.

C. The pattern of development into intensive agriculture in the Nile valley paralleled what we know of that development in the regions of the Tigris and Euphrates. However, as noted, cultivation in Egypt in this period was much easier than it was in Mesopotamia.

D. The Nile also promoted unity of the Egyptian people, starting around 3100 B.C. and lasting down to Alexander the Great. The Nile was the basis for all directions and the Egyptians' understanding of the world.

III. Up to 3100 B.C., Egyptian civilization consisted of sophisticated Neolithic villages that had formed into *nomes*, regional districts, ruled by *nomarchs*. Each *nome* had market towns and cult sites but no true cities. This situation changed dramatically when Narmer (probably Menes in Manetho's account) united Upper and Lower Egypt.

A. Narmer originally ruled in the southern regions of the Nile valley, called Upper Egypt; he conquered Lower Egypt, that is, the region of the Delta and the area around what is today Cairo. This unification is celebrated on a ceremonial object called the Narmer Palette. Henceforth, all the land north of the first cataract of the Nile was constituted as a single kingdom.

B. Narmer built the city of Memphis at the juncture of the two kingdoms, close to where modern Cairo is, and it became the political and religious capital of Egypt throughout most of antiquity.

C. The pharaohs of the First and Second Dynasties exercised power by establishing a great capital city that would attract the various *nomarchs* to royal service.

D. Egypt also advanced quickly to a literate stage, although scholars still debate how hieroglyphics were invented.

IV. The development of this early sacral monarchy reached its climax in the rulers of the Old Kingdom, particularly those of Dynasties III and IV. The greatest realization of this development was the pyramid.

A. Most of the pyramids were constructed from 2600–2300 B.C. The first was built by a pharaoh of the Third Dynasty, Zoser, at Sakkara. Its structure consists of a succession of diminishing mastabas.

B. Within 40 years, the classic sheer-faced pyramids were constructed. Two of these were erected by Snefru of Dynasty IV at Dahshur.

C. Snefru's successors, Khufu, Khafre, and Menkaura, built the three Great Pyramids at Gizeh.

V. The pyramid of Khufu sums up the achievements of the early Old Kingdom.

A. By the time Khufu built his pyramid, he was regarded as a living god—Horus. Since the First Dynasty, all pharaohs had also been associated with Ptah, the god of wisdom and the patron god of Memphis.

B. The tomb served as the burial place of not only the pharaoh but also his family, attendants, and loyal *nomarchs*. The complex was surrounded by an enormous temnos wall that encircled the sacred area.

C. The Great Pyramid of Khufu is a testimony to royal power and the ability to mobilize labor and resources.

D. The successors of Khufu, Khafre and Menkaura, also built pyramids, but these were considerably smaller. The pyramids represent the pinnacle of Egyptian civilization and the sacral power of the pharaoh, but they also probably resulted in the failure of the monarchy.

E. Thus, the god-kings in Memphis lost power in the Nile valley. Unlike their contemporaries in Mesopotamia, these pharaohs had not developed the institutions necessary to impose their authority.

  1. As Mesopotamia began to achieve unity under the Akkadian emperors, power in Egypt was divided among different *nomarchs*.

  2. The culmination of this process came in the Sixth Dynasty with the exceedingly long reign of Pepi II (2275–2185 B.C.). By the time of Pepi's death, the pharaohs in Memphis were no longer able to exercise authority over the Nile valley.

  3. For the next 150 years, Egypt was fragmented under the rule of independent *nomarchs*. Four regional powers ultimately emerged: in Memphis, in Upper Egypt at Edfu and Abydos, and in Thebes, home of the dynasty that would reunify Egypt and institute the brilliant Middle Kingdom.

Further Reading:

Dieter Arnold, *Building in Egypt: Pharaonic Stone Masonry.*

W. B. Emery, *Archaic Egypt.*

Questions to Consider:

1. What conditions in the Late Neolithic Age led to the emergence of an Egyptian kingdom under Narmer and his successors in the Archaic Age (3100–2700 B.C.)? Why were royal patronage and fiscal demands so important in directing cultural progress?

2. How did pharaohs exercise their power in the Nile valley? Why was the court at Memphis the center of Egyptian civilization? How were the pyramids a testimony to the success of royal power in the Old Kingdom?

Lecture Five—Transcript
Egypt in the Pyramid Age

In this lecture, I plan to look at developments in Egypt during the Bronze Age, even though Egypt did not acquire bronze until close to 2000 B.C. Nonetheless, we're going to look at Egyptian developments which were contemporary with those developments in Mesopotamian civilization from 3500 B.C. down to about 1200 B.C.—that is the period of the Bronze Age usually divided into an early, middle, and late period. After 1200 B.C., there will be a series of migrations; there will be an overthrow of the political order of the late Bronze Age. This will represent a major break in civilization, which is often compared to the break at the end of the Roman Empire when the Roman Empire begins to fragment in the 5th and 6th centuries A.D. So, that period of the end of the Bronze Age, the beginning of the Iron Age, is our stopping point on these next three lectures.

What I plan to do in this lecture is to lecture on Egypt in the so-called Early Dynastic or Archaic period and Old Kingdom, and that is a period running from 3100 B.C. to roughly about 2200 or 2100 B.C. Our chronology in early Egypt is a bit uncertain and, usually, these dates can be adjusted anywhere from 50 to 75 years.

Even so, the sequence is very well known because of several reasons; one is the archeology where we know the material culture very well. The other is there was a Greek author writing in around 280 B.C., Manetho, who wrote the *Dynasties of Egypt*, arranged them in their current form that we have today. One of the problems is that he uses a Greek rendition of the name and, very often, it's difficult to equate that Greek version of a name to an Egyptian pharaoh known from the hieroglyphic records. That's because Egyptian pharaohs had, literally, five different names for different ritual purposes; they had a personal name, which is known as an Osiris name, a Horus name, and two other ritual names. Even so, we do have a pretty good idea of the sequence of the dynasties and we will be looking at Dynasties I through VI in this particular lecture. Then, we'll deal with what is known as the Middle Kingdom and then the New Kingdom, or empire, which comes in the late Bronze Age.

First, it's important for us to recall some of the basic features of earliest Egyptian civilization and a point I made in the very first lecture of this series of comparing the Nile to the Tigris and the Euphrates. One of the reasons why I started with Mesopotamian civilization is that it is in Mesopotamia that the earliest intensive agriculture in cities emerged. It is also where literacy began and, therefore, the basis of an urban literate civilization emerged in Sumer between 3500 and 3100 B.C. In the Nile Valley, the conditions were different. I noted that the crops that were brought in from the Near East to the Nile—that would be cattle, sheep, barley, wheat—these are not native to the Nile Valley and they were brought into Egypt somewhere between 5000 and 4500 B.C., when movement across the Sinai was much easier. It's only with the drying up of the Sahara Desert—and that's a long process, perhaps beginning as early as 8000 B.C. and only ending somewhere around 4500 B.C., when the Nile assumed its current course, which is essentially a canyon. The riverbed is a canyon and the river's flowing through the middle of the desert with no tributaries of any note, until about 60 miles before the river reaches the Mediterranean Sea and then the river branches out into a series of tributaries. That region is known as a delta, which looks like the inverted Greek letter Delta or the equivalent of our D.

So, that river valley system of the Nile did not acquire its form until sometime between 5000 and 4500 and, as I mentioned, before that date, farming and habitation in the Nile Valley was very limited. I further noted that the pattern of development into intensive agriculture could be traced in the Nile, more or less, paralleling what we know in the Tigris and Euphrates. However, in the Nile, I noted that it was easier. The Nile is extremely predictable; its flood patterns can be learned very quickly. Greek authors, starting with the historian Herodotus in the 5th century B.C., wrote with envy of how easy it was to cultivate the Nile in comparison to other river systems. That it overflows and deposits this rich thick silt and the population can move in as the river recedes and plants and get a very high yield on its return.

However, the river has other important consequences. One is it promoted unity from the start. One of the features of Egyptian civilization is its homogenous unity that starts from 3100 B.C. and lasts down through the entire of the ancient period, down to Alexander the Great and beyond, into the Roman and Byzantine eras. The second important point about the Nile is it becomes the basis of all directions and understanding of the world. It's demonstrated very well in how the Egyptians give directions. To the ancient Egyptians, to go upstream, that is to go up the Nile, means to go south; to go downstream means to go north. The Egyptians could only conceive of the world as comprising the Nile in the middle, with all the other lands around them, and since Egypt doesn't receive rain, Egypt is favored by the gods and rain is sent to the foreigners. One of the curiosities for the

Egyptians is when the armies of Thutmose III in the 15th century B.C. reached the Euphrates, they encountered a river that flowed south instead of north, and the only way the Egyptians could express this was by saying that it was circling water, which goes downstream when it's going upstream.

So, it gives you some idea of the directional sense of the Egyptians. It also reveals the fact that Egypt was a society that was protected by deserts; it could not easily be invaded. There was only limited contact coming in from the north by sea through the delta. And that from the start, in Egyptian history, whatever the origins of these people, the Egyptians very quickly coalesced into a homogenous population speaking a single language, which is a Hamitic-based language that is still represented in its modern descendent, Coptic, which is a liturgical language of Christians in Egypt today.

From the start in Egyptian civilization, there was a base of unity; there was a base of cultural and linguistic homogeneity. There was the unity of the Nile. Some historians would go so far as to say that the Nile promoted a wider vision, that it influenced their worldview of a divine order that was eternal. The god Aton-Ra appears in the primeval muck; he orders the world. There are no creation epics in the Mesopotamian guise, where the gods must fight forces of chaos where you get the great heroes such as Gilgamesh. Quite the contrary, Egypt is an eternal order; it is one in which the divine and the mortal are intertwined and it has quite a different outlook from Mesopotamian civilization and that basis allows for the creation of, really, the earliest kingdom we know of in human history.

As I mentioned, again, in the very first lecture in this series, that Egyptian civilization up to 3100 B.C. could be characterized as very sophisticated Neolithic villages, which had formed into *nomes*, as they're called, these are regional districts. This is the Greek word for the name, *nomarch*—that is, the ruler of *nome*. In each *nome*, there were market towns and cult sites; these were essentially the villages and market towns of the region, but not true cities. They were nothing like the great walled cities of contemporary Sumer. Well, that changed dramatically around 3100 B.C. when a king called Narmer, probably Menes in the Greek account, united Upper and Lower Egypt. Upper Egypt consisted of the southern regions, the regions of mostly the Nile Valley. This King Narmer ruled at the city of Abydos and Edfu, which is very far up the Nile. He conquered the Lower Kingdom— that is, the region of the delta and the region around Cairo today and this is celebrated on a famous monument known as Narmer's Palette, which is some kind of ceremonial object. Also, he united the two kingdoms under his rule. He married a northern princess, a lady of the northern kingdom, and henceforth Egypt is ruled as a single kingdom that is all the land north of that First Cataract—that is, the great falls on the Nile are now constituted as a single kingdom. This is eight centuries before Sargon forged the first territorial empire in Mesopotamia. It is an extraordinary achievement. It is sometimes put by historians that Egypt leaped from a group of Neolithic villages to a colossus overnight, compliments of this royal conquest.

We call these Egyptian kings pharaohs; that's a tradition that goes back to the Hebrew Bible. It's a Hebrew rendition of a term *per-aa* which means "great house," and it's a term that technically applies to the rulers in later Egyptian history, where it was a term used instead of the name of the pharaoh because the pharaoh's name was too sacred to pronounce. It's a euphemism of a sort. It's a special royal title. The earlier kings in Egypt apparently might not have used this title, but for convenience, we designate all the monarchs of early Egypt pharaohs because it does denote very much the sacral powers that these kings had from the start. Narmer, in some ways, rules his kingdom as a composite of two realms; there are essentially two administrations, in some ways.

Nonetheless, he builds the city of Memphis, which is at the juncture of the two kingdoms close to where modern Cairo is today, and Memphis becomes the political and religious capital of Egypt through most of antiquity. That is the capital through which one will rule Egypt effectively. He takes the two crowns of Egypt—this is the white crown of Upper Egypt and the red crown of Lower Egypt—the two crowns are combined into a single crown. He goes through great efforts to use personnel from the lower kingdom at his court. The way these early pharaohs of this First Dynasty and the succeeding Second Dynasty—which is a family closely related to Narmer—the way they exercise power is by establishing a great capital city that attracts the various nomarchs, the regional lords from the districts to royal service.

The genius of early Egyptian civilization was that it centered around the god king, who in earliest times was seen as the son of Horus, the falcon god in Egyptian mythology. His destiny was to join the gods. There were all sorts of activities associated at court, and power and the favor of the kind enabled nomarchs to establish their power in their districts. So, the idea was to attract the local elites to the great court and rule Egypt through that personal connection. That meant that Egyptian pharaohs, from the start, did not need the types of bureaucrats and soldiers that are seen in Mesopotamia; it was done through personal connections. For instance, there were multiple marriages, a harem was kept by the pharaoh; titles of rank were awarded to these nomarchs. And, from what we can tell in this early archaic period or early dynastic period in the Old Kingdom, most of the nobles really made the effort to get to the court at Memphis and get in on the great patronage that pharaoh commanded as the god king of these two lands. That meant that the pharaoh became the lynch pin in cultural developments.

There's an argument to be made that the development of royal centers, and also the development of great shrines built with masonry architecture—that is, the great temple complexes such as at Heliopolis or Memphis or Abydos in Upper Egypt—all of that was fueled by the need of the pharaohs to project their royal sacral power, to gain the favor of the gods, and that forced economic development in Egypt. That is why Egyptian civilization advanced so quickly to an urban stage.

It also advanced quickly to a literate stage. In the lecture on writing, I noted that there is still a debate going on among Egyptian scholars about exactly how the hieroglyphics were invented. They go back to early pictograms of the Pre-Literate phase. Naqada pottery, too, around 3600–3300 B.C. showed totems that are symbols that evolved into symbols of the hieroglyphics. The system of writing in Egypt is different from Mesopotamian cuneiform because the signs represent consonantal clusters without vowels, so the principle is not the same, whereas in Sumerian, those pictograms represented a precise sound, vowel, and consonant. The argument that's often made by some scholars is that the application of these pictograms to writing was under the influence of the pharaoh who realized the value of writing because of the Sumerian communities that are known to have been in delta Egypt at the time, opening up trade connections with Narmer and his successors of the First and Second Dynasty, and the king was the one who propelled the development of the hieroglyphs in order to put up monumental inscriptions, to keep records. And, that the idea of writing, the applying, the extension of those pictograms to writing, it's sometimes argued that it was not only the initiative of the king, but also this Sumerian influence.

Furthermore, the kings put on enormous building projects in the First and Second Dynasties. These are the so-called mastaba; these are often limestone monuments, they are funerary monuments. There's a subterranean chamber, on top of it is built an elaborate rectangular building in limestone that is in masonry, not in mud brick, to protect the tomb. From the start, the pharaohs were awarded rich grave goods for the next lives. The development of this early sacral monarchy reaches its climax in the kings of the Old Kingdom, particularly of Dynasties III and IV, which are extremely well known. This saw its greatest development in the pyramid, and in some ways, the pyramid can be taken as the culmination, the epitomes of cultural development and royal power in early Egypt.

These are remarkable buildings; there was nothing like this at the time. Most of these pyramids are being constructed somewhere between, maybe, 2600 and 2300 B.C. In size, they absolutely dwarf anything being built in Mesopotamia. The first of these buildings was constructed by a pharaoh of the Third Dynasty, Zoser; his architect, in effect, adapted the construction of a mastaba. He superimposed ever declining, smaller mastabas on top of each other to create the great step pyramid at Sakkara, which is now a suburb of Cairo. That pyramid was the resting place of King Zoser. It is a stunning achievement in masonry architecture. Its dimensions alone are impressive. It's 411 by 358 feet at its base. It is over 204 feet high. There are millions of small blocks of stone that were used to construct it and within 40 years, classic pyramids are built—that is, the sheer-faced pyramids we usually associate with Egyptian pyramids. The first great achievement was by the first pharaoh of the Fourth Dynasty, one from the succeeding family to Zoser's family, King Snefru; he built two of them at Dashur. Then, Snefru's successors, particularly the pharaohs Khufu, Khafre, and Menkaura, built the three great pyramids at Gizeh, which are usually looked upon as one of the Seven Wonders of the Ancient World, and rightly so.

Let us take the pyramid of Khufu, as a way of summing up the achievements of the early Old Kingdom. By the time that Khufu came to build this pyramid in the Fourth Dynasty, he was already regarded as a living god, he was the god Horus. Since the First Dynasty when the capital was established at Memphis, all pharaohs were also associated with the powers of Ptah—that is, the god of wisdom, the patron god of Memphis—and that included the power of *ma'at*, justice, *hu*, utterance of authority, of logic, and *sia*, intelligence and perception.

Furthermore, the pharaoh was conceived as having, in effect, two souls. One was the body itself, *ba*. That was the body that would be laid to rest in the royal tomb. The other was the *ka*, or the soul, that joined the gods in the other world. Therefore, the burial of that body of the pharaoh—and that meant not only burying the pharaoh, but his family, his attendants, all pyramids, all royal complexes, even the mastaba—had this enormous, what the Greeks would call *temnos* wall, an encircling wall that cut off the sacred area. There were numerous burials and all those nomarchs and nobles who served loyally, the pharaoh expected to have their tombs there and were going to join the pharaoh in the next life. That was one of the reasons why these guys hung around Memphis and did the pharaoh's bidding. So, the pyramid was essentially the lynch pin of a much larger complex of royal burials and noble burials and they were all seen as religious sanctuaries.

Furthermore, Egyptians constantly stress—and, again, we're dealing with royal records on this, but it seems to reflect the society's attitude—the veneration and the maintenance of these tombs were very important. When these tombs were broken into and they were despoiled by thieves, that was seen as an act of sacrilege that occurred during a period of weakness, and many Egyptians would attribute the anger of the gods as visiting plagues and disasters on Egypt, as a result of that violation of those royal tombs. That is a thing that is repeated constantly in the literature.

In any case, Khufu constructed the great pyramid, the greatest of them all, and what is important to know about this pyramid is that it is a testimony to royal power and mobilization of labor and resources. He did not have to hire an army. He did not need a huge bureaucracy because Egypt was essentially protected; it had limited contact with the outside world. The trade was easily controlled in the delta, whatever outside contact came in there. And so, Khufu could put all of his resources on building this great monument, which doubled as a religious national monument, as well. It was the peculiar social structure of Egypt that allowed this to take place. Contrary to what many might think, these pyramids were not built by slaves; they were built by the peasant population of Egypt. This was possible because anywhere from five to six months of the year, the Nile flooded and the peasants didn't really have much to do except wait for the waters to recede and then move in and start planting wherever the silt was deposited. So, the period was not some sort of white elephant project; I mean there was lots of labor available and what the pharaoh was going to do was put that labor to work.

Furthermore, the number of men who would be engaged on the great pyramid, it's usually estimated that during the work season of three to four months, maybe a 100,000 men are put to work. This may well represent 1 out of 5 adult males in the Nile Valley. That is, the construction of pyramids had a powerful economic and religious impact on the population and is often compared to the construction of Romanesque or Gothic cathedrals in towns in Western Europe in the middle ages. It's an apt comparison in many ways. It is stunning what the mobilization of labor was and just to give a few statistics from Khufu's period, to give some sort of sense of the scale of these projects, if you have 100,000 men put to work during a building season, it's usually estimated that to build that great pyramid represented 24,000,000 man hours to put up that pyramid. The pyramid stood 480 feet high, it was 786 feet perfect square at its base, and it covered nearly 13 acres. The largest ziggurat in Mesopotamia isn't even a third of that size, maybe a quarter of that size for that great ziggurat in Ur. The hanging gardens of Babylon constructed in the 6th century B.C. are maybe about a half of the size of the great pyramid and they're only about 75 feet high, based on Herodotus's description. These were enormous undertakings.

Furthermore, they were done without any kind of advantages such as pulleys; there were no draft animals, there was no bronze. It is largely done by stone and copper tools, by breaking the rock off through clever ways of breaking them along the fissure, by using hot and cold water, sanding them down, and the quarries, both for the granite and for the limestone and sandstone, are all in Upper Egypt and had to be floated down the Nile to Gizeh outside of Memphis and then brought into position. The very construction of the pyramid to that great height was done in an incredibly simple form. They simply built huge incline planes of earth to move the blocks up to complete the pyramid and then removed the earth when the pyramid was finished. This was an enormous mobilization of labor and no monarch at the time could have commanded such resources. The great pyramid at Gizeh, the Pyramid of Khufu, still stands as the largest freestanding masonry building after the cathedral of Cologne in Germany— a truly stunning achievement. Napoleon claimed that the building blocks used, which averaged 2.5 tons of weight, that the building blocks in the great pyramid could build a wall 10 feet high and one foot thick and guard the eastern barrier of France against Germany. You could always see how Napoleon's mind was thinking of these things.

The son and grandson of Khufu—that is, Khafre and Menkaura also built great pyramids—theirs are considerably smaller. Menkaura's pyramid is really only about a quarter of the size of his granddad's Khufu's pyramid. As you go in the Fifth and Sixth Dynasties in succeeding families, the pyramids become increasingly smaller. Again, we have limited evidence, but it's a fairly good bet of what happened here—that is, the pyramids represented not only the pinnacle of Egyptian civilization and the sacral power of the pharaoh, they also, in the end, did the monarchy in. Well, how is that possible, given the great powers of the god king? In order to carry on pyramid construction, the only way you could summon the number of men, building materials, and the food necessary to feed 100,000 laborers, meant you had to work through the nomarchs, the local lords, the regional bigwigs, the men who served at the court of Memphis who expected to join the pharaoh in the second life.

There are clear indications already in the end of the Fourth Dynasty and, certainly, by the Fifth Dynasty, that these regional figures begin to assert their own power. That is, they gain power and privileges in their districts, their positions became hereditary and, increasingly, they did not have to pay as much attention to the directives of the pharaohs and later pharaohs could not demand as much from these nomarchs and the regions, as Khufu had been able to. It's a classic case of using power, in the end, consumes power. The greatest ability in the exercise of power is when really not to exercise it.

In any case, the nomarchs begin to assert their authority and this is seen in several ways. First, the nomarchs start building their own tombs in their hometowns. That we have a proliferation of noble tombs starting in the Fifth and Sixth Dynasties, and these run well into the Middle Kingdom, many of them probably felt that, "You know, I'm going to be entitled to the second life—there's no necessity for me to stay at the court of Memphis." So, what happens is that these regional lords become increasingly independent and increasingly confident. Furthermore, the pharaohs of Dynasties V and VI, in particular, felt a need to bolster their legitimacy and this is particularly true of the pharaohs of Dynasty V. They were not connected to the Fourth Dynasty, as far as we can tell; they were actually a family that originated in the delta.

In an effort to gain legitimacy in the Upper Kingdom, they went through great efforts to endow temples, to alienate property and royal rights to the priestly family, in particular, the temples of the god Ra who is the sun god of Lower Egypt, probably the premier god in the Egyptian pantheon. He's seen as the creator god. His temples emerged as great economic and political centers in local and regional life. The construction of the great obelisks that many are familiar with—they're usually hauled off to European and North American cities to act as the centers of parks—those are the rays of the sun; those are monuments dedicated to Ra. I always like to think that as the obelisks go up and Ra's monuments become increasingly large, pyramids become increasing small. I mean, architecturally, before your very eyes, you can see what's happening to the monarchy's power. When you get to the pyramids of the Sixth Dynasty and later, the later pyramids are so poorly constructed that some of them are collapsing before they're actually completed and these are far less impressive structures than the pyramids of the Third and Fourth Dynasties.

So, what happens is, the god king or pharaoh in Memphis is increasingly unable to make his will felt up and down the Nile Valley and, unlike his contemporaries in Mesopotamia, these pharaohs had not taken the effort to develop the sorts of institutions necessary to impose their authority. The Egyptian pharaohs do not have the kind of professional army or bureaucratic class that we would see in contemporary Mesopotamia. So, as Mesopotamia begins to achieve unity under the Akkadian emperors, this great pharaoh in Memphis is losing his power and the power in Egypt becomes increasingly divided up among different nomarchs. The culmination of this process comes at the end of the Sixth Dynasty with the last king of the Dynasty, and his name in the record is known as Pepi II, a really marvelous name. He's believed to have had a particularly long reign from 2275 to 2185 B.C, and if you do the math, that means he supposedly ruled for 90 years and if this record is at all correct, it's the longest reign on record and what it suggests is it was a very, very long regency before Pepi assumed his own majority, his right to rule, and there was a very long majority when Pepi was probably pretty much out of it.

That reign essentially caps a long development in the deterioration of royal power, and by his death, the pharaohs in Memphis are no longer able to exercise authority over the Nile Valley. They certainly can't summon the labor forces to build the kinds of monuments of the Third and Fourth Dynasty. What happens for the next 150 years is the independent nomarchs begin to assert their authority and, eventually, there are essentially four regional powers that emerge—one is at Memphis, the old capital that everyone ignores, the other is in Upper Egypt at Edfu and at Abydos. Abydos was the old capital of Narmer and the pharaohs of Dynasty I and II. Ultimately, the city or the Dynasty that will reunify Egypt comes from Thebes, which is on the remote southern frontier.

So, it's not any kind of foreign invasion, or outside danger, that brings about the collapse of royal power; it's within its own institutional weakness and what happens is Egypt fragments and it fragments for the next 150 years politically, but culturally and religiously, the basis is there to reunite Egypt and this will be carried out by the princes of Thebes who are the keepers of the south, who will reunite in Egypt an institute, the brilliant Middle Kingdom.

Lecture Six
The Middle Kingdom

Scope: Rival dynasts clashed during the First Intermediate Period in Egypt (c. 2200–2050 B.C.) so that *nomarchs* and priests looked for a return to order and justice (*ma'at*) under righteous pharaohs. Mentuhotep II (r. c. 2060–2010 B.C.), prince of Thebes in Upper Egypt, founded Dynasty XI and reunified Egypt. The usurper Amenemhet I (r. 1991–1962 B.C.) founded the illustrious Dynasty XII of the Middle Kingdom, which transformed Egypt into a well-governed imperial order. The pharaohs of the Middle Kingdom, who ruled from Thebes, reorganized royal administration, sponsored irrigation and drainage projects, and promoted trade. They, too, required lavish royal burials, but in subterranean tombs bored out of the cliffs of the Valley of Kings on the west bank of the Nile and opposite Thebes. Foremost, the pharaohs were warriors, and Senworset III (r. 1878–1843 B.C.) advanced the frontier to the second cataract in Nubia, founding military colonies and recruiting Nubian infantry into the royal army. The copper mines of Sinai were exploited, and Canaanite ports were brought into tributary alliance. Yet the pharaohs of Thebes faced hostility in Lower Egypt; under Dynasty XIII, rebellions erupted in the Delta. In the fighting, Egyptian pharaohs and rebels summoned Canaanite allies or mercenaries, known as Hyksos. In 1674 B.C., the Hyksos, experts in chariot warfare and fortifications, captured Memphis and ruled as foreign lords over Egypt for more than a century (1674–1544 B.C.).

Outline

I. In this lecture, we look at the Egyptian Middle Kingdom, a period that is roughly contemporary with the Babylon of Hammurabi. This period saw the expansion of Egyptian horizons and the beginnings of administrative and institutional changes characteristic of the earlier Mesopotamian Empire.

II. We shall begin by reviewing the conditions that brought the pharaohs of the Middle Kingdom to power.

A. As mentioned in the last lecture, royal power became ineffective shortly after 2200 B.C., and Egypt broke up into a series of competing kingdoms. The period from 2200–2050 B.C., called the First Intermediate Period, is often seen as a time of confusion.

B. *Lament literature*, from the period of the Middle Kingdom, was penned by members of the upper classes and describes the breakdown of *ma'at* ("justice"). In some ways, this literature was used to justify the position attained by the pharaohs of Dynasty XII, who attempted to style themselves as restorers of *ma'at*.

C. The princes of Thebes were minor figures, and the city itself served as a post for trade traveling into the Sudan. Prestige goods brought into Egypt lent authority to the pharaohs ruling at Memphis to impress the nobles and the *nomarchs* to serve the god-king.

D. As a frontier post, Thebes also gave its princes access to military power. Indeed, the pharaohs of Dynasty XII often recruited frontier peoples, including Nubians and Asiatic peoples, into military units.

III. The success of the pharaohs of the Middle Kingdom is owed to Mentuhotep II (r. c. 2060–2010 B.C.), who founded Dynasty XI and transformed Thebes into the capital of Upper Egypt.

A. His successor, Mentuhotep III (r. c. 2009–1998 B.C.), brought all of Egypt under his control, acquired Memphis, and imposed order throughout the Nile valley. His reign represents the end of the period of disunity.

B. Mentuhotep III was followed by weak successors, and the dynastic family was overthrown by a vizier, Amenemhet I (r. 1991–1962 B.C.), who established his own family as Dynasty XII.

1. Amenemhet carried the name of the patron god of Thebes, Amon ("hidden one"), not a particularly prominent divinity in the Egyptian cosmology.

2. The pharaohs of Dynasty XII linked Amon with the god Ra, the premier Sun god of Egypt. The Sun was regarded as the eternal organizing principle in Egyptian religion and, thus, in the kingdom's political institutions.

3. Through a process that scholars call *syncretism*, the god Amon in Thebes became the equivalent of the god Ra in the Delta.

They were seen as the same divinity but manifested in different ways.

4. The identification of the two gods was extremely successful; Amon became the protector god of the dynasty, and great temples were constructed to Amon in Luxor and Karnak.

C. The pharaohs of Dynasty XII also paid homage to Ra and endowed the temple to Ptah in Memphis. They promoted the cult of Osiris, lord of the underworld and judge of all Egyptians.

IV. The pharaohs of Dynasty XII were adroit not only in their religious policies but also in carrying out administrative and legal reforms that would transform royal government in Egypt.

A. As mentioned, the earliest pharaohs did not need to develop the kinds of political and military institutions that were seen in Sumer and Akkad. Starting with Amenemhet I, however, efforts were made to bring the independent *nomarchs* under control.

B. The royal administration was restructured. Egypt was divided into three parts (Upper, Middle, and Lower Egypt), and a new official, known as a *waret* ("recorder"), supervised each division.

1. The *waret* was appointed by the pharaoh and was required to report to the pharaoh regularly.

2. The *nomes* were kept in place, but the pharaohs now made a concerted effort to correspond with these districts.

C. The pharaohs also had to conduct what we might call public works projects to gain the reputation as upholders of *ma'at*.

1. The pharaohs of Dynasty XII started the tradition of building subterranean tombs. The opulence of such tombs can be seen in the exhibitions of artifacts from the tomb of King Tutankhamun.

2. Other projects included draining large sections of the Fayum area. By one estimate, the pharaohs of Dynasty XII reclaimed 17,000 acres for cultivation in this way over a period of two generations.

3. Prestigious expeditions were sent out, including one to the coast of what is now Somalia, known to the Egyptians as the Land of Punt.

4. Repairs were made to dikes and canals, and efforts were made to calculate the flooding of the Nile.

5. Litigation was recorded, and attempts were made to ensure that *ma'at* was administered uniformly for all Egyptians.

V. The pharaohs of Dynasty XII also had a policy of co-opting border peoples into the royal army—populations that might otherwise attack Egypt.

    A. Although the recruitment of a professional royal army was a major step, the equipment of these Egyptian armies was rather simple. Defense depended on a large wooden shield—there was no body armor—and infantrymen used a thrusting spear or a club in close combat.

    B. These armies were used by the pharaohs to extend Egyptian control up the Nile, deep into what is now northern and middle Sudan. Senworset III (1878–1843 B.C.) erected a boundary stone fixing the frontier of Egypt at the third cataract in Nubia.

    C. In the region that the Romans called Palestine (today Israel and the West Bank), Egyptians conducted limited military operations against the Canaanites.

VI. As a group, the pharaohs of Dynasty XII were an impressive family. They created the foundations of imperial and "classic" Egypt, and their institutions became the basis of the great imperial age under Dynasty XVIII. Given the record of these pharaohs, what went wrong?

    A. The pharaohs of Dynasty XII faced the problem that all pharaohs of Thebes faced; notably, the Egyptians of the Delta resented these southerners as outsiders.

    B. The fact that the pharaohs of Dynasty XII chose to rule from Thebes produced a great deal of resentment, particularly in the great priestly families of Ptah and Ra in the Lower Kingdom.

    C. Further, the regions of the Delta offered ideal conditions to carry out rebellions. The area is marshy and difficult to bring under control.

    D. Starting late in Dynasty XII, in the reign of Amenemhet IV, rebellions broke out in the Delta, and an independent set of kings set up a capital there. These would become the pharaohs of Dynasty XIII and XIV.

    E. In the civil wars that ensued after the fall of Dynasty XII, various candidates for the throne brought in mercenaries from Asia.

Starting in 1674 B.C., these outsiders, known in the sources as Hyksos ("foreigners"), overthrew Egyptian rule and reigned as Dynasty XV.

1. This conquest came in two parts: First, Hyksos mercenaries were brought in and settled in the Delta, where they established strongholds. Then, an organized invasion was carried out by a Hyksos prince, who probably had a fleet.
2. The invading Hyksos army had certain advantages that the Egyptians had never seen. Hyksos warriors had bronze armor, horse-drawn light chariots, and composite bows.
3. Egyptian resistance collapsed. The Hyksos overthrew the pharaohs ruling in Memphis, established their own capital in the Delta, and imposed their authority over the Nile valley for the next 100 years.
4. The shock of this outside invasion galvanized the princes of Thebes to overthrow the foreigners and restore prosperity and unity in the Nile valley, opening the New Kingdom, the imperial age of Dynasty XVIII.

Further Reading:

Donald B. Redford, *Egypt, Canaan, and Israel in Ancient Times.*

H. E. Winlock, *The Rise and Fall of the Middle Kingdom in Thebes.*

Questions to Consider:

1. How did lament literature reflect expectations of royal rule among the elite classes? How well did the pharaohs of the Middle Kingdom meet these expectations for restoration of *ma'at*? Why did the pharaohs of Dynasty XII choose to associate themselves with the cults of Amon, Ptah, and Osiris?

2. What pragmatic measures did the pharaohs of Dynasty XII take to make effective royal will? How did they promote royal revenues and general prosperity of Egypt? How important was long-distance trade?

3. What accounted for political instability after about 1785 B.C.? Why did the pharaohs at Thebes face hostility in Lower Egypt?

Lecture Six—Transcript
The Middle Kingdom

In this lecture, I plan to deal with what is known as the Egyptian Middle Kingdom and this is a period of Egyptian history that is roughly contemporary with the Babylon of Hammurabi, and I lectured about Hammurabi in an earlier lecture. The Middle Kingdom represents an important point in Egyptian history; it sees the expanding of Egyptian horizons. The pharaohs of especially Dynasty XII, the great dynasty of the Middle Kingdom, were the first to venture beyond Egyptian frontiers; this included a royal-sponsored long-distance trade and also, to a certain extent, imperialism. Conquests in the upper reaches of the Nile in which the frontiers were advanced as far as the Third Cataract, that's deep into what is Sudan today. Also, there are some limited expeditions into the Sinai, in part, to secure quarries and copper mines in the western Sinai, and the promotion of trade contacts with the cities of the Levantine shore, particularly Byblos, which is a city today in Lebanon that was long in contact with Egypt. Furthermore, these pharaohs will carry out some of the kind of administrative and institutional changes in Egypt that were characteristic of the earlier Mesopotamian empires we studied in a previous lecture.

So, the pharaohs of the Middle Kingdom are an impressive group and let's review the conditions that brought this dynasty to power. It's also important to stress that this dynasty not only transformed royal government, but in many ways, it set the pattern for the later pharaohs of the New Kingdom, the more famous Imperial Age, especially Dynasties XVIII and XIV, and it could be argued, to some extent, that the pharaohs of Dynasty XVIII in the New Kingdom are, in many ways, just a continuation of many of the policies and the cultural programs and religious programs of the pharaohs of the Middle Kingdom. So, if we recollect from the last lecture, royal power became ineffective shortly after 2200 B.C. The reign of Pepi II essentially marked the end of effective royal power in the Nile Valley and while kings continued to rule in Memphis, they really exercised little authority outside their immediate region and Egypt broke up into a series of competing kingdoms.

The Greek historian of this period who arranged the dynasties, Manetho, refers to one dynasty as comprising 70 kings ruling in 70 years. There are all sorts of tales about short-lived monarchs, the lack of justice in Egypt that would be *ma'at*. So, the period of roughly 2200 to 2050 B.C., about 150-year period, is often seen as a period of confusion and has the misfortune of being named by modern historians as The First Intermediate Period—a dreadful thought to live in The First Intermediate Period; it's really sometimes quite lamentable what types of terms historians apply to periods. There is a certain amount of literature and it was originally thought to survive from this period; it really comes from the period of the Middle Kingdom. It's often known as Lament Literature and it is literature penned by the upper classes lamenting the breakdown of *ma'at*, justice. *Ma'at* was one of the prime qualities of the god Ptah, the god of Memphis, the royal seat, and as I mentioned, when the pharaohs moved their capital to Memphis back in the First Dynasty, the pharaohs assumed many of the qualities of Ptah, the patron god of Memphis, and *ma'at* was supreme among them. That is, the pharaoh, by his utterance and by his authority, speaks justice; he is a god-king.

This literature is really largely retrospective, this lament literature. It can be compared to later Hebrew literature and Mesopotamian literature; there's a very long tradition in the Near East of writing this type of literature, protests calling for some types of justice. But it's, to some extent, created in the Middle Kingdom by the literate and upper classes as a way of justifying the position attained by the pharaohs of Dynasty XII, who went out of their way to style themselves as restorers of *ma'at*, of justice, and they had very good reasons to do this. For one, they were southerners; they came from Thebes. They were trying to rule the whole Nile Valley; they had to link themselves to the earlier pharaohs at Memphis and give some sort of justification for why these frontier princes should rule as the god-kings of Egypt. Nonetheless, this lament literature does represent what the upper classes expected of the monarchy, and that period of political division was something that most of the upper classes and property classes did not repeat. It prepared them for the acceptance of the pharaohs of Dynasty XI and XII, to carry out the types of institutional reforms we see in the Middle Kingdom, which augmented imperial power, royal power.

Well, the princes of Thebes—and Thebes is at the very southern end of Egypt—were always really rather minor figures. Abydos was really the capitol of Upper Egypt. Thebes was essentially a post for the trade going into the Sudan and this was a trade that's already being developed, certainly in the Third and Fourth Dynasties, and again, as most early Egyptian trade, the merchants came to Egypt. The Egyptians didn't go out and look for things. Egypt was a remarkably wealthy land; it's certainly regarded as the most wealthy land in the ancient world and so merchants came in bringing ivory, gold from the mine fields—Nubia is essentially the northern Sudan today—and various exotic animals, such as peacocks and ostriches; there's reports of dwarfs, though they probably mean pygmies being brought up from central Africa. These are all prestige goods, very important to the monarchy and extremely important for giving authority and opulence to the pharaohs ruling at Memphis, to impress the nobles and the nomarchs to serve the god king. Well, Thebes was the channel through which all these products came.

Furthermore, as a frontier post, the princes of Thebes had access to military power because one of the primary features of the pharaohs of the Dynasty XII, the pharaohs of the Middle Kingdom, was recruiting frontier peoples including Nubians, people who were not Egyptians, who were south of direct Egyptian control into military units and putting them under a royal authority and, essentially, creating a professional imperial army. This is a feature that climaxes in the reign of Senworset III, the great imperial pharaoh of the Middle Kingdom who ruled from 1878–1843 B.C. and his infantry becomes largely Nubians, which are black Africans who have been brought up and enrolled into elite infantry units. Furthermore, there's recruiting, apparently, of Asiatic peoples, on a limited basis, who are also brought in, and this starts a long tradition—that climaxes in the New Kingdom—of using frontier peoples and foreigners just outside the borders to do the real fighting. Egyptian peasants, who are the vast majority of the population, are just too valuable in farming and paying taxes. That's a feature of the Middle Kingdom that becomes a feature of Egyptian royal policy, thereafter.

The success of the pharaohs of the Middle Kingdom is really owed to a man by the name of Mentuhotep II, and between 2060 and 2010 B.C., he made Thebes into, effectively, the capital of Upper Egypt and managed to subdue a number of the obnoxious nomarchs and warlords of Upper and Middle Egypt. His eventual successor, Mentuhotep III, taking the same dynastic name, brought all of Egypt under his control, acquired Memphis, and imposed order throughout the Nile Valley. His reign represents the end of the period of disunity and the ushering in of the Middle Kingdom. Mentuhotep III himself, however, was followed by some weak successors and his family was overthrown by none other than the chief minister; we would call him a vizier, using the old Ottoman term. He was a man by the name of Amenemhet, who took his name from the chief god of Thebes, Amun or Amon, who overthrew Dynasty XI and established his own family as Dynasty XII.

This new pharaoh, Amenemhet, carried the name of the patron god of Thebes and that was the god Amen or Amun or Amon. The Egyptians never wrote the vowels in their hieroglyphic script; they never indicate what the vowel qualities were, so almost any vowel can be used for any Egyptian name and it's something of a guess whether Amun is Amon or "on." There are several different ways it could be rendered. But, the god Amon was regarded as the patron god of Thebes. The name actually means "the hidden one"—he was originally associated with the upper air. He is the protector of the princes of Thebes and he was not a particular prominent divinity in early Egyptian cosmology; he has no place to play in the cosmology of the Old Kingdom. He's not even numbered among the important gods in, what is known very often as, the theology of Memphis, which is a very detailed record of creation starting with Aton-Ra and ending with the creation of the god Horus, who is the son of Isis and Osiris and the opponent of Osiris' brother Set and his wife. Amon is essentially a newcomer, a local god.

The pharaohs of Dynasty XII went out of their way to link Amon with the god Ra—that is, the premier sun god of Egypt who had a great sanctuary at Heliopolis, who was seen as the protector of the kings, and the sun is regarded as the eternal organizing principle in Egyptian religion and, ergo, in Egyptian political institutions, as well. So, what happens is that in the text we often get a hyphenated Amon-Ra—that is Amon assumes the qualities of the solar divinity of the delta and the pharaohs of Dynasty XII begin this process of assimilation. Sometimes, historians of religion like to call it syncretism, which is rendered from two Greek words, which means, "mixing together." With that, the god Amun in Thebes is the equivalent to the god Ra in Delta; it is the same divinity, but manifested in different ways. Some would like to see this type of religious approach as a first step to monotheism and, essentially, culminating of the pharaoh of the eighteenth Dynasty, Akhenaton, who ruled from 1352–1335 B.C., who establishes a solar monotheism around the sun god Aton—and we will be getting to that whole religious reform in the next lecture. In any case, this identification is extremely important because Amon—and the priests of Amon particularly—with great temples at Karnak and Luxor in Upper Egypt, becomes the protective god of the Dynasty and the temples of Amon prosper under the pharaohs of Dynasty XII.

But, the pharaohs of Dynasty XII are also shrewd guys and they know that Egypt is a land of many gods. They pay homage to Ra. The temple to Ptah in Memphis is very well endowed. They also promote the cult of Osiris and it seems to be in the Middle Kingdom that the tradition emerges of Osiris as

Lord of the Underworld, as the judge of all Egyptians who have had a moral life, the great famous judgment that's depicted in much later texts known as the Book of the Dead. These come much later in Egyptian history, but that scene where the scales are brought out before Osiris and Anubis weighs the heart of every Egyptian and if the heart is lighter than a feather—that is, it has no sins—it passes into the other world; if it's heavier than a feather, then you've lived an immoral life and you're condemned to the outer reaches. That notion of a moral life associated with acceptance into the other world, into a permanent afterlife, for all Egyptians takes hold in the Middle Kingdom. It's promoted by the pharaohs of Dynasty XII, who liked to associate themselves with Osiris, and really pushed the connection that pharaohs become Osiris in death. And, why not? Osiris becomes the guarding of *ma'at*, justice, the very quality that was missing in that period of disorder and which the pharaohs of Dynasty XII have restored.

They're also keen on promoting much lesser cults and these are cults that often had just local importance. In the region of the Fayum—and that is that great lake system just to the west of the Nile, which is a combination of lake and marshes and is a very rich area; it's a region where there's excellent fish and fowl to hunt—in that marsh area, there's a local sacred god to the crocodile. That cult shrine is ennobled by the pharaohs of Dynasty XII and you can go through most of the sanctuaries of Egypt in the Middle Kingdom and see endowments, the expansion of temples, the granting of privileges to local divinities, and, again, this an effort by these princes of Thebes who are seen as many Egyptians as interlopers; they're from the far south, in what we would call the Thebaid, attempting to link themselves with every cult within the realm and gaining the favor of the gods.

The pharaohs of Dynasty XII are not only adroit in their religious policies, they also carried out a number of important administrative and legal reforms that transformed royal government in Egypt and really made the imperial order of the New Kingdom possible. In some ways, the Egyptians were catching up with their Mesopotamian contemporaries in terms of law and administration. As I mentioned, the earliest pharaohs did not need to develop the kinds of political and administrative institutions, or military institutions, that were seen in Sumer and Akkad. But, starting with Amenemhet I, the first ruler of Dynasty XII—and all the pharaohs either bear that name or the name Senworset; they're names associated with the god Amun, a dynastic name—there was an effort to crack down on the nomarchs and the independent warlords who had gotten out of hand in that period of the First Intermediate Period, that period of disorder. That took different forms. One was to restructure the royal administration, and it's under the pharaohs of Dynasty XII that Egypt is essentially divided into three parts. A new official known as a *waret*, which essentially means a recorder or super accountant, if you will, is put in charge of these three divisions and those divisions don't correspond with the old division of the Upper and Lower Kingdom.

They're essentially three new divisions of what are known as Upper, Middle, and Lower Egypt and that official survives into the Roman and Byzantine Age. It's translated into Greek as *epistrategos*, in the Thalamic administration. That reporter is directly appointed by the pharaoh, he's removed by the pharaoh, he's a professional bureaucrat, and he has to report to the pharaoh at regular intervals. Below the pharaoh, the nomes are kept in place—that is, the local districts—but there's no real effort to correspond with these areas, to start creating the kinds of documents that you would have in Mesopotamia. It is only in the Middle Kingdom that we get the proliferation of royal letters and law codes and missives—the types of government, documents of a government, that we had much earlier in Mesopotamia. The pharaohs can no longer rule through the utterance of sacral power in Memphis; they have to have a professional bureaucracy and the pharaohs of Dynasty XII create it.

They also find that they have to conduct various activities that gain them reputation and gain them good PR as upholders of *ma'at*; this includes a number of, what we would call, public projects. There are still royal funerary monuments and great temples being constructed and the pharaohs of Dynasty XII, they're really a savvy lot; they realize there's no point in bringing back pyramids. It's a debate how much did pyramids directly contribute to the demise of the pharaohs of the Old Kingdoms. But, the pharaohs of Dynasty XII are not about to summon up 100,000 guys and have them work for 20 years on one of these great pyramids. For one, they don't have the powers to do that and two, building a pyramid is, essentially, announcing to grave robbers, dig here; you know where it is. It depends very much on keeping the guards around the pyramid to prevent gravediggers from getting into those pyramids and the depressing fact is over that 150-year period of disorder, they got in and robbed all the main graves in the pyramid age.

This meant they destroyed the pharaohs' bodies; they disrupted the rites. Many Egyptians would have said that the reason we've lost *ma'at* is that the tombs had been despoiled; the pharaohs, the gods of the earlier period, had been destroyed. So, the pharaohs of Dynasty XII start the tradition of building these subterranean tombs in which they go for concealment. This will climax in the great tombs of the New Kingdom in the Valley of the Kings, and the opulence of these tombs must have been spectacular; you can get some sort of sense of what the opulence of a real royal burial would have been like by seeing the various exhibitions for King Tut, which are in the Cairo museum and have recently traveled to the United States. Keep in mind that King Tut's tomb is a cheap royal burial. This is the most insignificant king of the Eighteenth Dynasty and probably one of the reasons why they missed it, it wasn't important enough to plunder. It gives you some idea of what these tombs might have been like. They certainly are prepared with the afterlife with their goodies. So, there are these royal burials that continue and there is the veneration of pharaoh as Horus in life and Osiris in death.

Nonetheless, the pharaohs of Dynasty XII really go out of their way to publicize their public works. This includes draining large sections of the Fayum area and, by one estimate, over a period of two generations, those pharaohs reclaim something like 17,000 acres of prime real estate, which was put under cultivation and, of course, yielded taxes. There are repairs to the dikes in the canal systems. There are big prestige expeditions that are sent in several directions; one of them is sent along the Red Sea to the coasts of what are now Somalia—which to the Egyptians was known as the land of Punt, delightful name—and there they got all sorts of products, such as ivory and exotic animals, and they made contact with these local rulers. Then, these products were brought back to Thebes, again to grace to the court; nonetheless, this was a big PR diplomatic mission. It's publicized as bringing prosperity into Egypt. There are measures taken to calculate the flooding of the Nile, trying what's known in Greek sources as a nilometer—that is, a way of determining what the flood patterns will be. Will the flooding be particularly high this year? Will it be low this year? There is a great deal of documentation and legal decisions—that is, the writing down of the legal systems and getting involved in putting in writing, litigation, what the rules are. You don't produce the kind of coherent code as Hammurabi, but the pharaohs are going out of their way to make sure that their subject are getting *ma'at*, that this is administered uniformly by royal officials, this is taken in tandem with all of these public projects, and it does show a new tone of this monarchy. It is not resting solely on those sacral powers. It has to deliver and it has to deliver to the subjects of the pharaoh.

I also mentioned that these pharaohs were extremely good in co-opting border peoples into the royal army. This made sense. You're taking in populations who otherwise might be attacking Egypt, who are from a society in which the profession of arms is expected of all free men. There is recruitment of Nubians—that's actually the classical name for this region and, very often in the Egyptian texts they seem to call them Nehsi, which they seem to be the same people of the northern Sudan. Also, the recruiting of a royal army, which is apparently professional and paid all the time, is a big step. As far as we can tell, after Narmer, pharaohs did not maintain very large royal forces.

Furthermore, even in the Middle Kingdom, the equipment of these Egyptian armies is really rather simple. Defense depends on, essentially, a large wooden shield and this is true of most Egyptian infantry. There's no body armor to speak of. They depend on a thrusting spear and a variety of different types of clubs, should you get up close to an opponent. The bow, such as it is, is a very weak hunting weapon. There are no horses, mules— there are no draft animals in Egypt; they don't even know the wheel. You're dealing, essentially, with infantry armies that are being trained to fight in dense formations and bowl over less organized opponents.

These armies are used by the pharaohs to extend Egyptian control up the Nile—that is, deep into what is now northern and middle Sudan. And, we have, for instance, a remarkable boundary stone set up by Senworset III, who is really the great pharaoh of the dynasty, and this boundary stone set up in his eighth year—which would be the equivalent of 1871-1870 B.C.— states his intentions and it reads as follows:

> Southern boundary made in year eight under the majesty of the King of Upper and Lower Egypt, Senworset, who is given life forever and ever [This is a common title that you use with the pharaoh.]—in order to prevent any Nehsi [that is the Nubians] from passing it, either by water or by land, with ship or with Nehsi herds; except Nehsi who cross for purposes of trade…or by proper authority.

This is the first type of boundary stele we have from an Egyptian ruler.

There's been a very long tradition of this in Mesopotamia, going back to the earliest kings of Sumer where I read an earlier passage that the ensi of Umma tears up the boundary markers of Lagash and Sargon and Naram-sin and Hammurabi, the kings of Ur III; all of them set up boundary markers in different parts of the world to mark the limits of their empire and their intention to rule. Now we have a pharaoh falling in this tradition, marking the limit of Egyptian rule. Furthermore, archeology has borne out this boast very successfully, although now many of these sites are essentially washed away with the construction of the new Aswan Dam. But, in a region in Nubia, which is often known as the Belly of Stones, we have a number of sites, which represent Egyptian military colonies. Families of 200 to 300 Egyptian men were sent in there as a permanent garrison and this was, again, a typical policy; you move in Egyptian soldiers, you recruit the locals, the Nubians, move them into Egypt, and of course they're going to stay loyal to you because in Egypt they're foreigners and they don't have identity with the Egyptian peasants. This effort to bring Nubia under control will again climax in the New Kingdom with direct Egyptian incorporation of Nubia. Nubia will be incorporated into the Egyptian Kingdom and Egyptian rule will be extended even farther south into the region known as Kush, which is deep into the Sudan.

There are also efforts into, what the Romans would call, Palestine, which is today the West Bank in Israel, and I use that term in the Roman sense—that is, it designates the region between the Mediterranean and the Jordan Valley. In that area, there are limited military operations against people that are best designated Canaanites. There are reports of military demonstrations in there. There's the promotion of a great deal of trade along the Levantine shore, particularly at the ports of what are known as Lebanon, later known in antiquity as Phoenicia—the port of Byblos, which had long had a trade contact, but these pharaohs of Dynasty XII really promote that connection and the trade increases substantially.

So, as a group, the pharaohs of Dynasty XII are an impressive family. They really create the foundations of imperial, and in many ways, what we think of as classic Egypt. It's their institutions that become the basis for the creation of the great imperial age under Dynasty XVIII. Well, with such an impressive set of pharaohs the question comes up, what went wrong? I mean they seemed to do everything right and, in some ways, they really caught up with their Mesopotamian contemporaries in administration and law. Well, there seems to have been a problem that all pharaohs in the Thebaid faced—that is, all the southerners who come to rule all of Egypt. That is that the Egyptians in the Delta and the area around Memphis always resented those southerners as outsiders. Above all, the pharaohs in Dynasty XII chose to rule from Thebes; and as much as they honored the other gods of Egypt, that produced a great deal of resentment, particularly in the great priestly families of Ptah and Ra in the Lower Kingdom.

Furthermore, the regions in the Delta were ideal conditions to carry out rebellions. It is an extremely marshy area, it is difficult to bring under control, and starting late in the twelfth Dynasty in the reign of Amenemhet IV, rebellions broke out in the Delta and an independent set of kings declared themselves as pharaohs in the Delta setting up their own capital there. These are the pharaohs of the next dynasty, Dynasty XIII, as they're often designated and later of Dynasty XIV, and it was very difficult to bring these people under control.

In the process of putting down this rebellion and the civil wars that ensued after the fall of Dynasty XII, different Egyptian pharaohs or candidates to the throne brought in outside mercenaries. These were people from Asia, they were Canaanite speakers; they spoke a west Semitic language related to the other Semitic languages of what are now Syria, Lebanon, Israel, and Jordan—that whole area—the Levant. There were a series of dialects known as Canaanite and these guys were brought in as mercenaries and as allies and starting in 1674 B.C., these outsiders—known in the sources as Hyksos, which is the Greek rendition of an Egyptian name that means "foreigner," that's all it meant; sometimes they were called the Shepard Kings, but that's not really a correct translation—overthrew Egyptian rule. It was a dramatic conquest and it has to be seen as coming, essentially, in two parts—that is, these Canaanite mercenaries were brought in, settled into the Delta, established strong points there, and then in 1674, an organized invasion was carried out by a Hyksos prince coming out of Asia. He probably had a fleet because there's no way you can bring an army; he had to have a fleet. There's no way you can bring an army across Sinai without a fleet.

This Hyksos army brought certain advantages that the Egyptians had never seen; for one, they were well armed in bronze armor. They had the military technology of Mesopotamia and the wider Near East. They also had horse-drawn light chariots armed with composite bows. One wonders what the first Egyptian armies must have thought when they ran into these weapons. These are people who had no draft animals and no wheel. Egyptian resistance collapses. The Hyksos manage to overthrow the pharaohs ruling in Memphis. They establish their own capital at Avaris in the Delta and impose their authority over the Nile Valley for the next century or so, and rule without Ra, without Ptah, without *ma'at*. That invasion, the shock of an outside invasion for the first time in Egyptian history, galvanized the princes of Thebes, once again, to overthrow the foreigners who had invaded Egypt and restore prosperity and unity in the Nile Valley, and open Egypt's greatest period—the New Kingdom or the Imperial Age of Dynasty XVIII.

Lecture Seven
Imperial Egypt

Scope: Khamose (r. 1570–1550 B.C.) founded Dynasty XVIII at Thebes and challenged the Hyksos kings of Avaris. Ahmose (r. c. 1550–1544 B.C.) forged a new royal army of chariots and Nubian infantry to expel the Hyksos and restore *ma'at* in Egypt. The pharaohs of Dynasty XVIII styled themselves as conquerors in memorial reliefs and painting and endowed the shrines of Amon, Ptah, and Ra with rich offerings of thanks. Hatshepsut (r. 1489–1479 B.C.), the first queen to rule in her own right, halted expansion in favor of building projects and diplomacy. But she alienated the military elite at Thebes, and her nephew, Thutmose III (r. 1479–1426 B.C.), seized power. Thutmose III waged 17 campaigns in Asia and organized an Asiatic empire. The transformation of Egyptian values and material life climaxed in the religious reforms of Akhenaton (r. 1352–1335 B.C.), who aimed to exalt his majesty as the oracular voice of the sole god Aton. Akhenaton sought to break the aristocracy at Thebes and imposed his monotheistic cult by force. Religious reform at home put the Asiatic empire in jeopardy, as the Hittite emperor Šuppiluliumaš (r. 1344–1322 B.C.) conquered northern Syria. Akhenaton had compromised his dynasty and the empire, and his heirs would abandon the cult of Aton. Warrior pharaohs of Dynasty XIX met the Hittite challenge in Asia, but Rameses II (r. 1279–1212 B.C.) achieved a stalemate at Kadesh and was forced to recognize Hittite supremacy in northern Syria. Rameses II and Merneptah (r. 1212–1200 B.C.) restored Egyptian rule in Palestine, but their heirs faced new invaders, the "Sea Peoples," who ended Egyptian rule in Asia.

Outline

I. This lecture looks at the New Kingdom (c. 1550–1150s B.C.), the period when the Egyptian monarchy came to play a dominant role in the Middle East and Egypt reached its political and cultural zenith.

II. We shall begin by looking at the pharaohs of Dynasty XVIII (1570–1293 B.C.).

    A. As you recall, Egypt had fallen under the control of Hyksos invaders, but the Hyksos ruled as a small military caste and never truly controlled the Nile valley.

    B. The princes of Thebes again emerged as a force of unity in the Nile valley. The pharaohs of Dynasty XVIII, starting with the founder of the family, Khamose (r. 1570–1550 B.C.), adopted the military technology of the Hyksos and overthrew these foreign rulers. His successor, Ahmose (r. 1550–1544 B.C.), stormed Avaris and expelled the Hyksos.

    C. The immediate successors of Ahmose, Amenhotep I (r. 1544–1520 B.C.), Thutmose I (r. 1520–1500 B.C.), and Thutmose II (r. 1500–1489 B.C.), conducted massive attacks into the region between the Mediterranean and the Jordan valley.

    D. The Egyptians also pushed deep into the Sudan. The region known as Kush, south of the third cataract, was organized as a viceroyalty, and Nubia was incorporated into Egypt. The territorial extent of Egypt was greatly enlarged from what it had been in the Old or Middle Kingdom.

    E. Imperial expansion halted briefly in the early 15th century B.C., during the reign of Queen Hatshepsut (r. 1489–1479 B.C.), daughter of Thutmose II, who ruled with the trappings of a male pharaoh.

        1. Hatshepsut halted imperial expansion for a good reason: She was married to a royal consort, a nephew or half-brother, the future Thutmose III. He was proclaimed as a joint ruler, although he was considerably younger than Hatshepsut. Any military operations launched by Thutmose III would benefit him, not Hatshepsut, who risked losing her throne.

        2. For this reason, she pioneered methods of promoting the monarchy that prefigured the policies of the heretic pharaoh Akhenaton (r. 1352–1335 B.C.). She promoted arts, building and irrigation programs, and high-prestige trade.

      3.   We are not quite sure what happened to this remarkable woman, but she probably died of an illness in 1479 B.C. In her final years, however, she was already losing power, and Thutmose III was able to assert himself.

III. The victories won by the early pharaohs of Dynasty XVIII transformed the Egyptian monarchy.

    A. Henceforth, the Egyptian pharaohs would be depicted in war garb; this iconography is seen in the tombs of later pharaohs, such as King Tutankhamun (r. 1335–1325 B.C.) and Rameses II (r. 1279–1212 B.C.), as well as on boundary markers proclaiming the power of the pharaohs.

    B. Thutmose III (r. 1479–1426 B.C.) has been called the Napoleon of the Near East. He created the Egyptian Empire in Asia.

        1. Egyptian armies reached as far as the northern banks of the Euphrates and brought the various Canaanite princes of the Levant under Egyptian control.

        2. Egyptian governors were established in Asia, and the Asiatic provinces were ruled in much the same way that earlier pharaohs had ruled the *nomes*; that is, by co-opting the elite and cementing ties of friendship, hospitality, and marriage.

        3. Thutmose III was also heir to the administrative apparatus of the Middle Kingdom. The vastly expanded royal bureaucracy in Memphis was staffed by Asiatics who conducted international correspondence in Akkadian.

    C. The Asiatic empire created by Thutmose III became the pillar of Dynasties XVIII and XIX, because it brought enormous wealth to the monarchy in the form of slaves, tribute, and commodities. This wealth transformed the monarchy by enabling the pharaohs to employ a professional army and bureaucracy.

    D. The great national shrines also profited immensely, especially the shrines of Ptah, god of wisdom; Ra, the great Sun god of the Delta; and Amon, the protector of Dynasties XII and XVIII.

IV. As noted in the previous lecture, pharaohs from Thebes faced opposition in Middle and Lower Egypt. Thus, the pharaohs of Dynasty XVIII had to prove themselves as upholders of *ma'at* and the traditional cults.

A. Hatshepsut had transferred the capital from Thebes to Memphis, a move that was resented by the great families of Thebes. Thutmose III maintained the capital at Memphis; indeed, his successors made a concerted effort to develop the monarchy there and to support cults other than that of Amon, notably Ra.

B. The focus on Ra reflected the efforts of the pharaohs of Dynasty XVIII to make themselves presentable to their subjects in Lower Egypt and to break the power of the priestly families of Amon in Thebes.

C. This policy had important consequences: The monarchs became more dependent on imperial resources in the form of bureaucrats, scribes, and soldiers paid with the wealth of the Asiatic empire.

D. The pharaohs of Dynasty XVIII also promoted solar cults, which became more uniform and what some scholars would call *henotheistic*; that is, the Sun god was worshiped as the ultimate divine power manifested in many ways.

V. The pharaoh Akhenaton (r. 1352–1335 B.C.), who came to the throne as Amenhotep IV, is perhaps the most intriguing figure in the New Kingdom.

A. Until recently, we knew little about Akhenaton other than the fact that in the sixth year of his reign, he proclaimed a solar monotheism and ended the worship of other gods in Egypt. With the groundbreaking work of Professor Donald Redford, however, we have come to understand more about Akhenaton.

B. The pharaoh's shrines were destroyed after his death, in the reign of Horemheb (r. 1322–1293 B.C.), and his relief sculptures were smashed and used as fill for other monuments. When these 20,000 fragments (*talatat*) were recovered in excavation, Redford was able to reconstruct them into Akhenaton's wall relief.

C. Akhenaton changed his name from Amenhotep soon after he took the throne to celebrate and honor the god Aton, an early solar divinity. He also declared a new capital 300 miles north of Thebes. The site is now known as Tel el-Amarna but at the time was called Akhenaton ("the place effective of the glory of Aton").

D. In concentrating on religious reform, Akhenaton neglected the empire, which proved fatal for Dynasty XVIII. The Hittites arose as a new power in Asia Minor (modern Turkey); they invaded the

Asiatic provinces and threatened to strip away the monarchy's imperial power base.

E. Akhenaton's successor, Tutankhamun, distanced himself from the solar cult of Aton and restored the worship of the ancient gods. Horemheb, a general who became successor to the throne, obliterated the solar cult.

VI. Besides launching a succession crisis in Egypt, Akhenaton also put the empire in jeopardy. Fortunately for Egypt, a series of generals contested the efforts of the Hittites to appropriate the Asiatic empire.

A. These pharaohs of Dynasty XIX, particularly Rameses II (r. 1279–1212 B.C.), attempted to beat back Hittite attacks and restore Egyptian frontiers in Asia. This climaxed in the Battle of Kadesh in 1275 B.C., a draw with the Hittites that marked the limit of revived Egyptian power.

B. The successors of Rameses II faced not only the Hittites but the great migrations and changes that would come at the end of the Late Bronze Age. In our next lecture, we shall turn to the Hittites and the Mitanni, who would challenge the imperial power of Egypt and change the face of Near Eastern culture and politics.

Further Reading:

K. A. Kitchen, *Pharaoh Triumphant: The Life and Times of Ramesses II.*

Donald B. Redford, *Akhenaten: Heretic King.*

Questions to Consider:

1. What motivated Egyptian imperialism under the pharaohs of Dynasty XVIII? What were the benefits of Egypt's imperial experience? In what ways did the transformation of society and culture lead to the religious changes in the reign of Akhenaton?

2. How did Queen Hatshepsut and Pharaoh Thutmose III establish the policies expected for later pharaohs? How did Akhenaton break with these policies by promoting his solar monotheism? What were the costs of religious revolution for the monarchy and Egyptian society?

Lecture Seven—Transcript
Imperial Egypt

In this lecture, I plan to deal with the New Kingdom of Egypt, which is Egypt's great Imperial Age, and it's a time when the Egyptian monarchy came to play the dominant role in the Near East. From approximately 1550 B.C. with the success of the pharaohs of Dynasty XVIII who originated in Thebes, through the end of the so-called Bronze Age—that is, into the period of the 1150s, more or less—Egypt was the great power in the Near East. Egypt presided over a wider political order and, in many ways, at least in terms of the political and cultural achievements, Egypt reaches zenith under these pharaohs of Dynasty XVIII and XIX. The empire will come to an end with the attacks that are associated with the so-called Sea Peoples; these are invaders coming out of Libya, as well as the Aegean world, and they are part of a wider set of migrations that bring an end to the entire late Bronze Age political order, and we'll be discussing that in a later lecture.

But, during the period of the late Bronze Age, there's no question that Imperial Egypt was the dominant power. The Egyptians enjoyed this position, in part, because when Egyptian power emerged in the mid-16th century B.C., there was no great territorial state in Mesopotamia. As we'll see, Mesopotamia was divided between two foreign dynasties—the Kassites ruling in the south centered at Babylon and a rather mysterious group known as the Mitanni, who held sway in the north. And so, the Egyptians did not encounter any major resistance from a Mesopotamian monarch and many of the kingdoms they encountered in the Levant—that is, on the western arm of the Fertile Crescent were rather small or medium size Canaanite realms, which didn't pose the type of opposition a great empire would have been capable of. Later in this period, they will encounter the Hittites, who revive under their King Šuppiluliumaš in the 14th century B.C. and Hittite power will actually threaten Egyptian primacy at the end of this period.

Let's look at the pharaohs of Dynasty XVIII and, as I mentioned in the last lecture, in many ways they owed a great deal of their policies to the pharaohs of Dynasty XII—that is, the great pharaohs in the Middle Kingdom and the pharaohs of Dynasty XVIII, however, were going to be better armed. As you recollect, Egypt had fallen under the control of invaders, known from the Greek rendition of the name the Hyksos, which means "foreigners," sometimes loosely translated as Shepard Kings, a very deceptive title. These were invaders who spoke a Canaanite dialect—that is, a West Semitic dialect. They ruled from their fortress city of Avaris in the Delta; they had the up-to-date military technology of the Near East. That included the light chariot drawn by horses, the composite bow, which is a very powerful bow that can penetrate armor, they had the bronze arms and heavy armor of the Near East, and they also had excellent techniques in fortification and siege warfare, all of this unknown to the Egyptians. However, they ruled as a small military caste. They were invaders and they never really controlled most of the Nile Valley and so, the princes of Thebes, as in the case of the resurgence of royal power in the Middle Kingdom, the princes of Thebes, the keepers of the gates to the south, again emerged as the force of unity in the Nile Valley. It is the pharaohs of Dynasty XVIII, starting with the founder of the family, Khamose, who overthrows the power of the Hyksos in the Nile Valley, ends the tributary status of Thebes. Then, his successor, Ahmose, who comes to the throne in the late 16th century B.C., storms the city of Avaris, scatters the Asiatics, as they call them, and expels the foreigners forever from the Nile Valley.

Now, these pharaohs were able to achieve this because they adopted the military technology that the Hyksos had brought into Egypt. That is, they were able to field armies of light chariots and they had acquired horses; they also had to rearm their infantry with the heavy arms of the late Bronze Age. Again, as I noted, the pharaohs ruling in Thebes had the advantage that they could draw on the military personnel of the boarder peoples. These included the Nubians in what are now northern Sudan and ever more important in Egyptian armies would be the nomadic peoples to the west, the so-called Libyans, as they're called by their Greek name. These border peoples increasingly form an important element in the royal army, especially in the infantry corps.

The immediate successors of Ahmose are Amenhotep I, and then Thutmose II and Thutmose I, conducted massive attacks into Asia. This would be the area of Palestine and, again, I stress that I use the Roman designation of the area and that refers to everything between the Mediterranean and the Jordan Valley, and the name is actually derived from the Philistines; the people who come to settle on the seaboard of "Palestine" at the end of Bronze Age and the term does not carry any of the modern political connotations it carries today. It's essentially a geographic term, and it's used as such by most archeologists and that would essentially be today the Gaza Strip, Israel, and what's called the West Bank, formerly attached to Jordan. So, in these areas, the pharaohs waged campaigns and, in part, these were in retaliation because the people in these regions were related to the Hyksos;

they apparently all spoke a common Canaanite dialect. This was a matter of conducting, what I would call prestige campaigns.

Even so, these campaigns represented a substantial level of organization that you had not seen in previous Egyptian armies. No army, no large mass of people, can cross the Sinai without naval support. It's just not possible, given the desert conditions. That meant that the pharaohs already had the cooperation of the cities of the Levantine shore; these are the future Phoenician cities such as Byblos, Tyre, and Sidon, who had come to acknowledge the pharaoh and were long in contact with Egypt through trade connections going back to the first dynasty, and in many ways, the Phoenicians are Egyptianized Canaanites of the shore. So, already the pharaohs of Dynasty XVIII were able to draw on the naval services of these people in the Levant, who had a favored status in Egypt as merchants. The pharaohs also pushed deep into the Sudan and the regions known as Kush, south of the Third Cataract, were organized as vice royalty. Nubia, the northern sections of the Sudan, was incorporated into Egypt. That is, the territorial extent of this kingdom was greatly enlarged from what had been in the Middle Kingdom or the Old Kingdom.

Imperial expansion halted briefly in the early 15th century B.C. in the reign of a really remarkable lady; her name was Queen Hatshepsut, the daughter of Thutmose II, who reigned from 1489–1479 and I'm using what is known as the low chronology. This is a new chronology that's been pioneered by recent scholars looking at the documents; it's 25 years later than older textbooks would have been, so if there's any confusion between the so-called high and low chronology, I am going with the low chronology, as advocated by Donald Redford and his colleagues.

In any case, Hatshepsut was the full daughter and successor to Thutmose II and she succeeded as Pharaoh, in every sense. She did not rule as queen and she presided over all the religious ceremonies expected of a pharaoh and in the art, she is shown with the attire of a male pharaoh, including the fake beard that all pharaohs wear. The Egyptians who were passionate about cleanliness always shaved themselves and the elaborate hairdos that are seen, particularly on Egyptian women, are all wigs. They shaved themselves bald; they removed all the hair for sanitary purposes and pharaohs wore fake beards because that's how the gods were depicted and a pharaoh is a god, so he has to have a beard and Hatshepsut, in official, art wore a beard like every pharaoh.

She called a halt in imperial expansion for very good reason. She was married to a royal consort, always a dubious prize for anyone to receive as a title, and this was probably a nephew—some would argue it's a half-brother of Thutmose, that is, a son from a concubine to Thutmose II. In any case, Hatshepsut's credentials were better; she was descended from royal blood on both sides and her consort, the future Thutmose III, was proclaimed as a joint ruler, and he was considerably younger than his aunt or half-sister and kept in the background, rightly so. Any military operations to be launched by Thutmose III would benefit him and not Hatshepsut, who could end up essentially losing her throne. Therefore, she pioneered a number of ways of promoting the monarchy that, in some ways, prefigure the policies of the famous heretic pharaoh, Akhenaton, which we'll be discussing shortly in this lecture. That is, she went with promotion of arts, of building programs, high-prestige trade; her great temple at Deir el-Bahri, which is in Middle Egypt cut out of living rock by her brilliant architect Senmut, depicts on the wall paintings another one of those great prestige diplomatic trade missions to the land of Punt, which today would be the Somalian coast, where all sorts of exotic animals are obtained in trade. She conducted a number of impressive building programs, irrigation programs, really in terms of her interest in architecture.

Of all the rulers, she impresses me as having the same inclination that the later Roman Emperor Hadrian would show. On the other hand, this did not mean she was pacific or weak in her policy. She would brook no rebellion in Nubia and if there was any acting up on the frontier, Egyptian armies went barreling into the Canaanite zones to make sure that there was proper respect paid to Egyptian arms. But, she did halt expansion; this frustrated Thutmose III. We're not quite sure exactly what happened to her; the most likely result was that she died of an illness in 1479 B.C., which is equivalent, I think, to year 22 or 23 of her reign. But, in her closing years, she was already losing grip over affairs and Thutmose III was able to assert himself.

We know by year 20 that Thutmose was able to lead an enormous Egyptian army into Asia, defeat a coalition of Canaanite kings at the so-called Battle of Megiddo in 1482 B.C., and that victory opened up a whole new era of Egyptian expansion in Asia. That battle is now thought to have occurred in the joint reign of Thutmose III and his consort Hatshepsut, not in the sole reign; it's sometimes dated some 20 years later and the best guess is that the queen was failing and that Thutmose had taken over. Thutmose represented more than just his personal ambitions. The victories won by the early pharaohs of Dynasty XVIII transform the Egyptian monarchy henceforth, and this goes back with Amos, the first pharaoh to wage campaigns against the Asiatics and expel them from the Nile Valley. Henceforth, the Egyptian pharaohs are not depicted in the white and red crown of Upper and Lower Egypt; they're depicted in war garb, often driving chariots, and shooting arrows into the fleeing Asiatics.

This iconography is extremely well represented on the works of later pharaohs, such as King Tutankhamun, the boy king whose tomb is the subject of all sorts of displays because it happens to survive. And, as I noted, it's a really insignificant burial, though he's not a very important pharaoh; he was probably 18 years old at the age of his death. Or, in the colossal victory programs on the reliefs of Rameses II, the great pharaoh of the 13th century B.C. who ruled a very long time from 1279–1212 B.C. All of this marshal iconography is part of what is now expected of the pharaoh. It even comes down to great inscriptions, stele boundary markers set up proclaiming the triumph of the pharaohs and, above all, we have even what are known as curse tablets—that is, writing curses of the various Canaanite foe and then taking the pottery, the ceramics, and smashing them as a part of magical ceremony to crush the power of the hated Asiatic. I stress this point, especially from the previous lecture, because Egyptian civilization had evolved without an outside threat. The humiliation of that conquest and rule by the Hyksos really did galvanize the Egyptian elite classes, at least, never to allow this to take place again and, also, not only to drive out the Asiatics, but now trod the empire.

Well, Thutmose III, whose known in the older textbooks as "the Napoleon of the Near East," had an extremely long reign from 1479 to 1426 B.C.; that is much of the 15th century and he creates the Egyptian Empire in Asia. He not only moves in and defeats the Canaanites, he comes to stay. And Egyptian armies reach as far as the northern banks of the Euphrates, and I told you they get very confused up there because they encounter a river that's flowing south instead of north the way the Nile does, and they really don't know how to express this. He establishes boundary markers; he encounters the kings of the Mitanni to the east of the Euphrates, these mysterious Indo-Aryan ruling elite, who pose a certain amount of opposition, the first serious organized kingdom. But, he brings the various Canaanite princes of the Levant under Egyptian control. The result is the imposition of Egyptian governors. Very often, the princes of the Canaanites are taken to Memphis, they are reared at the great court of a pharaoh, and they are trained to be Egyptians; they're often given Egyptian wives and so the way the Asiatic provinces are ruled are very similar, in some ways, to the way Egyptian pharaohs had ruled the nomarchs—that is, the nomes, the local districts of Egypt going back to earliest time and that is by co-opting that elite, taking them to a great court, cementing personal ties, friendship, hospitality, marriage alliance, and this system works extremely well. However, Thutmose III is also heir to the administrative apparatus of the Middle Kingdom and there is a vastly expanded royal bureaucracy in Memphis and the significant point is all international correspondence and imperial correspondence is conducted not in Egyptian, but in Akkadian staffed by Asiatic scribes who've been captured in the great wars.

Well, that empire that is created by Thutmose III, this great Asiatic empire, becomes the absolute essential pillar to the monarchy of the XVIII and XIX Dynasty because that empire brings an enormous amount of wealth in the form of slaves, in the form of tribute, silver, grain, commodities. For instance, Thutmose himself reports, after the Battle of Megiddo, that he captured 1,000 chariots, 2,000 cattle, 2,000 goats, 20,000 sheep, and stocks of grain and oil so that his army could live for a whole year, as if on festival. Regular taxation followed and this yielded revenues on an order that no other pharaoh had seen before and that vastly transformed the monarchy. It enabled the pharaohs to hire a professional army and bureaucracy and that army increasingly became to be staffed with frontier peoples, the Libyans and the Nubians, as infantry, but above all, many of the Asiatics. Many of the very people the Egyptians were fighting in Asia were recruited into the chariot army and the Egyptian pharaohs could launch 4,000 to 5,000 chariots in their great armies. These were overwhelmingly staffed by professionals, usually non-Egyptians.

Thousands of slaves entered in Egypt to be distributed among the population and the way the Egyptians usually handled this is to take small groups of them and hand them out to the nobility, hand them to out to the great sanctuaries, to use them for specialized plantation work, to work on the great monuments, and it's anyone's guess how many Asiatics were brought into the general Egyptian population. This was the first massive infusion of a new set of people into Egypt; many of these are Canaanites or Hurrians, or people from Asia. There are a number of loan words, changes in Egyptian art, in tastes of aesthetics, painting styles, jewelry styles, that suggest that numerous Asiatics have been put to work as craftsmen, as shipbuilders, as masons, and they are profoundly influencing, also, the material culture of Egyptian life and contributing words into the Egyptian language. We do not have the kind of statistical information we do as in the

Roman Empire, but this was a significant move of people into Egypt, who are all ultimately assimilated into that general Egyptian population.

Furthermore, the great national shrines profited immensely. These included, particularly, the shrines of Ptah at Memphis, the god of wisdom, traditional patron of the pharaohs; it included Ra at Heliopolis, the great sun god of the Delta; and, above all, it included the god Amon at Thebes, who was the protecting god of the XII Dynasty and just as much the protecting god of the XVIII Dynasty. The great priesthood became, in effect, a national, even an imperial, aristocracy. The high priest of Amun at Thebes—or actually his temple is at Karnak—essentially became the chief administrative official of Upper Egypt. A small clique of powerful families served the pharaoh and, particularly at Thebes, these great families insisted on having a say in policy, and all pharaohs, as part of their expectations of the elite and the armies and the upper classes, rewarded the shrines with great endowments of slaves and wealth in thanks for the victories on the foreign battlefields. So, the result is the monarchy is transformed even more along with the shrines; increasingly, Amun is the protector of the pharaoh.

As I noted in the previous lecture, dealing with the kings of the Middle Kingdom, any pharaoh who came from the south, who came from Thebes, always faced opposition in Middle and Lower Egypt. They were seen as interlopers, as tough border frontier types. So, the pharaohs of Dynasty XVIII really had to go out of their way to prove their legitimacy as upholders of *ma'at*, of justice, and of the traditional cults. Hatshepsut transferred the capital from Thebes to Memphis; that was one of her most important actions. It probably was one reason why she was losing power in her later years; the great families at Thebes resented this. Thutmose III continued to keep the capital at Memphis and used the court at Memphis as the way of training all those Syrian princes he would send back to the Asiatic provinces. There is a concerted effort by the successors of Thutmose III to develop the monarchy at Memphis and to support the other cults other than Amon, notably the cult of Ra, the great sun god of the Delta. Ra is often praised as the soul god who made myriads of himself; all gods come from him. There's this hyperbole and exaggeration in the traditional creator solar divinity of Egypt that is promoted by the heirs of Thutmose III and we believe, in part, this represented not only legitimate thank offerings, but it also reflected part of the efforts of Dynasty XVIII to make themselves presentable to their subjects in lower Egypt, who constituted the majority of their population. That's where the traditional capital is, that's where the trade is. Egypt always faces on the Mediterranean, it always faces towards

Asia, but it was also an effort to break the power of those powerful families back in Thebes, the great priestly families of Amon.

This policy has a couple of consequences to it. For one, the monarchs become ever more dependent on those imperial resources in the form of bureaucrats, scribes, and wealth coming in from the Asiatic Empire. That is, monarchical power is directly dependent on the empire; they must have it if they are to run their own policy and to maintain an independence vis-à-vis of the great priestly families at Thebes. Another important point is that they promote solar cults—notably the cult of Ra—but other solar cults that increasingly become uniform and, what some scholars would call, henotheistic in their thrust. That is, they worship the sun god as the ultimate divine power, manifested in many ways. This type of outlook, which grows out of traditional Egyptian worship, will lead to the solar monotheism proclaimed by the Pharaoh Akhenaton in the mid-14th century B.C.

This brings us to, perhaps, our most intriguing figure in the entire New Kingdom and a man who's been subject to all sorts of novels and psychoanalysis; Sigmund Freud actually wrote a book trying to link this pharaoh with the monotheism of Moses, and it's a very ill-founded argument. But, the Pharaoh Akhenaton, who came to the throne as Amenhotep IV—you know Amenhotep is carrying the name of Amun; it's a traditional dynastic family name—turns out to be one of the most remarkable individuals ever to sit on the Egyptian throne. Until fairly recently, we knew very little about him other than that we believed in the sixth year of his reign, he proclaimed a solar monotheism and ended the worship of the other gods in Egypt. It is only the groundbreaking work by Professor Donald Redford, who wrote a book, *Akhenaten: The Heretic King* and then has gone on to write another even more important work on Egyptian history, really the most important works in Near Eastern history in the last 50 years, in my opinion, that we actually understood who Akhenaton was. His great shrines were smashed after his death, particularly by a general pharaoh named Horemheb. His main relief sculptures were actually smashed into over 20,000 pieces and used as fill for later monuments, and when these were recovered in excavation, they were known as the *talatat*, which is an Arabic word for fragment. It was only Redford who had his graduate students go through and sort all these damn things out and run them through an early computer program, whereby we're able to reconstruct the wall reliefs of Akhenaton's great shrine that we actually understand what this religion was all about. He carried out these reforms not in his sixth year, but immediately at the opening of his second year.

Akhenaton changed his name immediately from Amenhotep to Akhenaton, and the name Akhenaton celebrates and honors the god Aton, an early solar divinity from the Delta who was seen as an avatar of Ra, as a benevolent creator god. In Akhenaton's mind, this was the sole god. The sun was the sole god in the universe and the iconography in his reign is peculiar; it shows the rays of the sun coming down in the form of a hand, touching Akhenaton, who is standing with his wife, Nefertiti, and their children, and he acts as the sole, oracular voice of Aton.

He immediately declares a new capital some 300 miles north of Thebes, represented by the current site of Tel el-Amarna; hence, it's sometimes known as the period of Tel el-Amarna. It's Akhetaton in Egyptian, which is a place of effective glory of Aton; that is what the name means. It's now just a village and it is in the hottest part of Middle Egypt. Akhenaton holds sorts of ceremonies to Aton in the blazing sun. There are actually some reports by his Syrian envoys, who think the pharaoh was probably crazy to keep envoys waiting in this blazing sun. Akhenaton goes so far as to reform the hieroglyphics; he removes the plural for gods. He shuts down all the great sanctuaries, especially the sanctuary of Amun. Now, in part, Akhenaton is following traditional policy, he's upholding solar divinity. He's moved the capital out of Thebes and he's trying to break the power of the priests of Thebes, but he goes far beyond that proclaiming this solar monotheism, trying to break the old cults, and this essentially puts Egypt virtually into a position of civil war. He is able to get away with this because he has the bureaucracy and army behind him. He has the professional pillars, those two pillars of a great monarchy, to impose his will and he rules for 17 years and, as far as we can tell, dies of natural causes. There is no uprising or rebellion against this, although there is widespread resentment throughout the Nile Valley.

In so concentrating on religious reform and all of its repercussions, Akhenaton neglects the empire and this almost proves fatal for the monarchy. It certainly proves fatal for the XVIII Dynasty and it almost proves fatal for Egypt. This is because that allows the emergence of a new power, the Hittites—who are based in what is now Asia Minor and Turkey, and we will be discussing the Hittites in the next lecture—to invade the Asiatic provinces and threaten to strip away that Asiatic Empire so important to royal power. Akhenaton's successors cannot keep control. We believe that King Tut, King Tutankhaton, who was then forced to change his name to Tutankhamun and actually move the capital back to Thebes at one point, that he has to distance himself from the great solar cult of Aton; he has to restore the worship of the ancient gods. Eventually, the last pharaoh in the dynasty, who's a really a general who seizes power and marries a daughter of King Tut, Horemheb, who was commander of the chariot arm, he obliterates the solar cult entirely. That's when the great reliefs of Akhenaton are smashed and used as fill. This brief experiment in solar monotheism is forgotten. There's really no historical memory of it in later Egyptian accounts and it proved a very brief experiment in royal monotheism.

It's hard to get a handle on Akhenaton. I always think he represents a peculiar mix between the Emperor Caligula and Constantine, but that's just a Roman historian looking at the problem. Akhenaton, besides putting Egypt into a succession crisis, insuring the end of his own family, as the XVIII Dynasty was bankrupt, also put the empire in jeopardy. Fortunately for Egypt, a series of generals starting with a man named Rameses I, who established a new dynasty, the XIX Dynasty, intended to contest that effort of the Hittites to take away the Asiatic Empire. It is these pharaohs of Dynasty XIX, particularly the third pharaoh in that family, Rameses II, who make an effort to beat back the Hittite attacks and to restore Egyptian frontiers in Asia. That will climax at a great battle at Kadesh in 1275, which will be a draw with the Hittites and, in many ways, Rameses II goes on to consolidate his empire, but Egyptian power has reached its zenith. In fact, Egyptian's power is on the wane. It is the successors of Rameses II who must face not only the Hittites, but above all, the great migrations and changes coming in the wake of these wars and those are the migrations that bring down the old order of the late Bronze Age. And, to understand that transformation, it will be necessary for us to stop our lecture here on Egypt, leaving Egypt in the reign of Rameses II, and go back and look at who were the Hittites, the Mitanni, these new players in the Near East who came to challenge the imperial power of Egypt and were to rewrite the face of Near Eastern culture and politics.

Lecture Eight
New Peoples of the Bronze Age

Scope: By trade and immigration, Sumerians carried their cuneiform writing and culture west into the Levant and eastern Anatolia and east into Elam, today southwestern Iran. At Elba in northern Syria, excavations have revealed the palaces and archives of West Semitic-speaking kings who ruled over an urbanized kingdom by 2600 B.C. By the Middle Bronze Age, great cities dotted the plains of northern Syria and the Levantine shores, sustained by trade with Mesopotamia and Egypt. In the upper Euphrates and Khabur valleys dwelled the Hurrians, who adapted and disseminated Mesopotamian mores, letters, and visual arts to the Hittites of Asia Minor. Under Indo-Aryan warrior kings, the Mitanni, Hurrian, and Canaanite cities were welded into a major kingdom by 1550 B.C. In central Anatolia, the Hittite kings of Hattušas fielded the first chariot armies, and Šuppiluliumaš I (r. 1344–1322 B.C.) and his heirs battled the pharaohs of Egypt for domination of the Levant. By seaborne commerce, the Minoans of Crete, too, learned of the writing and arts of Near Eastern civilization. By 2100 B.C., the fleets of the kings at Cnossos dominated the Aegean Sea, and in Minoan Crete were the cultural foundations of Classical Greece. In 1600–1400 B.C., Greek-speaking lords of central and southern Greece adopted Minoan arts and aesthetics, overthrew Minoan Cnossos, and clashed with the Hittite emperors.

Outline

I.   This lecture completes our examination of the Bronze Age. We shall look at three areas that came under the influence of the civilizations we have been discussing—those in Mesopotamia, Sumer and Akkad, and in the Nile valley.

   A.   The first of these areas is the western arm of the Fertile Crescent, including the Levant and sections of the middle and upper Euphrates, especially the valley of the Khabur River and the al-Jazirah.

   B.   The second area we shall explore is Anatolia, or Asia Minor, what is today Asiatic Turkey.

C. Finally, we shall briefly look at the Aegean world, that is, central and southern Greece, the islands of Greece, and the island of Crete.

II. The primary agent of this outward influence was long-distance trade.

    A. The region called by Roman historians Greater Syria, that is, the region stretching from the northern frontiers of Syria today down to the Red Sea, was broken up into diverse zones.

        1. The northern sections bordered on the upper Euphrates.

        2. The long coastal strip of Phoenicia, most of which is Lebanon today, was defined by the sea and high mountains.

        3. The interior is watered by two important rivers, the Orontes, flowing north and emptying into the Gulf of Alexandretta, and the Litani, which cuts across Lebanon and southern Syria.

        4. In the far south is the Jordan valley, flowing into the Sea of Galilee and ending at the Dead Sea.

        5. The highlands to the west of the Jordan valley were the traditional home of the Hebrews.

        6. The coastal plain is notable for the city of Gaza.

    B. Evidence of early urban civilization (c. 2600 B.C.) is found in the northern reaches of Syria, in the Orontes valley. This civilization was ruled over by West Semitic kings, and its citizens used cuneiform script for their Semitic dialect. By the Middle Bronze Age (2000–1550 B.C.), northern Syria was dotted with walled cities.

    C. The ports of northern Syria and Phoenicia acted as the conduits to connect Egyptian civilization with early Mesopotamian civilization. At one of those ports, Ugarit, at the mouth of the Orontes River, the first syllabary was devised around 1850 B.C.

    D. The ports of northern Syria and Lebanon were also in touch with the Aegean world, and through these ports, many of the influences of the Near East would pass to Crete and, ultimately, to Greece.

    E. By the Middle Bronze Age, when the Egyptian armies began to appear, there was a series of powerful kingdoms in Greater Syria, notably, Megiddo, Hazor, Tunip, and Kadesh.

III. The region of the al-Jazirah was occupied by the Hurrians.

    A. The Hurrians moved into the region between 2500–2000 B.C. and settled in what are now eastern Syria and western Iraq.

    B. They adapted the institutions of Akkadian and Sumerian civilization and transmitted them to Asia Minor and points west. In that sense, they played a vital role in the formation of the Hittite civilization.

    C. The Hurrians came chiefly as merchants; they were, however, mobilized into an effective military force shortly before the emergence of Egypt as a great kingdom in the 16th century B.C.

    D. This mobilization was carried out by Indo-Aryan speakers of obscure origin called the Mitanni. These people seem to represent a warrior elite and were experts in chariot warfare.

    E. By 1550 B.C., the Mitanni had organized the Hurrians into the main political order dominating Mesopotamia.

    F. The Mitanni proved to be tough opponents for the Egyptians. The immediate successors of Thutmose III negotiated an understanding with the kings of the Mitanni to share rule of northern Syria and maintain the Euphrates as a common frontier.

IV. The second major area to examine is Asia Minor, which also came under the influence of Mesopotamian civilization through trade.

    A. Trade goods have surfaced at two royal sites of the Early Bronze Age in this region: Troy II, site of the Trojan War, and Alaça Hüyük, perhaps the later Hittite city of Arrina or Zippalanda.

    B. The Akkadian emperors waged wars in this region, and starting from 1900 B.C. on, Assyrian merchants moved into the cities of central Asia Minor and established merchant communities.

    C. Influences from Mesopotamia stimulated the Hittites to coalesce into kingdoms around 1700 B.C.

    D. The early Hittite kings unified central Asia Minor into a powerful confederation known as the Hittite Old Kingdom. This kingdom was centered on the capital of Hattušas (Bogazkale), east of the Halys River.

    E. Two of the early Hittite kings, Hattušiliš I (r. 1650–1620 B.C.) and his son, Mursiliš I (r. 1620–1590 B.C.), carried out a methodical conquest of southeastern Asia Minor and advanced into the lands of Syria.

F. Mursiliš I, third of the known kings of the Hittite dynasty, conducted a raid into Babylon around 1595 B.C., recorded in literary accounts of the Near East. The sacking of the city proved how unsuccessful Hammurabi's heirs had been in maintaining imperial defenses.

G. Mursiliš I was murdered upon his return, and the Hittite kingdom experienced a series of succession crises for the next several generations. The Hittites only managed to reemerge as a power through the efforts of several remarkable rulers late in the Bronze Age.

    1. The first of these was Šuppiluliumaš I (r. 1344–1322 B.C.). Through him, the Hittites were able to capitalize on Egyptian weakness and overrun the northern and central provinces of Syria, stripping the Egyptian monarchy of vital imperial possessions.

    2. Šuppiluliumaš was succeeded by two sons, Mursiliš II (r. 1321–1295 B.C.) and Muwatallis (r. 1295–1272 B.C.), both of whom proved to be able campaigners, and both understood that Hittite power could be maintained by conquering the wealthy cities of the east.

H. In many ways, the Hittites represented a preview of the types of imperial institutions that would later be used by Rome. They established military colonies, constructed road systems, and were adept at imposing vassal treaties.

I. Muwatallis clashed with Rameses II, the pharaoh of Dynasty XIX who sought to retake Egyptian possessions. This climaxed in the Battle of Kadesh which was, essentially, a draw. Rameses III later had to sign a treaty with Hattušiliš III acknowledging his loss of Egypt's northern and central possessions.

V. The third area we shall discuss briefly is the Aegean world, which also had a basis in the earlier river-valley civilizations.

A. Evidence from excavations in the Greek world reveals that many of the cultural forms, aesthetic traditions, and material culture of Classical Greece arose in the so-called Bronze Age of Greece (2800–1200 B.C.).

B. Civilization emerged in the Aegean world on the island of Crete. The people of Crete devised a hierarchical society comparable to what we saw in the Near East. By 2100 B.C., the kings of the city of Cnossos had united the island and established control of the sea.

C. The people of this civilization, the Minoans, were responsible for spreading their literacy and arts across the Aegean and into mainland Greece. From 1600 B.C., the people in southern and central Greece, that is, the Mycenaeans of the Greek heartland, adopted much of the civilization of Minoan Crete.

D. What emerged in southern and central Greece was a series of about 12 kingdoms, each ruled by a *wanax* ("lord"). These rulers controlled hierarchical societies, adopted chariot warfare by 1500–1400 B.C., and acquired expertise in shipbuilding and ship warfare from the Minoans. Indeed, around 1400 B.C., Mycenaean Greeks sacked the palace of Cnossos. Thereafter, Crete was incorporated into a wider Mycenaean, Greek-speaking world.

E. These Mycenaean or Achaean warlords had quite a different record from the Minoans, but they, too, were the heirs of the urban, literate tradition that can be traced back to Sumer and Akkad. As we'll see in upcoming lectures, however, all these civilizations would come tumbling down in the decades after 1200 B.C.

Further Reading:

T. Bryce, *The Kingdom of the Hittites.*

———, *Life and Society in the Hittite World.*

Questions to Consider:

1. What was the role played by the Hurrians in transmitting Sumerio-Akkadian culture to Asia Minor? Why did later Hittite kings admire Hurrian culture?

2. How were Minoan and Mycenaean civilizations part of a wider Near Eastern civilization in the Bronze Age? What elements of Minoan and Mycenaean civilization were transmitted to Classical Greece?

Lecture Eight—Transcript
New Peoples of the Bronze Age

In this lecture, I plan to complete the discussion of the Bronze Age and the ambition in this lecture is to cover three areas that came under the influence of the old river valley civilizations—that is, Mesopotamia, the early civilizations of Sumer and Akkad in the lower Tigris and Euphrates, and the Nile Valley. We'll be looking at three distinct areas; one of them will be the western arm of the Fertile Crescent, as I would like to call it. That would comprise the regions of the Levant, everything running from today's Israel and Jordan to Lebanon and Syria. Also, that includes sections of the middle and upper Euphrates River and, especially, the valley of the Khabur River and the great grasslands known as the al-Jazirah today. That whole area acts as a land bridge of sorts between lower Mesopotamia and Egypt, although most travel to Egypt is going to be by sea; there's very limited travel across the Sinai due to the desert conditions.

The second important area we shall look at is the region of Anatolia, Asia Minor—today, Asiatic Turkey. This is a region that is, essentially, a mini-continent in itself. The peninsula of Asia Minor, the interior, is essentially part of Central Asia that is put in the middle of this Mediterranean peninsula—the shores are very Mediterranean in climate, the interior is very much a high central Asian climate with steppes, and it's cut off by mountains—and that peninsula is also important; it will be the home to Hittite civilization. We will also briefly look at the Aegean world and by that I mean what is now central and southern Greece, the islands of Greece, notably the Cyclades, which are the southern islands and, above all, the island of Crete. All three of these areas came under the influence of the older literate civilizations and in all of these regions, new societies were built based on literacy, on cities, on commerce, in the case of the emerging or the incipient Greek world, as you will, that is the civilizations of Crete and Greece in the Bronze Age. This would be sea borne commerce and they became part of a wider civilized late Bronze Age world, of which I spoke in the previous lecture and over which the pharaohs of Dynasties XVIII and XIX presided. So, what this lecture plans to do is to explain how the civilization moved out from those core areas, those two great river valley systems, into this wider arc of related civilizations.

Well, the primary agent, at least in its earliest stages, was trade. Above all, I stress the importance of trade in the development of the first cities of Sumer and then, of the great territorial empires that developed in Mesopotamia—

that is, the Akkadian empire of Sargon and Dynasty III of Ur. That long-distance trade brought merchants from the Mesopotamian world into the Levant, into the upper reaches of Mesopotamia, Asia Minor, and ultimately, even to Egypt. As I noted, there's a very early Sumerian settlement at Buto in the western Delta dating from the very start of Egyptian literate history—that is, around 3100 B.C. That trade stimulated the growth of cities and the region that comprises greater Syria, as Roman historians like to call it, and that would be the whole region stretching from the northern frontiers of Syria today, down to the Red Sea.

That region is a very diverse land; it's broken up into different zones. The northern sections of it border on the upper Euphrates. There is a long coastal strip, most of it, today, the country of Lebanon or in antiquity, Phoenicia, which has a whole tradition of its own. It's cut off by the great mountains of Lebanon and it faces toward the sea. The interior is in its northern and central zones watered by two important rivers; one of them is the Orontes that flows north and empties into the Gulf of Alexandretta. The other is the Litani River that has been making headlines recently, that is often a traditional boundary line in different political orders starting in antiquity down to the modern age. That's the major southern river cutting across Lebanon and southern Syria. Then, in the far south, there's the Jordan Valley flowing into the Sea of Galilee and then dead-ending into the Dead Sea, and that valley is capable of sustaining farming. There are the highlands immediately to the west of that valley; this is the traditional home of the Hebrews, and then there's the coastal plain notable for the city of Gaza in both ancient and modern times. So, what you have is a very mixed zone.

It's in the northern reaches of Syria on the Orontes Valley and in the regions between the Orontes and the Euphrates, where we begin to get the evidence of first urban civilization. This has now been demonstrated dramatically by Italian excavations at the city of Ebla in northern Syria, where as early as 2600 B.C.—far earlier than previously believed—a full urban literate civilization had emerged ruled over by west Semitic kings, employing the cuneiform script for their own Semitic dialect—there are Sumerian merchants settled among them and many of the institutions we'd associate with Akkadian-Sumerian civilization were already in place, centuries earlier than anyone imagined. Ebla is probably not unique. We can detect the same at Mari on the middle Euphrates and so our conception of early Mesopotamian history has been greatly widened and much of what is northern Syria, certainly by the period of middle Bronze Age, running approximately from 2000 to 1550 B.C., was dotted with cities, to be sure not quite as large as those of the great river valleys, but substantial cities, walled cities based on that Mesopotamian model. Most of the people dwelling in those cities spoke various Semitic dialects, which we call for convenience Canaanite, and the best guess is that whole Levant at this early period, as early as we can tell, perhaps 3000 B.C. or earlier, spoke a series of related Canaanite dialects later represented as Phoenician or Hebrew in the Iron Age.

The areas are important for several reasons. One is the ports of northern Syria and of Phoenicia acted as the conduits connecting Egyptian civilization to early Mesopotamian civilization. At one of those ports, Ugarit south of the Orontes, the mouth of the Orontes that enters into the Mediterranean, was devised the first syllabary—that was the simplification of cuneiform into a more manageable script of some 75 to 85 symbols; you're representing syllables. From those syllabaries, eventually an alphabetic system was devised by Phoenicians in the early Iron Age—that is, approximately after 1000 or 1100 B.C. It's also clear that the cities on the ports of northern Syria and of Lebanon, today, were in touch with the Aegean world and it will be through these ports that many of these influences will pass to Crete and, eventually, to the Greek world.

By the middle Bronze Age, certainly by 1550 B.C. when the Egyptian armies begin to appear, and certainly in the reign of Thutmose III in the 15th century B.C., there are a series of very powerful kingdoms in northern and central Levant, or greater Syria. Notably, there is Megiddo, Hazor, Tunip, and Kadesh—all cities replete with important histories in the late Bronze Age with numerous battles and sieges occurring there.

In addition to these regions of greater Syria, there was also a region immediately to the east of the Euphrates—I mentioned it in passing—I call it the great grasslands of the al-Jazirah, the Khabur river valley, which flows into the Euphrates. This region is now divided between Syria and Turkey, and a bit of it is also in Iraq, but most of it is in Syria and Turkey today. In this region, a people that we know very little about in terms of their origins, known to us as the Hurrians, occupied much of this area.

The Hurrians speak a language that is otherwise unrelated to any other language we know, and again, the reason we're able to read Hurrian is that the Hurrians employed the cuneiform script and they also used Akkadian. So, since we can read Akkadian, we got some sense of Hurrian; some progress has been made in reading the Hurrian language and we know that a later people of the Iron Age in Lake Van in Eastern Turkey—which becomes the core, the cultural foundations of classical Armenia, that is the Kingdom of Van, Tushpa as it's called—that they, too, are somehow related to this Hurrian language. The best guess is that these people had moved into the area sometime between 2500 and 2000 B.C. and they settled in the grasslands and the towns of what are now eastern Syria and western Iraq. They became the great educators of civilization. They adapted the institutions of Akkadian and Sumerian civilization and transmitted it to Asia Minor and points west. In that sense, they played a very vital role in the formation of the Hittite civilization in Asia Minor.

The Hurrians themselves arrived largely as merchants, some of them came as immigrants; they settled in towns and even in the towns of Assyria—that is the northern Tigris Valley, the center of the future Kingdom of Assyria. Many of the residents were actually Hurrian in origin and they did not represent any kind of military invasion or even a migration of a new people muscling their way into the Near East. It seems that the settlement was a case of small numbers of immigrants; they very often mixed with Canaanite speakers and Akkadian speakers. They were, however, mobilized into an effective military force shortly before the emergence of Egypt as a great kingdom—that is, in the 16th century B.C. That had to do with the arrival of a new people, Indo-Aryan speakers, as they're called, and these are people of obscure origin; they're called, in the records, the Mitanni. They seem to represent a warrior elite and they're also expert in the new chariot warfare that was evolved about this time and that is the light chariot pulled by two horses, which enables either two or three men to be in the vehicle. One of them is a bowman armed with a composite bow; the other is often a spearman, and then the charioteer is the guy who actually takes care of the horse. These chariots were devised somewhere between 1700 or 1800 and 1600 B.C. in Eastern Asia Minor, in Armenia, in areas where you had horses and you had the grasslands. They were very complicated vehicles to build; you had to have very good expertise in woodwork. There are all sorts of wood that need to be used; the wheels are open spoke wheels. The chariot is built for flexibility and strength. A very strong man can actually carry the vehicle over his head. It was usually pulled by two horses. The horses have to be bred to handle this weapon and all light chariots required, essentially, an elite warrior class sustained by estates and peasants, comparable to what you would think of medieval knights in Western Europe. This is a whole military system with social implications.

It seems the Mitanni came in and organized these Hurrians on the upper Tigris into an effective kingdom and, by 1550 B.C., this is the main political order dominating Mesopotamia. They are perhaps no more than 5 percent of the population. From what we can tell of the names of these rulers, they were speaking a language closely related to the later historic language of Sanskrit and worshipped the gods known from the *Rig Veda* such as Indra, Varuna, and Mithra, gods known in the later Sanskrit Hindu tradition. What we think they are, are a branch of this group that moved into the Near East as other members of that linguistic group, moved into the Indus Valley and eventually made their way to the Ganges and founded the basis of later Hindu civilization. They proved to be tough opponents to the Egyptians. It is really the immediate successor of Thutmose III who negotiated an understanding with the kings of the Mitanni, essentially, to share rule in northern Syria, keeping the Euphrates as, more or less, a common frontier with a certain no man's land between the two of them. We don't really know much about the Mitanni. I think the largest text we have is actually a horse-training manual that survives in Hatusha.

The second major area I want to look at is Asia Minor—and that's an area that has been brought into our discussion with the pharaohs of Egypt—and today that is Asiatic Turkey. That region came under influence of Mesopotamian civilization, again, through trade. Sumerian merchants undoubtedly had an effect on the great peninsula of Asia Minor. We know this from trade goods; they've surfaced at two early royal sites of the early Bronze Age. One of them is Troy II, which is the famous Troy of the Trojan War; it's a much earlier version of the city, it's about 2600 B.C. The other is a site called Alaça Hüyük, perhaps the later Hittite city of Zippalanda or Arrina. We know the Akkadian emperors waged war in this region and later on Assyrian merchants, starting from 1900 B.C. on; they moved into the cities of Central Asia Minor and set up those merchant communities I've described. They're known as a *karum*, which is sort of merchant consortium, which survives today in modern Turkish as the word for shopping center, actually, which is a pretty good use of that old Akkadian word.

These influences from Mesopotamia stimulated a group of people we know as the Hittites, whose ancestors had entered the peninsula of Asia Minor centuries earlier to coalesce into kingdoms starting around shortly after 1700 B.C. The Hittites seem to have been in the forefront of developing chariot warfare. There are good reasons for this; in part, they had the kind of pastures and real estate necessary to maintain those herds, the horses were native to the area, and one of the items that we know which Syrian merchants so desperately wanted in Asia Minor were horses and mules. Usually, horses were obtained in Mesopotamia in an early age to breed with the donkeys to create mules; the mule was the main pack animal. No one rode a horse; it was just too difficult to deal with. It was probably the Hittites, perhaps the Hurrians—the Mitanni—who broke horses and hooked them up to these light chariots and turned them into an animal of war. Calvary will only come much, much later in the Iron Age; that's a whole later development in the future.

It was the early Hittite kings who unified central Asia Minor. They unified the various subkingdoms and states into a powerful confederation; we often call it the Hittite Old Kingdom. This kingdom was centered on a city known as Hattušaš, today known as Bogazkale, which is east of Ankara. It's east of the Halys River, the great river that bisects the Anatolia, the Kizilirmak or Red River, as it's said in Turkish today. The Hittites' state was really quite a precocious state. Two of the early kings of the Hittites, Hattušiliš I was the first whose name is given to the capital—he built the initial capital—and then his son Mursiliš I carried out a methodical conquest of southeastern Asia Minor and advanced into the lands of Syria. This would occur between 1650 and 1590 B.C., about two generations before the emergence of the Egyptian Empire, and after the death of Hammurabi of Babylon.

In these regions were these very prosperous Sumerian style cities that had been built in Syria, and the Hittite kings moved into this region because to them, the cities of Syria populated by Canaanites and Hurrians represented the most civilized part of the world. That is where the urban-based civilization was. The Hittites had received writing in the form of cuneiform, legal institutions; they redefined their gods very much along the lines of the Hurrian pantheon. They also obtained the various myths of Mesopotamia, such as the legend of Gilgamesh and the myth of creation—the *Enuma Elish*; all of these were adapted and written both in an Akkadian version and then eventually applied to the Hittite language in cuneiform text, that have come down to us from Hattušiliš. Sumerian civilization had this remarkable extension of this influence deep into the peninsula of Asia Minor, in a landscape totally different from the Delta conditions of the great cities of the flood plain of lower Iraq today, on these steppes and these high tablelands of Anatolia. It's really a testimony to the Hittite kings that they could organize the diverse peoples of Asia Minor under their aegis and then project that power east into Syria and northern Mesopotamia.

The first instant of the projection of this power came from a king named Mursiliš I, third in the known kings of the Hittite dynasty; we really can't trace him much back beyond Labarnas I, the founder of the dynasty. He conducted a massive raid into Babylon around 1595 B.C. It was an event that was recorded in all the literary accounts in the Near East because it was such a dramatic event. I stress that Babylon, by that time, was really the premiere cosmopolitan city of the Near East, it was the great nexus of trade routes; it was the center of culture and learning. Hammurabi had turned Babylon into a capital more than lower Mesopotamia, but for the whole of the Near East, had made Akkadian the literary and diplomatic language of the Near East. And, that event probably proved how unsuccessful Hammurabi's heirs had been in maintaining imperial defenses, the fact that the Hittites could get 300 miles down the Euphrates, appear rather unexpectedly, take the city, and then retreat. The attack didn't do the Hittites much good. Mursiliš I came back to a welcoming committee of nobles, angry over his long absence; he was murdered and the Hittite kingdom went into a series of succession crises for the next several generations. The attack on Babylon weakened Babylon to such an extent that the family of Hammurabi lost power and these Kassites, these people from western Iran, moved in and took over as military elite in Babylon. Hence, that situation I described earlier in a previous lecture, when the Egyptians moved into the Near East, Mesopotamia was ruled by two foreign dynasties—the Mitanni in the north, those mysterious Indo-Aryan chariot warriors, and the Kassites in the south, who apparently also had access to that new military technology of the chariot.

The Hittites went into a period of decline and really managed to reemerge on the scene, largely due to the efforts of several remarkable rulers late in the Bronze Age. The first of these is a man known as Šuppiluliumaš, who came to the throne in 1344 and died in 1322, during a great plague that ravaged the Hittite Empire. He was the Hittite emperor, more or less, contemporary with Akhenaton the great heretic pharaoh of Egypt, who was pushing his solo monotheistic reforms. The Hittites were able to capitalize on Egyptian weakness and overrun, at least, the northern and central provinces of Syria and strip the Egyptians' monarchy of those vital imperial possessions, those possessions so important to maintaining the bureaucracy and army in imperial Egypt that allowed a pharaoh such as Akhenaton to carry out his solo reforms.

Šuppiluliumaš was succeeded by two sons, Mursiliš II, and then his brother, Muwatallis. Both of these kings proved able campaigners; they understood, as all Hittite emperors understood, that the way Hittite power could be maintained is to conquer the wealthy cities of the east, to gain the resources and institutions that would allow you to construct an effective monarchy in central Anatolia, and to gain those areas you had to build a series of coalitions and alliances with the rather war-like people of Asia Minor, stretching to the Aegean and recruit all your western neighbors who would otherwise be a problem for you, and turn them loose on the unsuspecting Syrians, Hurrians, and Canaanites, which is the whole principle of Hittite power.

The Hittites, in many ways, represented, to me, a sort of preview of the types of imperial institutions Rome would use. They used military colonies, they used road systems, and above all, they were extremely good in posing vassal treaties. The Hittite emperor was very punctual about that tribute being paid in chariots and manpower. The great capital of Hattušaš was essentially a ritual capital to summon various vassals to the presence of the great king of Hatti, as he was known to impress upon them the need to render tribute and military forces and whatever else was necessary. The excavations going on at Hattušaš, conducted by Peter Neva and the German team, have revealed that the city was just studded with temples. There was a vast expansion of the capital in the 14th and 13th century B.C. and all of this was to create the sort of ritual theatre necessary to exalt the power of the great king. It was a remarkable achievement because the King Mursiliš clashed with Rameses II, the great pharaoh of the Dynasty XIX, who sought to retake the Egyptian possessions back from the Hittites. This climaxed in the battle of Kadesh, which was essentially a draw.

While celebrated on the magnificent reliefs of Abu Simbel in northern Sudan, a world monument, a first class monument known to most, you're looking at the official PR version by the Egyptian pharaoh, and Rameses later had to sign a treaty with the King Hattušiliš III, the later Hittite emperor, acknowledging his loss of all those northern and central possessions. That is, Egypt had suffered a major check, the first of a series of reverses that will result in the Egyptians withdrawing from their Asiatic possessions sometime shortly after 1050 B.C. Well, the Hittite achievement is stunning and, as I say, it represents the achievements of these great kings of Hatti, who were working with institutions and resources far less than either the river valleys of the Mesopotamia or Egypt.

There's one third area I want to bring in briefly and, again, because this course acts as something of a gateway course to other courses in The Teaching Company, I think it's important to say a few words on that third area—that is the Aegean civilizations that, too, had their basis in these earlier river valley systems. This is because it's increasingly evident from excavations going on in the Greek world that the so-called Bronze Age of Greece, which is usually regarded as extending from about 2800 to 1200 B.C., that many of the cultural forms, aesthetic traditions, perhaps many of the important sanctuaries of classical Greece, material culture, go back to this Bronze Age. Also, there is a lot more continuity between this Bronze Age and the later so-called Iron Age—that is, the period after 1000 B.C., which eventually sees the emergence of classical Greek civilization, and there's very little doubt that classical Greek civilization represents the foundations of the western tradition and so, classical Greece has deep cultural roots in the Bronze Age. And these civilizations emerging in the Bronze Age, in turn, have important links with Egypt in the Near East.

Civilization emerged in the Aegean world on the island of Crete, in some ways, the most unlikely of islands for anyone who has visited it; it's volcanic, it doesn't have nearly the resources as the more eastern island Cyprus, which is close to the Syrian shore and has been a home to Greek speakers for a very long time. Nonetheless, it's in Crete that the first sea borne civilization really emerges. Crete could only succeed by taking to the sea. The people who dwelled on the island of Crete in these earliest days are unknown to us. They devised a palace structure, a hierarchical society comparable to what we saw in the Near East. By 2100 B.C., we believe kings ruling from the city of Cnossos had united the island and imposed, what the later Athenian historians called a thalassocracy—that is, control of the sea. Certainly, these southern islands of the Aegean, the Cyclades, were under the influence of this brilliant Cretan civilization or Minoan civilization, as we prefer to call it, named after the legendary King Minos, associated with the Minotaur Greek legend. The Minoans were responsible for spreading their literacy and their arts across the Aegean and into mainland Greece. That was a very, very important role played by the Minoans because from 1600 B.C. on, the people in southern Greece, today Peloponnesus, central Greece, the region of Attica where Athens is, Boeotia, the island of Euboea—that is the heartland of what becomes the later Greek world, the center of the Greek city-state.

These areas that were occupied by early Greek speakers, we call them Achaeans based on the term used in Homer or Mycenaean, based on the main site excavated in Peloponnesus known as Mycenae. These people came into contact with the Minoans and adopted much of the civilization of Minoan Crete; that included the arts and that also included literacy. The

Minoans had devised a syllabary of their own, probably based on models from the Near East; it's now called Linear A. We cannot read it. There have been numerous efforts to crack it; we just don't know what it is.

These early Greeks devised their own version of that syllabary and employed it for keeping royal records and the like. We can read that, the script is called Linear B and is an early form of East Greek or South Greek. That was demonstrated by a brilliant case of decipherment by Michael Ventris in 1953. So, what emerges in southern and central Greece are a series of, maybe, 12 kingdoms ruled by dynasts who would be known as *wanax—wanakes* in plural—lord, a title that appears early in Homer, a title that appears on Linear B tablets. They ruled very much the kind of hierarchical societies we would see in the urban cities of the Near East. They adopted the chariot warfare by 1500 or 1400 B.C. They actually got so good at learning seafaring and shipbuilding from the Minoans, that they knocked off Cnossos somewhere around 1400 B.C. There is very little doubt that Cnossos was burned and the burning was done by an invading army. That was probably a group of Greeks coming from the mainland that came to Crete and stayed. Thereafter, Crete was incorporated into a wider Mycenaean or Achaean Greek-speaking world. That is, Greek-speaking lords ruled from the throne of Cnossos, which most people visit today as a major tourist attraction at Crete. When you come into Iráklion, they always take you up to Cnossos.

The Mycenaeans or Achaeans, these war lords were quite a different outfit from the Minoans and they are known, in the records, as attacking the outlying possessions of the Hittite Empire on its western and southern shores, especially Hittite allies, and their activities are in some ways connected with the emergence of the later legends of Troy. But they, too, were part of the heirs of this great bureaucratic literate urban-based tradition that goes back to Sumer and Akkad, and so were members of that wider late political and cultural order, the late Bronze Age. The question then comes up—what happened to this incredible expansion of civilization by 1200 B.C.? Because in many of these areas I've just discussed, civilization will take a step backwards after 1200 B.C. and the great empire of Egypt, the empire of Hittites—the Mitanni, the Kassites—these empires will come tumbling down in the decades after 1200 B.C.

Lecture Nine
The Collapse of the Bronze Age

Scope: Between 1225 and 1050 B.C., the great empires of the Late Bronze Age fell in the wake of migrations and barbarian invasions usually associated with the advent of iron technology, but the imperial order of the Late Bronze Age did not collapse so much as fragment. Civilization in Egypt and Babylonia exhibited continuity between the Bronze and Iron Ages, whereas urban, literate civilization was disrupted in the Levant, Anatolia, and the Aegean world—all regions that adopted alphabetic writing in the Iron Age. In the Late Bronze Age, kings of the Near East and petty dynasts of the Aegean world, facing rising administrative and military costs, had recruited greater numbers of barbarian warriors. Innovations in weapons and tactics undermined the dominance of the chariot and shifted the military balance to the frontier peoples. In the Aegean world, the palaces of Achaean lords were sacked; in Asia Minor, the Hittite Empire fell. The Sea Peoples swarming out of these regions ended Egyptian imperial rule in the Levant by 1050 B.C. The ensuing world of the Early Iron Age was politically divided and culturally diverse. The great palaces of Mycenaean Greece disappeared in favor of small communities destined to evolve into the city-states of Classical Greece. Phrygians dwelled in central Anatolia, while Neo-Hittite kings ruled over the former southeastern Hittite provinces. The Levant was shared between the Aramaeans, newcomers, and the Canaanites, who had redefined themselves as Phoenicians and Hebrews. Even in Egypt and Babylonia there was change, for Libyan and Nubian military elites dominated the Nile valley, and the Assyrians aspired to rule Babylon.

Outline

I. This lecture looks at the collapse of the political and cultural order that had emerged by about 1550 B.C. in the Near East. The collapse occurred shortly before 1200 B.C. and is connected with the migration of new peoples, the emergence of new societies, and the introduction of iron technology.

A. The collapse of the Bronze Age is often compared to the fall of the western Roman Empire in the 5th century A.D.

B. This lecture discusses some of the explanations that have been put forth for why the collapse occurred and examines some of the changes in civilization that took place in the Early Iron Age.

II. Archaeologists have advanced a number of explanations for the collapse of the imperial orders in the Near East.

    A. Efforts have been made to link the collapse of organized civilizations with natural catastrophes, such as changes in climatic conditions or a pandemic, but these theories cannot be sustained by evidence. Most of the population decline that can be detected is the result of the destruction of cities brought on by war.

    B. Older textbooks theorize that various invaders wielding superior iron weapons moved in and overthrew the earlier civilizations. For example, the Dorians, a group of West Greek speakers, are said to have invaded the Aegean world and overtaken the Mycenaean palaces of the Late Bronze Age. Again, no documented evidence attests to battles with newcomers armed with superior weapons. In fact, iron weapons did not come into general use until about 900 B.C.

    C. The answer probably lies in the weaknesses of the institutions and cultures of the Late Bronze Age.

        1. All of the great political and cultural orders of the Late Bronze Age—imperial Egypt, the Hittite Empire, the kingdom of the Mitanni, and even the petty dynasts who ruled under the title *wanax* in Greece—faced high costs of government.

        2. The rulers of these civilizations had a great appetite for money. The pharaohs in Egypt and the Hittite kings, in particular, felt the need to display the power of their courts through elaborate ceremonies and the construction of great palace-temple complexes.

        3. The costs of maintaining royal bureaucracies and professional armies were also significant. As we've said, Egyptians led the way in recruiting frontier peoples for military service: The Libyans became all-important to the Egyptian infantry, and vast numbers of Asiatics were recruited into chariot armies.

The Hittites followed suit: Their armies comprised numerous allies from western Asia Minor and other regions.

4. Warfare was no longer a matter of minor clashes. For example, in the campaign that climaxed at the Battle of Kadesh in 1275 B.C. between the Hittite and Egyptian armies, at least 5,000 chariots were pitted against each other in a battle involving 75,000 men.

5. In conducting these campaigns, the great monarchs armed the very frontier peoples who would ultimately seize power for themselves. Robert Drews has pointed out that changes in warfare were not brought about by the shift from bronze to iron technology but by changes in tactics and weapons associated with the frontier peoples. At the end of the Bronze Age, warfare required skilled, agile warriors who could fan out in light infantry formations and break up chariot attacks.

III. The extent of the collapse of the Late Bronze Age varied in different civilizations.

A. In the newer areas, the zones where civilization was received from the earlier river-valley cores, the destruction was at its most violent.

B. In contrast, in Egypt and Babylonia, urban, literate civilization survived. We find linguistic, cultural, and demographic continuity between the Bronze and the Iron Ages.

C. To some extent, we can determine which areas went under and which came through the collapse based on the writing systems used in the Iron Age. In Egypt, hieroglyphics continued, as did cuneiform script in Mesopotamia. In the Levant, Asia Minor, and the Greek world, however, the Early Iron Age saw a period of illiteracy, during which writing was lost. Literacy later reappeared, with the adoption of an alphabetic system invented by the Phoenicians around 1000 B.C.

IV. Migrations at the end of the Bronze Age led to a profound rearrangement of the political and cultural landscape.

A. In the Greek world, the great palaces of the warlords and royal centers were burned, with the exception of Athens, around 1225–1200 B.C. With the destruction of the palaces came the end of long-distance trade, the complicated bureaucracy, and the elite warrior class that had sustained the monarchs. After 1000–900 B.C., the organization of Greece returned to scattered communities that would eventually evolve into the *poleis* ("city-states") of Classical Greece.

B. In Asia Minor, the Hittite Empire fragmented. The western and central sections fell, and new peoples emerged, primarily the Phrygians, who occupied central Anatolia. Excavations of their capital at Gordian reveal that the society there had adopted the alphabetic system and was in touch with the Greek world. Political order returned to Asia Minor after a period of almost 350 years of disorder and disruption.

C. In the southeastern sections of the old Hittite Empire, some of the imperial traditions held on. Noble families who claimed descent from the great emperors of the Bronze Age ruled over small regional states in what is now northern Syria and southwestern Turkey. The Neo-Hittites were also linked to the Urartians, a people located immediately to their east in Armenia around Lake Van, who had their capital at Tushpa.

    1. The Neo-Hittite kingdoms are the equivalent of medieval Byzantium—the political heir of Rome but culturally Greek.

    2. The eastern sections of the Hittite Empire, which had been the most urbanized and civilized, survived. They were culturally part of the Hurrian-Mesopotamian world but claimed to be the political and legal heirs of the old Hittite kings.

D. Reconfigurations in the political and linguistic landscape also took place in the Levant. Two peoples emerged: One group was Semitic speakers from the desert known as Aramaeans, who were the first people to domesticate the camel in the 9th and 8th centuries B.C. This development changed the trade routes in the Near East, launching the caravan networks that we think of in the Middle East today.

    1. The Aramaeans took over important cities in Syria, notably Damascus, and Aramaic became the commercial language of the caravan trade from the 8th century B.C. to the Muslim conquest.

    2. The pioneering of caravan routes by the Aramaeans led to the revival of trade and city life and sustained the reemergence of civilization in the Early Iron Age.

E. The Phoenicians settled as far as Gades (modern Cadiz) in southern Spain and Carthage in North Africa.

    1. In the collapse of Bronze Age civilization, the "Sea Peoples" attacked the shores of the Levant and invaded Egypt. These invasions disrupted the Egyptian Empire, although the pharaohs were able to beat back the invaders. The price was the loss of the Asiatic empire for Egypt after 1040 B.C.

    2. The Egyptians' loss allowed Phoenician cities to emerge as commercial centers. Starting from 1000 B.C., the Phoenicians were responsible for the revival of sea routes and their extension into the western Mediterranean.

    3. Phoenicians invented the alphabet and, above all, pioneered marketing in the Iron Age; they sold manufactured goods from the Near East to North Africa, the Greek world, Italy, and Spain.

F. Among all the "new peoples," the ones who would have the most significant impact after 900 B.C. must have seemed to contemporaries to be the least important. This would be the Hebrews, dwelling in the highlands between the Jordan valley and the coastal plain occupied by the Philistines. We shall turn to these people in the next lecture.

Further Reading:

Robert Drews, *The End of the Bronze Age: Changes in Warfare and the Catastrophe ca. 1200 B.C.*

N. Sandars, *The Sea Peoples: Warriors of the Ancient Mediterranean, 1250–1150 B.C.*

Questions to Consider:

1. What led to the collapse of the political and cultural order of the Late Bronze Age after 1200 B.C.? How did conditions in the Aegean world, Anatolia, and the Levant differ from those in Egypt and Babylonia?

2. Who were the important newcomers in the Near East of the Early Iron Age? Why did the Aramaeans and Phoenicians play such a crucial role? What was the political situation in Asia Minor? Why did these new societies act as intermediaries between the Near East and the nascent Greek world?

Lecture Nine—Transcript
The Collapse of the Bronze Age

In this lecture, I plan to look at the end of the Bronze Age, the collapse of the great political and cultural order that had emerged in about 1550 B.C. with imperial Egypt presiding over that wider world, and the collapse of the political institutions that allowed these complicated monarchies to exist that occurred shortly before 1200 B.C. That decline is also connected with the migration of new peoples and the eventual emergence of new societies and, also, the introduction of iron technology; which is seen as a very important break, between the so-called Bronze Age and the Iron Age. I mentioned this at the start of this course about this period, which is often known as the end of the Bronze Age or the collapse of the Bronze Age, running anywhere from 1200 to 900 B.C., depending on where one was living.

In Egypt, there's a lot more continuity; it's much shorter than it would be in the Greek world or Asia Minor, but nonetheless, in this period sometimes characterized as a Dark Age, many of the conditions and changes in society are often compared to the type of changes wrought with the breakup of Roman power between the 5th and 6th centuries A.D.—that is, the transition from antiquity into the medieval world. And, some of the comparisons do hold up. I must admit in giving this lecture, I am primarily a historian of the Roman world and therefore, I instinctively see these problems through the eyes of a Roman historian, which has a certain amount of value, I hope, because it allows me to look at what is very limited body of evidence—nothing like what we have for the Roman Empire—in order to piece together these great changes. Therefore, what I plan to do is to discuss some of the arguments that have been proposed on why the political and cultural order of the late Bronze Age collapsed.

There's a number of theories that have been proposed on this and I'm going to give my own take on what the situation might have been, and then look at the way civilization changed in that early Iron Age, in the immediate aftermath of the collapse of the Bronze Age. We will look at the changes in the river valley systems—that is, the old core areas of the Nile, and the Tigris and the Euphrates, but also in those wider areas, in the Levant, in Northern Mesopotamia, in Asia Minor, and a little bit in the Greek world, to get some sort of sense on how the changes occurred in these areas, areas where civilization had arrived at a later date. Furthermore, I want to stress that this lecture acts as a transition not only from the Bronze Age into the Iron Age—and the next three lectures will deal with three of the most important people coming out of the Iron Age, the Hebrews, the Assyrians, and the Persians—but it is also a very, very important gateway for classes and lectures dealing with Classical Greece and other courses, because Classical Greece will emerge out of this dark age. Out of all the civilizations that collapsed in the Bronze Age, by everyone's agreement, the darkest of the dark ages, the darkest of almost any Dark Age anywhere, is the Greek Dark Age, that intervening period between the Bronze Age and the Iron Age, which eventually saw the emergence of a new civilization, Classical Greece. Part of my responsibility is to set up the wider world that came after the collapse of the Bronze Age and a bit how Classical Greece fits into that world that follows in the Iron Age. Even though Classical Greece is not really the subject of this course, at least it will give you an entrée into some of the problems of early Greek civilization.

Let's look at the first part of this lecture, which is the collapse of the imperial orders in the Near East. Explanations have often been advanced by archeologists—and, again, I must stress the information is quite limited. We do know, for instance, of vast burning of sites, especially in the Greek world, in Asia Minor, parts of the Levant. There have been efforts to link the collapse of organized civilization with natural catastrophes. Some have tried to see resumption of volcanic activity; there are the famous excavations at Santorini or Thera, where all the cruise ships go in the Aegean Islands. This is a volcano that erupted somewhere around 1570 B.C. Efforts to deduce from looking at changing climactic conditions based on pollen samples and wood samples, that perhaps the Near East went into a period of ecological decline or there were a series of bad harvest, brought on with draught, famine, disease. Various references in the Hittite, Egyptian, and Ugaritic texts have been culled in order to argue that, perhaps, there was some kind of pandemic—that is, a wide-ranging disease—that carried off the population. None of these theories really can be sustained by the evidence.

The evidence is very select; most of the population decline, which we can detect by archeological survey, is a result of the destruction of cities and the movement of people, which caused hardship and the collapse of agriculture, and those cities were sacked by humans, not by natural catastrophe. There's no evidence of widespread earthquakes or volcanoes; there's no real evidence of a major disease sweeping through them. Ultimately, famine and death and disease were the results of war, rather than the actual causes of the collapse of these civilizations. There have been, in older textbooks, efforts to note that invaders came in and overthrew the earlier civilizations.

These were invaders wielding superior weapons, notably iron weapons that invaders known as the Dorians—these were a group of Greeks speaking, what is known as, a west Greek dialect—they moved into the Aegean world and overthrew the Mycenaean palaces of the late Bronze Age. The palaces are remembered distantly in the Homeric poems. That Phrygians and the so-called Gasga people of Anatolia again overthrew the Hittite Empire; that Iranian peoples moved in from the east to overthrow some of the civilizations in Mesopotamia; and again, there is no documented evidence of such types of battles or invasions in which newcomers were armed with superior weapons.

These were all surmises based on a very limited record of evidence and while iron technology comes in, again it seems much more to be a result rather than a cause of the end of the Bronze Age. Iron weapons and tools—and it's mostly weapons, really; bronze is still used for most tools—but iron weapons do not come into general use until around 900 B.C. There are early efforts going back as early as the 13th century B.C., primarily among the Hittites, one of the empires to lose in the Bronze Age, there are references to the Hittites forging the earliest iron. They're probably doing it because they have a lack of tin to alloy with their copper to create bronze and its metallurgists working on contract for the great King of Hatti, who is creating the first iron weapons that have to be forged. What you have to do is temper the iron so you can pound out the impurity because you can't achieve the temperatures necessary to forge the iron the way we can in a modern Bessemer process. That's just not available to these people. And so, you have to temper it; you create the image of the smith, especially when you think of Hephaestus in Greek mythology. In any case, there doesn't seem to be a sort of technological change, where barbarians wielding iron weapons, mounted on horses—everyone's worst nightmare, something out of *Conan the Barbarian* and one of those types of movies—moving in and overthrowing these settled communities, these great civilizations. It just didn't happen that way.

Instead, I think it's important to look at, the institutions and cultures in the late Bronze Age. There were weaknesses in those states that already prefigured that the descendants of the great kings of the Bronze Age were to face in the 12th and 11th and 10th centuries B.C. I think, again, I'm bringing a perspective from the Roman world to bear on this, but ultimately, all of the great political and cultural orders of the Bronze Age—Imperial Egypt, the Hittite Empire, the kingdom of the Mitanni in northern Mesopotamia, the Kassites of the Babylon, and even those petty dynasts who ruled by the term lord or *wanax* in Greece—all of them faced very high costs of government in order to sustain those societies and those organizations. Furthermore, these kings from 1500 B.C. faced, as all kings did, rising costs, and kings always have an appetite for money. They need it for displaying the great power of their courts; one thinks of how the ceremony at the Court of Memphis, starting with Hatshepsut, was articulated into the elaborate types of ceremonial and burial practices that one would see in the tomb of Tutankhamen or the great war reliefs at Abu Simbel of Rameses II.

The Hittite kings, too, had to keep up with the Egyptians on this. And starting with Šuppiluliumaš I and ending, certainly, with the last well-known Hittite king, Tudhaliyas IV at the end of the 13th century B.C., the Hittite kings developed their own great palace at Hattušaš and also satellite capitals—one at Carchemish on the Euphrates, the other at Hamath on the lower Orontes, those two vital river systems that gave the Hittites control of those vital Syrian possessions. Near Hattušaš, for instance, remarkable work has been done on the great rock relief sanctuaries of Yazilikaya, which was commissioned by Hattušiliš III and his queen, Pudahepa, carried on by his sons Tudhaliyas IV and Šuppiluliumaš II. And, what the Hittite kings attempt to do is to pioneer a major religious reform to link their monarchy with the types of sacral kingships you would see in Egypt, and to create the high ceremonies and religious institutions that would give the Hittite kings legitimacy and parity with Egypt. I mean they're obviously putting in an enormous amount of expense in maintaining this capital Hattušaš, which is really becoming increasingly remote and difficult to defend since the gravity of Hittite power was shifting southeast and to Syria.

Besides all of those costs, there were also the administrative costs, the great bureaucracies that had to be maintained to collect the taxes and, above all, armies. Probably the biggest expenditure all of these kings were facing, all of these lords, was military expenditures and it's important to stress that armies were professional. That, increasingly, kings recruited not their own subjects, but the frontier peoples, the people who were on the borders and the fringes, who would otherwise be a problem into these professional armies. Again, the Egyptians led the way. The Libyans became all important to their infantry—that is, the nomads immediately to the west of Egypt. Many of them were already being brought in at the end of the Bronze Age, particularly in Dynasties XIX, XX, XXI, as military colonists in the Delta—the vast recruitment of Asiatic peoples into the chariot arm. The Hittite kings did the same; their armies comprised numerous allies from western Asian Minor and from the so-called Luvian kingdoms, these were people who spoke a related language to the Hittites. The Kassites, the Kings of the Mitanni, likely did the same and we believe—and there's a good argument to be made on this—that the Mycenaean or Achaean lords of Greece actually brought those Dorians in initially as mercenaries and allies and armed them as tribal regiments in their own wars, faintly remembered in the later Greek legendary tradition. So, all of these kings went to recruiting the border regions in these zones and that meant high expense. Warfare became increasingly expensive when the great kings went to war; these were no longer minor clashes.

The campaign that climaxed at the Battle of Kadesh in 1275 B.C. between the Hittite and Egyptian armies, that campaign represents the type of warfare that went on starting from the time of Thutmose III and ending with the collapse of these great political orders. That required fleets, it required logistics; at Kadesh, alone, there were at least 5,000 chariots pitted, total about 2,500 on the side, perhaps 75,000 men clashed in the great battle, a battle of which we have a considerable number of details. These types of wars, wars of siege and position, these were expensive. All of the monarchies engaged in these types of wars, along with the complicated and expensive diplomacy that went with it and that meant higher taxes, higher costs, and ways of trying to cut corners on meeting those military expenditures. Part of the problem was that the great monarchs armed the very frontier peoples so important to their defense, and eventually what happened is that those frontier marshal peoples went into business for themselves and knocked over a number of these states or seized power.

There were also changes in warfare and there has been some very significant arguments made by Robert Drews on this regard, in his work on *The End of the Bronze Age*, and he's pointed out that it wasn't so much a question of technology—iron as opposed to bronze weapons. But, in part, it was a change of tactics and weapons very closely linked with that shift increasingly over to frontier peoples. He was the one to note that the real key was not that iron swords were being made, but now, long slashing swords, and that the frontier peoples, such as the Dorians or the Libyans or the allies of the Hittite Empire, these were all being recruited from people accustomed to hunting, men who came from societies in which every free man was a warrior. They were able to use javelins; they could throw them on the run. They used large slashing swords and with it, a short shield and articulated armor, so tactics changed significantly. Prior to these tactics of the late Bronze Age, armies really comprised dense infantry formations. The large shield and the spear, they clashed, the chariots acted on the wings, the charioteers would ride in and shoot areas, trying to flank the infantry formations, take them in the rear in the confusion of battle.

The type of warfare that develops at the end of the Bronze Age among these frontier peoples, is just the type of warfare requiring skilled, agile warriors, men who could actually take out chariots, who could fan out in light infantry formations, open formations, throw their spears at chariots, break up chariot attacks, come smashing into infantry formations with these slashing swords, and kill at a deadly close range. And, the change in tactics meant whole new changes in warfare; you had to have these types of soldiers. Increasingly, those soldiers were on the fringe, and so part of the change was simply the fact that the best soldiers available were in the frontier zones and these are the people who bring down the Hittite Empire and the Achaean city-states. In this sense, there's a certain similarity to what happens in the Roman world, which is that, essentially, the Romans arm first their defenders and, ultimately, the people who do them in, and that is the German tribal armies of the 4th and early 5th centuries. What happens is the frontier peoples, in effect, bring a marshal society into the interior, into the civilized core.

So, that seems to be part of the problem, along with fiscal difficulties, rising costs of government, and all of that conspires to lead to the collapse of some of this political order. And here, the extent of the damage and the extent of the loss of contact with the Bronze Age, depended very much on where one lived. In the newer areas, in the zones where civilization was received from the river valley cores, we believe that the destruction was at its most violent and most profound. That makes sense. Civilization was much newer there, there weren't as many cities, the population was smaller; institutions did not survive to the same degree. In Egypt and Babylonia—that is, in southern Mesopotamia and Babylonia is the heir to Sumer and Akkad—there, our urban literate civilization survived and continued. There is great cultural continuity, linguistic, and even demographic continuity between the Bronze and Iron Age. I always put it this way; one can tell, more or less, what areas went under and what areas got through the Bronze Age collapse, based on the writing systems they used in the Iron Age. In Egypt, hieroglyphics continued; in Mesopotamia, so did the cuneiform script.

But in the areas of the Levant and the areas of Asia Minor, in the areas of the Greek world, there was usually a period of illiteracy where writing was lost; the syllabaries and the cuneiform script of the Bronze Age went out of use and when literacy reappears, it reappears in the form of the alphabet, a peculiar script invented by the Phoenicians somewhere around 1000 B.C.

and adopted in those regions where the collapse had been the greatest. That is where continuity had been the least, where in many cases urban institutions, literate-based institutions, had disappeared. That's a pretty good way of seeing the extent of the damage at the end of the Bronze Age.

Those changes—those migrations—led to a profound rearrangement of the political and cultural landscape. And, again, without getting too much into the very vexed details of the migrations themselves, I think it's best to start from west to east and look at who was there and then who emerged after about 1000 B.C. How did the world change? Well, the most profound change was in the Greek world. This is seen in the destruction of all the palaces in the Greek world. They were all burned at some point between 1225 and, maybe, 1200 B.C. There was one exception and that is Athens, and the Athenians themselves in classical times had a tradition that Athens had escaped the destruction and that seems to be borne out by the archeology. That meant a break in continuity. The great palaces of those warlords or *wanax—wanakes,* as they would call themselves in early Greek—were brought to an end. With the collapse of those palaces, went long-distance trade, the complicated bureaucracy, and that elite warrior class that sustained the monarchs, and as a result, what we get in Greece after 1000 or 900 B.C. is a very different society.

It's not organized along regal lines, not organized along palaces with overseas trade, but rather scattered communities. There is a whole new linguistic pattern in Greece; the dialects have changed. The speakers of what were to become east Greek had largely been pushed east, people who spoke west Greek had pushed into central Greece, and Peloponnesus and the destiny of Greece would not be in the kind of hierarchical urban order that you saw in the Bronze Age, but in new institutions that would evolve, and those would be the institutions of the *polis* or the city-state of Classical Greek—a very profound change, indeed.

In Asia Minor, the changes were almost as dramatic. The Hittite Empire did not so much collapse as fragment. The western and central sections fell. New people emerged; foremost among them, the Phrygians who occupied central Anatolia, their capital city at Gordion, had been excavated by a very important team of archeologists since 1950. The finds at Gordion that continue to this day are revealing the remarkable transformation of society in central Asia Minor. The capital of Hattušaš was abandoned, power now moved west. The Phrygians developed a new society in central Asia Minor; now, excavations indicate that this society had emerged perhaps as early as the 9th century B.C. They adopted the alphabetic system, they're in close touch with the Greek world, and political order returns to Asia Minor after a period of almost 350 years of disorder in local cultures. In the southeastern sections of the old Hittite empire, some of the old imperial traditions hold on, particularly in the cities of Carchemish and Hamath; these were subsidiary capitals in the late Bronze Age and become the royal capitals of what we call the Neo-Hittites.

These are royal families claiming descent from the great emperors of the Bronze Age, ruling over small regional states in what is now northern Syria and southeastern Turkey. They were also connected with these people known as the Urartians immediately to their east in Armenia around Lake Van at their city of Tushpa. They are linked, certainly culturally, even though linguistically, they're not. Most of these so-called Neo-Hittites really don't speak Hittite; what they speak are various so-called Luvian dialects, Hurrian languages, and you can think of these Neo-Hittite kingdoms as sort of the equivalent of medieval Byzantium as the political heir of Rome, but essentially culturally Greek. That's what you have. That is, the eastern sections of the Hittite Empire, which were the most urbanized and cultured and civilized, and were based most directly upon Mesopotamian civilization, and continued to use the old writing systems—those areas survived, culturally, very much part of the Hurrian-Mesopotamian world, but claiming to be the political and legal heirs of the old Hittite kings. Whereas the Hittite homeland fell apart and new peoples moved in and organized new states in that period of the dark age, notably, the Phrygians and later the Lydians.

Farther south in the Levant, there were important reconfigurations in the political and linguistic landscape. Two peoples emerge who will have a very important role to play in the succeeding centuries; one group were newcomers. These are Semitic speakers, emerging from the desert known as Aramaeans. This was the first time we could actually begin to speak of desert nomads, starting around 900 B.C. The Aramaeans seem to be more, again a result rather than a cause of the Bronze Age collapse, but there are several innovations that change the situation in the Fertile Crescent and this is the first domestication of the camel. The Aramaeans are the first people to begin use of the camel in the 9th and 8th centuries B.C. and that changes significantly the trade route patterns in the Near East. They begin to acquire, what we think of as, the caravans and the networks of the Middle East today; those did not exist before 900 B.C. Furthermore, the Aramaeans and the other Semitic peoples in the desert have mastered oasis farming, particularly the date trees, and so there is a network of communities, at least on the fringes of the Arabian Desert, that now can be linked by these caravan trades, and this will eventually evolve into the classic pattern of the Bedouin that we know from the Islamic period; it's already even known in the Roman period for that matter.

So, the Aramaeans move in and they take over important cities in Syria, notably Damascus, the cities along the Euphrates; their kinsmen, the Chaldaeans, migrate into Babylonia. What they develop is the caravan networks and, above all, they popularize their language, which becomes the major commercial language of caravans and commerce starting in the 8th century B.C. and really running down to the Muslim conquest. Aramaic will become the *lingua franca* of the Near East; it will displace Akkadian cuneiform. It's already occurring in the time of the Assyrian Empire. The Neo-Assyrian kings of the 8th and 7th centuries B.C. actually publish their documents both in cuneiform and in the more adaptable, alphabetic Aramaic script. So, the Aramaeans are extremely important in pioneering the caravan routes that lead to the revival of trade and city life in the early Iron Age, and sustained the reemergence of civilization in the early Iron Age. And, they are newcomers. Their language, while closely related to Hebrew and Phoenician, is not the same; it is a distinct west Semitic dialect and Phoenician and Hebrew and the Canaanite languages descend from the languages of the Bronze Age. The Aramaeans represent a group of newcomers who have arrived off the desert.

That gets us to the Phoenicians and the Phoenicians are settled along the coast of what is now Lebanon and parts of Syria, and when the Greeks apply the term, they actually also include people living in southeastern Asia Minor. There are Phoenician colonies there, in Cyprus, and eventually, Phoenicians settle as far west as Cadiz, or Gades as it would be called in the ancient world. Gades is Cadiz, too, in Spain. Carthage, which means new city in the Phoenician language, is in North Africa. What the Aramaeans achieve on the desert, the Phoenicians achieve on the sea. In the collapse of the Bronze Age civilization, especially in the Aegean world, numerous people, called in Egyptian accounts the Sea Peoples, attacked the shores of the Levant and invaded Egypt. Those invasions disrupted the Egyptian Empire. The Egyptian pharaohs fought for their lives to beat back the invaders and they succeeded. The success of Egypt was well served by the successors of Rameses II, but part of the price was the loss of the Asiatic Empire after 1040 B.C. That allowed the Phoenician cities—some of those newcomers among the sea peoples, the Philistines, who settled father south along what is now the coastal areas of Israel—that allowed those cities to emerge as commercial centers.

The Phoenicians took to the sea starting from 1000 B.C. on. They are responsible for not only the revival of sea routes, but for their extension into the western Mediterranean. It was Phoenician merchants who created the alphabet, who perfected the marketing of glass and the purple dye, which is sort of a crimson, and above all, what I admire about the Phoenicians is that they really pioneered the market logic of the Iron Age and that is—don't sell what the customer wants, sell what you have. And, they were excellent at marketing all sorts of manufactured goods, mass manufactured goods, from the Near East to North Africa, to the Greek world, to Italy, and to Spain. They have an important economic and, even, cultural role to play in the emerging Iron Age. The Phoenician cities, independent city-states ruled by dynasts, were very adroit; they always aligned with whoever was the major political power. Once Egypt had declined, they could assert their independence, but when the Assyrians emerge on the scene, they deal with the Assyrian kings, after them, they deal with the Neo-Babylonian kings, and finally, the Persian Emperors. And so, the Phoenician cities come to play a major role in the commercial life of this new political order of the Iron Age and they will prosper under the great political orders that are constructed, starting from about 911 B.C. on, when the Assyrians begin to build the first major political orders in almost 500 years.

Finally, I should mention that among all of the "new peoples," the ones that would have the most important impact in the world after 900 B.C. must have seemed, to contemporaries, the least important. That will be the Hebrews, who are dwelling in the highlands between the Jordan Valley and the coastal plains occupied by the Philistines, but their impact will not be political or economic or military; their impact will be theological and intellectual and they will be the subject of the next lecture, dealing with the emergence of the Hebrews and their religious vision that is to have such a profound impact in shaping the western tradition.

Lecture Ten
From Hebrews to Jews

Scope: The Hebrews are first documented in contemporary sources of the
Near East in the 9th century B.C., when cuneiform and Aramaic
texts report the kings of Israel and Judah, who claimed descent
from King David. The two Hebrew kingdoms were united in their
common worship of Yahweh, although each had its own
sanctuary, and many Hebrews worshiped the Canaanite gods on
the "high places." The dynasty of King Omri (884–873 B.C.) and
Ahab (873–852 B.C.) forged a state with institutions comparable
to the Neo-Hittite and Aramaic kingdoms, but their heirs ran afoul
of the Assyrian kings, resulting in the sack of Dan by Sennacherib
and the breaking of Israelite power. Population and prosperity
shifted to the southern kingdom, Judah, where the kings Hezekiah
(727–698 B.C.) and Josiah (640–609 B.C.) conducted a reform of
the worship of Yahweh. In 586 B.C., King Nebuchadrezzar II
(605–556 B.C.) sacked Jerusalem and deported the city's ruling
classes to Babylonia. During the Babylonian Captivity (c. 586–539
B.C.), Hebrew priests and psalmists defined the transcendence of
Yahweh and initiated the editing of the Torah. In so doing, they
also defined Judaism as a faith detached from place and, thus,
altered forever the conception of religion in the Western tradition.

Outline

I.   This lecture deals with the evolution of the Hebrew peoples into the
     Jews, a transformation that occurred in the Iron Age.

II. The first five books of the Christian Old Testament constitute Torah,
     the law of Moses. The narrative books that follow, such as Joshua,
     Judges, and so on, continue the story of the Hebrews and are the result
     of composition in the period after the so-called Babylonian Captivity
     (c. 586–539 B.C.).

     A. Scholars designate the editorial traditions of the Hebrews as E, J,
     P, and D, each of which offers a unique conception of the
     godhead.

1. E represents the earliest tradition in the Old Testament, evidenced by references to God using the term *Elohim* ("Lord" or "Lords").
2. The J, or Jehovah, tradition was clearly passed on by authors who had a powerful sense of the monotheistic God.
3. The P, or Priestly, tradition is usually thought to come from authors in Babylonia and later. These authors, writing in Babylon after 535 B.C., put together the documents in their final form, a brilliant religious vision of the evolution of the people of Israel from earliest times through the covenant with Moses, the Divided Kingdom, the restoration from Babylon, and the fulfillment of God's promise.
4. Finally, the D, or Deuteronomy, tradition, gives yet another vision of the godhead that influenced the later narrative books.

B. These traditions do not represent a coherent historical narrative, but they do hint at what society must have been like for the Hebrews.

III. The Bronze Age collapse was decisive in the destruction of the Egyptian Empire.

A. The Sea Peoples coming out of the Aegean assaulted Egyptian possessions in the Levant, including the historic kingdoms of Israel and Judah. The weakening of Egyptian rule on the Levantine shore was significant in shaping the Hebrew kingdoms and identity.

B. The Philistines, who are believed to have originated in Crete, were driven onto the shores of Israel sometime between 1100–1150 B.C. They are remembered in the Old Testament as interlopers. They forced the Hebrews to organize themselves into effective kingdoms.

C. We have no written documentation of the Hebrews from contemporary Near Eastern records before 1200 B.C., but the core of the Hebrew kingdoms has been the subject of intense archaeological work.
1. There was probably always a distinction between the northern zone, Israel, running along a line near Jericho, and the southern zone, Judah, around Jerusalem.

      2. The northern zone was more densely populated and wealthier and would become the kingdom of Israel, with cult centers at Dan and Shechem (Samaria).

  D. The Hebrews clearly had a memory of the kings Saul, David, and Solomon. In 1993, excavations at Dan uncovered an Aramaic inscription naming a victory over a king of Israel, perhaps King Omri (884–873 B.C.) or his son, Ahab (873–852 B.C.). Significantly, the Aramaic inscription notes that this king was of the house of David.

  E. The Hebrews also faced competitors to the east, in the Jordan valley. There, we have the inscription of King Mesha of Moab, which again, tells us of wars with Israel and highlights the position of Israel as sandwiched between dangerous rivals to the east and the west.

IV. The development of the Hebrews into effective kingdoms came quite late.

  A. Cities first appeared in the northern kingdom under King Omri and his successors. Omri was a tough mercenary general who had extinguished the line of David. Ahab, the second in the Omrid line, is the first named biblical king, recorded in a cuneiform text as participating in the Battle of Qarqar (853 B.C.) against the Assyrian king Shalmaneser III. Ahab's military resources in the battle point to Israel's position as the third most important kingdom in a coalition of 10 states.

  B. Archaeology bears this out: In the 9th and 8th centuries B.C., Israel experienced major urban development. The Hebrews embarked on building programs and promoted the worship of Yahweh at cult centers.

  C. The dynasty in Israel, although politically and economically far more significant than Judah, was too prominent in Near Eastern politics. In the 8th century, Israel became caught up with its neighbors in the imperialism of the Assyrian kings.

  D. Eventually, the Israelite kingdom submitted to the Assyrians as a client state. Several rebellions followed, ending in a colossal failure around 724–721 B.C. with the Assyrian deportation of the "Ten Lost Tribes."

V. The fall of the kingdom of Israel is an important factor in the Hebrew self-identity and religious conceptions.

    A. Power shifted to Jerusalem abruptly. The Assyrians reduced Judah, or Judaea, to a province. The kings ruling in Judah paid tribute to the Assyrian kings but were fundamentally left alone. Thus, Jerusalem began to emerge as the capital of an effective kingdom.

    B. Under the kings Hezekiah (727–698 B.C.) and Josiah (640–609 B.C.), Judah became the political and religious center of the Hebrews. These two righteous kings imposed strict monotheism on the population, and Judah asserted itself as the successor to the Davidic kingdom.

    C. This position is confirmed by economic and social developments; under the Assyrian kings, Judah prospered. The kingdom also managed to stay outside of the destructive wars waged at the time by the Assyrian kings.

    D. After the Assyrian Empire collapsed, the kings of Judah ran afoul of its successors, the Neo-Babylonian kings, including Nebuchadrezzar II (605–556 B.C.). In 587/6 B.C., Nebuchadrezzar besieged Jerusalem and deported the upper classes to Babylon in the so-called Babylonian Captivity.

    E. This deportation was another important step in the development of Hebrew monotheism. The ruling, literate classes were exiled for a period of about 40 years, down to 539 B.C. In that year, the Persian king Cyrus the Great conquered Babylon, returned the Hebrew exiles to Jerusalem, and permitted the rebuilding of the Temple.

    F. During the exile, monotheistic Judaism as we understand it today was defined. The monarchy of Judah had been destroyed, and the Hebrews were unable to perform their religious rites, yet they did not become assimilated into Babylonian society. Instead, they redefined the powers of Yahweh; this God was universal, omniscient, and omnipotent, and his worship did not depend on any particular location or rites.

    G. When the upper classes were returned from Babylon to Jerusalem, they carried with them a powerful conception of the godhead. Further, they now emphasized the importance of the written word in understanding the godhead.

VI. The Hebrew prophets and poets composed psalms and conceived of the God of Abraham, Yahweh, as lord of the universe.

    A. These poets described the covenant with Abraham, the arrival of the Hebrews in Egypt and their liberation by Moses, and the conquest of Canaan as the delivery of the promise of Yahweh. The Hebrew kingdoms came together under Saul, reached their pinnacle under David and Solomon, then broke into the Divided Kingdoms.

    B. What comes through in this powerful religious vision are the traditions encapsulated in Exodus in the Ten Commandments, primarily the first one: "Thou shalt have no other gods before me."

        1. The Hebrew religious vision was fundamentally at odds with all other religious visions that we know of in the Near East: God is transcendent and not part of nature.

        2. Efforts have been made to link this Hebrew monotheism with other such conceptions in the Near East. The Hebrew poets, however, clearly had a transcendent vision of the godhead.

        3. Further, the God of the Hebrews was conceptualized with human personality but without human limitations. He is not defined or limited in myths, as are the other gods of the Near East.

        4. Finally, the Hebrew God acts through human affairs, making the struggles of humans important in and of themselves.

    C. The religious vision of the Hebrews ultimately became the religious, ethical, and philosophical perception of the West.

Further Reading:

I. Finkelstein and N. A. Silberman, *The Bible Unearthed: Archaeology's New Vision of Ancient Israel and the Origin of Its Sacred Texts.*

A. Mazar, *Archaeology of the Land of the Bible, 10,000–586 B C.E.*

Questions to Consider:

1. What were the literary and religious traditions of the Pentateuch (Genesis, Exodus, Leviticus, Numbers, and Deuteronomy)? What were the religious objectives of these works, and how does each conceive of the godhead?

2. What were the political and economic conditions of the Early Iron Age that contributed to the development of monotheism? How important were the roles of the prophets and the righteous kings of Judah? What was the importance of the Babylonian Captivity?

Lecture Ten—Transcript
From Hebrews to Jews

In this lecture, I plan to deal with the question of the evolution of the Hebrews into the Jews, as I like to put it. That is the movement from a group of Canaanite speakers who worshiped Yahweh— which is Yahweh, the word for God in the Hebrew, Old Testament, as Christians call it—to Jews who were a people with a faith, Judaism. It was a monotheistic faith, no longer attached, necessarily, to a particular location or even ritual, and that is a very, very important evolution that occurs in the Iron Age and, very often, the term Hebrews is used by scholars to designate the ancestors of the Jews, dwelling in their homeland at the time of David, at the divided kingdoms. The term Jew is really a term that comes out of the administrative text of the new Babylonian Empire and the Persian Empire; it's their name for the province of Judea, the southern kingdom, and it comes to designate the religion of those who believe in Judaism, whether they're residents in the homeland or not. That's one of the important aspects of the religious vision to which we are heirs from Judaism of these ancient times—that is, religion is not necessarily attached to place. It is attached to one's perceptions, one's ethical beliefs, and one's worship of the transcendent God.

In starting this lecture, it's necessary perhaps to give some of my own perspective on this issue. I'm going to approach it as a historian, a historian of the Near East with an interest in archeology and documentary evidence, and this course is only a preview of the very complicated question of Hebrew origins, the evolution of the Bible; there are numerous courses that handle that topic and that's a whole subject in and of itself. What I should start out with is the fact that what Christians would call the first five books of the Old Testament, or Torah, the law of Moses—Genesis, Exodus, Leviticus, Numbers, and Deuteronomy—and then the narrative books that follow usually designated by scholars as the Deuteronomist historian— these would be the narrative books such as Joshua, Judges, Samuel I and II, Kings I and II, which continue the story of the Hebrews through the divided kingdom, the conquest by the Babylonians—these narrative works of the Old Testament are a result of composition in the period after the so-called Babylonian captivity in 587 B.C. or 586 B.C. That is one date; another date is ten years earlier.

The date is sometimes disputed of exactly when the Babylonian king took Jerusalem and deported the Jewish populations to Babylonia. Scholars working in the 19th century have seen the production of these works as the result of editorial traditions and perspectives, religious perspectives that are usually designated by abbreviations, and each of these is a unique perspective on the godhead. People working in biblical text usually identify these as E, J, P, and D; E represents the oldest traditions in the Old Testament, as we have it. These are references to god by the term *Elohim*, meaning "Lords" or "Lord"; these go back very early in Hebrew history in the praise of God. There is a tradition known as J, or Yahweh, or Jehovah, as it was rendered in Latin, and those represent a tradition by editors who clearly have a very powerful sense of the monotheistic god. These traditions are particularly evident in the accounts dealing with David, also in the accounts dealing with Moses and the conquest of Canaan. There is a P tradition, a Priestly tradition, as it's called, and this is usually thought to be those authors in Babylonia and later, who put together the documents in their final form and have cast this work as a brilliant religious vision of the evolution of the children of Israel from earliest time through the covenant with Moses, through the trials and tribulations following the death of Solomon, the divided kingdom, the restoration from Babylon, and the fulfillment of God's moral experiment and his promise.

Finally, Deuteronomy, that very, very critical book that is sometimes thought to be the law that is reported to have been found in Jerusalem in the 7th century B.C., gives yet another vision on the godhead and that's seen as distinct and as a vision that influences those later narrative books I spoke of earlier. So, these literary traditions, these religious outlooks, stand behind the production of the biblical accounts and they present an incredibly powerful and very poignant religious vision. It's a vision that has come to dominate western thought and really has defined what religion is in the western tradition. Ultimately, the notions of religion in the west go back to the conceptions of these Hebrew prophets and the people who spoke these inspired words, which were then cast in the literary form that we have them today.

They do not represent a coherent historical narrative, in any sense, and I don't believe that reading the text as a history in the sense of Egyptian annals, the king list of Sumer, or the historical accounts that come to us from the Greek world, is the proper way of understanding what the message and moral worth of the Bible is. On the other hand, there are many historical traditions preserved in it. What we can tell is that starting in the Iron Age, these traditions give us a window into what the society must have been like for those Hebrews who came under considerable stress with the collapse of the Bronze Age civilization. They came to redefine themselves religiously by a religious conceit that they were a distinct people who worshipped Yahweh and that differentiated them from everyone else in Near East, despite the common cultural, linguistic, and artistic heritage they had with these earlier civilizations, particularly the influence of Egypt, which is very early in the Levant, as well as the many associations that can be traced through Biblical texts that show parallels with Mesopotamian literature. I mentioned in the last lecture that the Bronze Age collapse was decisive in the destruction of the Egyptian Empire.

A multitude of people who came out of the Aegean, known as the Sea Peoples, assaulted the Egyptian possessions in the Levant. That included the areas that were the original homelands of the Hebrews, which came to become the historic kingdoms of Israel and Judah, and Israel is already clearly known to the Egyptians; it's named on the Stele of Merneptah somewhere shortly after 1210 B.C. Apparently, it's part of the Egyptian Empire. There was a rebellion in which Israel, along with others, were defeated by the pharaoh. In any case, that weakening of Egyptian rule, the whole of the Levantine shore, was decisive in shaping those Hebrew kingdoms and the Hebrew identity.

For one, the Philistines who are believed to have originated in Crete now—this is told in the Old Testament and it seems to be borne out by the ceramics and some of the linguistic evidence—they were people driven out of the Aegean by the collapse of those great palaces of Greece. They arrived on the eastern shores of the Mediterranean, they invaded Egypt along with other sea peoples; these are people coming from the Aegean from western Asia Minor and Libya. They wear a very distinct headdress and they are defeated by the Egyptian pharaohs, and they are eventually driven into the shores of what became the Philistine city—that is, today, the shores of Israel—sometime between 1100 and say 1050 B.C. and are remembered in the Old Testament tradition as interlopers. They were newcomers; they did not speak Canaanite. They eventually were assimilated, but the Hebrews, as well the Phoenicians and the other Semitic-speaking peoples in the areas, saw the Philistines as interlopers and from the descriptions, for instance, the arming of Goliath in his contest with David—and I always feel that David had an unfair advantage with that sling. The sling is an extremely effective weapon, can knock anyone out, if you know how to use it, but the arming of Goliath does show a lot of similarities with the type of weapons of the Aegean world. It seems to be a memory of that.

Those Philistines forced the highland zones, the traditional regions of Hebrew settlement—that is, Israel and Judah—to organize themselves. There has been extensive survey carried out in what we believe to have been the core of the Hebrew Kingdoms. This has been done by Israeli archeologists and they've demonstrated several facts that the archeology tell us and I should note, we have absolutely no written records from contemporary Near Eastern sources on these people before 1200 B.C. The one we have is a very brief reference on Egyptian Stele. The first figures of the Old Testament to be mentioned in contemporary documents come from the 9th century B.C. and there's been a spectacular recent find in 1993. So, in terms of what we know from the historical record based on archeology, we really have a very, very limited record. What the society is, as far as we can tell, is a society based on mixed agriculture and stock-raising. There's already evidence as early as 3000 B.C. that these people probably did not consume pork, which later becomes a prohibition, one of a number of prohibitions that separates them from their neighbors, and that seems to be borne out in the archeology, that these people had always dwelled there speaking a Semitic language, as far as we can tell, and that there was probably always a distinction between the northern zones and that northern zone, more or less, runs along a line near Jericho. That is, there were a group of tribes that clearly were in the more densely populated and wealthier areas, later to be the kingdom of Israel, with its cult centers at Dan and Shechem, quite distinct from the southern zone that was less populated around Jerusalem.

There clearly was a memory of these kings of Saul, David, and Solomon. They're remembered and the stories on them are absolutely some of the most beautiful literature ever written and really inspiring. In 1993, there were excavations conducted at Dan, or Tel Dan as its called, which is one of the capitals of the later northern kingdom of Israel and uncovered there was an Aramaic inscription, probably set up by King Hazael of Damascus, and it names a victory over a king of Israel; we're not sure who he is—it could be either King Omri or his son Ahab, well-known as rulers of the 9th century B.C. But, what is significant is that Aramaic inscription says that whoever this Hebrew king is—the name is lost—he was of the house of David and that already, in the 9th century B.C., both the northern kings of Israel and the kings of Judah, in our contemporary records, already claim to be kings of ruling, as some kind of descendent going back to David and this Davidic kingdom. So, the best guess is that these Hebrew tribes were forced, in part, to organize into more effective states to battle the Philistines of the coast.

They also faced competitors to the east in the Jordan valley; there we have another inscription found in the 19th century that bears out some of what we're told in these conflicts, going back to the time of David and Solomon. That is the inscription of King Mesha of Moab. Moab is constantly referred to in the Biblical text. The Moabites are seen as relatives of the Hebrews; they worship Moloch as their national god and Mesha's inscription tells us of wars he had with the kings of Israel. And, again, that is a very good 9th-century B.C. document that gives a sense of the position of where the Hebrews were; they were really sandwiched between very dangerous rivals, both to the east and to the west. The development of these kingdoms into effective kingdoms is really quite late. We know that it was under the king of Omri and his successors that the cities first appeared in the Northern Kingdom. This makes sense, considering what we know of the early Iron Age and the end of the Bronze Age. There had been a period of loss of literacy, there had been a collapse of urban life, and that this revived starting from 900 B.C. from a combination of the pioneering of the caravan trades by the Aramaeans, as well as the development of sea borne commerce by the Phoenicians. And Israel, the northern kingdom, was ideally placed to exploit these advantages.

Omri was a tough mercenary general who had seized power, according to the Old Testament. He had extinguished the line of David and in the religious perception of what went on, the kingdom of Israel—which essentially broke off from Solomon's family—had a very brief time as, perhaps, being the new Davidic kingdom, but essentially blew it under these kings of the 9th and 8th centuries B.C. who gave such concern to the prophets, Elija and Elisha. That is because these kings were caught up in the vortex of Near Eastern politics. We know from very good Biblical testimony that King Ahab, the second of the line, sometimes known as the Omrid kings—that is, the kings descended from Omri; that's using a Greek rendition of the name, a Greek patronymic—that he married the Princess Jezebel of Tyre. He sponsored the worship of Baal—that is, of other gods—and he had connections with Phoenician cities. Ahab is the first Biblical king named in a cuneiform text. He shows up at the Battle of Qarqar in 853 B.C., fighting the Assyrian King Shalmaneser III. What is impressive about the account, we're told that the he fielded 2,000 chariots and 10,000 infantry, which means if this is correct, Israel was the third most important coalition in a coalition of ten kings and right on par with the Neo-Hittite state of Hamath and the Aramaean state of Damascus.

The archeology, especially some very good Israeli archeology, has borne this out; in the 9th and 8th centuries B.C., Israel takes off. There is major urban development, the centers at Dan and Shechem are developed architecturally; in fact, Shechem is later to be named as Samaria from which we get the Samaritans, renamed in the Roman Age, Neapolis, and today the modern city of Nablus. They apparently promote building programs. They also promote the worship of Yahweh at their own cult centers. These kings are not particularly good monotheists and it is their presiding over this combination of rites that really provokes Hebrew prophets of the 9th and 8th centuries, in this tradition of trying to bring the kings back to proper worship to cast down the idols; the most dramatic, of course, is Elisha's contest with the priests of Baal. That tradition seems to be very much borne out from what we can tell of the material culture of Israel at this time.

The dynasty in Israel, while politically and economically far more significant than Judah, really has the misfortune of being too much in the forefront of Near Eastern politics. These kings of Israel can prosper in the 9th century because of the fact that conditions are revising to some sort of notion of political normalcy, but in the 8th century B.C., Israel gets caught up with a number of its neighbors in the imperialism of the Assyrian kings, who will be brought on in the next lecture. It's the misfortune of the Israelite kings that they stood right in the path of Assyrian kings and, as so often will be unfortunate in the history of this area, the area was also strategic for securing routes so the Assyrian kings could invade Egypt, which was their opponent starting in the 8th century and 7th century B.C. What happens is the Israelite kingdom first submits to the Assyrian kings as a client state. There are several rebellions backed by the Egyptian pharaohs; these are very well remembered in the Hebrew tradition and it ends in a colossal failure sometime around 724 to 722 B.C., when the Assyrians have had it and they ruthlessly move into the northern kingdom and carry out the deportation of the Ten Lost Tribes. They were apparently deported over to the upper Tigris and settled as military colonists on the Iranian frontier.

They didn't remove everyone. They brought in a number of colonists from other parts of the Assyrian Empire, who were settled in the cities of the kingdom of Israel, and the resulting fusion of the Assyrian-sponsored colonists and the Hebrews, who remained in the old northern kingdoms, produced the Samaritans that won encounters in the time of King Herod or in the New Testament. The Samaritans maintain a separate identity well through the Roman age. They are certainly a separate group in the 6th century A.D. and beyond. They are worshippers of Yahweh, worshippers of the monotheistic god, but at their own sites in Dan and in Shechem.

The fall of the northern kingdom of Israel is a really important development not only for the southern kingdom, Judah, but also for the whole development of the Hebrew self-identity, which expresses itself in its religious conceptions. Power shifted to Jerusalem abruptly; the Assyrians reduced Judah, or Judea to use the Roman name, to a province. Their kings ruled there as clients of the Assyrian kings. They had to pay tribute, but fundamentally, they were left on their own and what happens, from what we can tell in the archeology, is that Jerusalem begins to emerge as the capital of an effective kingdom. It is under the Kings Hezekiah in the late 8th century B.C. and Josiah in the 7th century B.C. that Judah really begins to emerge as the religious and political center of the Hebrews. It is these two righteous kings, always favorites of medieval kings of France, for instance, who really impose monotheism on the population—that conception of a single transcendent god, which is preached by the prophets and linked back to David and to the great traditions into the distant Hebrew past.

Hezekiah, for instance, prohibits the worship on the high places—that is, the ancient Canaanite gods. It is in this period that Judah can assert itself as the successor to the Davidic kingdom, to the successors of the purified worship of Yahweh, and Jerusalem, as the temple of the Hebrews, as the center, emerges around the priestly caste. That position is confirmed by economic and social developments; that is, under Assyrian kings, Judah does prosper a great deal. There are several embarrassing situations when Sennacherib shows up and blackmails the kings of Jerusalem, but fundamentally, the kingdom of Judah stayed outside of the destructive wars that were waged under the time of the Assyrian kings. It is only afterwards, when the Assyrian empire collapsed, that the kings of Judah fell afoul of the successor of the Assyrian empire and that was the Neo-Babylonian kings, King Nebuchadrezzar, or Nebuchadnezzar—Nebuchadrezzar is his Akkadian name—who either in 597, or maybe ten years later in 587 or 586 BC, besieged Jerusalem, captured the city, and deported the upper classes to Babylon.

That was another important step in the development of Hebrew monotheism for several reasons. First, the ruling classes and the literate classes were removed to Babylonia and the tradition remembers 40 years, meaning a generation, and that's about right. Down to 539 B.C., Babylonian kings reigned in Babylon. In 539 B.C., Babylon was conquered by the Persians, by King Cyrus the Great of Persia. Cyrus returned those Hebrew exiles to

Jerusalem and permitted the rebuilding of the temple in Jerusalem, which had been destroyed by the Babylonian king earlier. Furthermore, in that exile—and that exile was extremely important—monotheistic Judaism, as we understand it today, was defined. The old kingdom had come to an end. The monarchy had been destroyed, there were no more kings ruling in Judah; even the rites could not proceed in the temple.

What was remarkable about the Hebrews under these circumstances was that they did not become assimilated into the Babylonian society—that is, they did not simply conclude that our god was weak, so we should then worship other gods or whatever. Instead, they redefined the powers of Yahweh and were able to understand that the powers of God were universal, omniscient, omnipresent, and omnipotent. That the worship of Yahweh did not depend on any sort of particular location or even rites; of course, they longed to be restored to Jerusalem and the Babylonian captivity and the restoration of Israel was compared instinctively to the story of Exodus. That is, the captivity in Egypt and its restoration under Moses, so the Babylonian captivity was the second time that Israel had been tested in its long history.

As a result, when those upper classes were returned from Babylon to Jerusalem and rebuilt the temple, sometime at the end of the 6th century B.C., they carried with them an incredibly powerful conception of the godhead. This leads to the interpretation of the traditions of Yahweh as a great omnipresent, transcendent god, beyond time, beyond place, universal in his powers, and that is carrying to the logical conclusion, the images seen in the great prophetic utterances of the prophets during the divided kingdom. Furthermore, they arrive from Babylon with a new emphasis on writing, on the written word and its importance in understanding the godhead. They also come with, essentially, a new name because Judea was the term for this area used by the Babylonians, used by the Persians, and from which Jews—and it is from that point that I always say—Hebrews have turned into Jews at the end of the 6th, the beginning of the 5th century B.C., when they've retuned from Babylon bringing this new tradition.

The political importance and the political account of the two Hebrew kingdoms in the early Iron Age is not particularly impressive, nor are the physical remains that have come through the result of incredibly intense archeology. No part of the Near East, probably no part of the world, has been subject to more archaeology than the Holy Land. Yet, it isn't necessarily political institutions, cultural achievements, or economics that determine the importance of a people. The Hebrew prophets and poets composing the psalms and giving the conception of the God of Abraham,

Yahweh as lord of the universe, presented a powerful image based on ancient tradition stretched back to the patriarchs, to the very creation and how God had originally made his covenant with Abraham. It was based on how the Hebrews had come into Egypt and how they had been liberated by Moses through the wandering in Sinai, the conquest of Canaan, as the delivery of the promise of Yahweh to establish the new society. These Hebrew kingdoms that come together under Saul, reach their pinnacle under David and Solomon, and then break into the two divided kingdoms that we can document in the early Iron Age that lead to that very bitter political history of brother against brother, leading to the destruction of the northern kingdom and the deportation of the Hebrews in the southern kingdom.

Yet, what comes through this powerful religious vision, are the traditions encapsulated in Exodus with the Ten Commandments that Moses receives from God. The foremost commandment is that first one, "Thou shalt have no other gods before me." The religious vision of the Hebrews is fundamentally at odds with all other religious visions that we know of in the Near East. God is transcendent and not part of nature. Efforts have been made to link this Hebrew monotheism with other such conceptions in the Near East; the most common one is, for instance, the Aton heresy I spoke of in the New Kingdom in Egypt that was pioneered in the 14th century B.C. If one could translate the Egyptian translate of Praise to Aton into language, it would sound very similar to Psalms. That would give you sort of a deceptive image that one might have influenced the other and, furthermore, one could also see where certain images and notions go back deep in the Near East that the Hebrews are drawing on an old and rich tradition.

But, there's absolutely no question that the writer of Psalm 104, for instance, which is usually compared to the Hymn to Aton, has an absolute transcendent vision of the godhead, whereas Pharaoh Akhenaton believes that the sun is god. That notion of a transcendent god is one of the great perceptions, one of the great religious visions that come in the western tradition. Furthermore, that god is a god who is conceptualized with human personality, but is not in any way conceptualized as with human limitations. There are no myths about Yahweh. He can rise to anger. He will punish his people as they fall away, his chosen people in this moral experiment, but there are no myths. He's not defined and limited, as are the other gods of the Near East. And furthermore, what is all-important, he acts through human affairs, and human affairs become important in and of themselves.

Perhaps, what is most wonderful about reading of the figures of the Old Testament is not the actual historical details about them, but the beauty of the stories and the powerful images of these people who come across to us. Moses, David, Solomon—all of these figures jump out at you on the pages and it is because they are human figures struggling with the task put before them and trying to reach these moral standards. This tradition is carried on by the later kings of Judah, by the prophets and beyond. So, what comes out of this Hebrew tradition is not only this transcendent godhead, but a notion that human affairs are part of this overall moral plan, that human affairs matter, and that the Hebrews were never dualists; they never rejected the importance of the physical world. The physical world is part of God's creation, even though it is not divine in and of itself, and as a result, the Hebrews give a very powerful sense, also, of progress in linear time, in understanding one's relationship to God, and that is another powerful intellectual force in the western tradition. Time is linear, time is significant, and that religious perception—that is certainly encapsulated. By the 5th century B.C., it becomes, ultimately, the religious ethical and philosophical perception of the entire west. One could argue that every vision—political, religious, or otherwise—in the west, from St. Augustine to Karl Marx, is ultimately Hebrew.

Lecture Eleven
Imperial Assyria

Scope: The Neo-Assyrian kings (911–612 B.C.) forged the first imperial
order in the Near East since the collapse of the political order of
the Late Bronze Age. The kings of Ashur, who saw themselves as
the political and cultural heirs of the Akkadian Empire, acquired
iron technology and fielded a formidable imperial army. In the 10th
and 9th centuries B.C., Assyrian kings brought to heel the
Aramaean princes on their borders and battled Neo-Hittite kings
under the leadership of Hamath and Carchemish. Setbacks and
civil war after the Battle of Qarqar in 853 B.C. nearly undermined
the Assyrian kingdom, but Tiglath-Pileser III (745–727 B.C.)
forged new institutions; hence his heirs, from Sargon II (721–705
B.C.) to Ashurbanipal II (669–631 B.C.), ruled the first imperial
order embracing both Egypt and Mesopotamia. The Assyrians
transmitted to later empires their provincial administration, use of
highways and military colonies, and taxation in silver. Assyrian
kings promoted prosperity, arts, and Akkadian literature. Yet
Assyrian kings were remembered for their ruthless treatment of the
defeated and the rebellious. In 612 B.C., Babylon, under
Chaldaean kings, and the Medes of Iran allied to overthrow
Assyrian rule and sack Nineveh.

Outline

I. The Assyrians are among the most important people to emerge out of
the end of the Bronze Age and the beginning of the Iron Age. Around
911 B.C., they began to launch out into a series of campaigns that
culminated in the unification of the entire Near East, including both the
Nile valley and the Tigris–Euphrates valley.

II. First we shall look at the background of Assyria in an attempt to
answer the question: Why was it the Assyrians who would unite the
Near East? Why not the Egyptians or the Babylonians?

  A. The Egyptians and Babylonians found themselves in a peculiar
  situation by the opening of the Iron Age. By 1040 B.C., the
  Egyptians had lost their Asiatic empire, and Egyptian political and

military power increasingly rested in the hands of border peoples, notably Libyans.

   1. The Libyan pharaohs were primarily concerned with maintaining their position in the Nile valley.
   2. Further, they faced the disappointing fact that Egypt did not have iron deposits nor easy access to such deposits, at a time when iron was becoming the metal of choice for the manufacture of weapons.
   3. Thus, Egypt was not in a position to play the same role that it had played in the Late Bronze Age.

B. The situation in Babylonia was also complicated, divided between a foreign military elite that had moved in at the end of the Bronze Age and the native population. The newcomers here were the Chaldaeans, kinsmen of the Aramaeans who had seized control in Babylon. This region, too, lacked access to iron deposits.

C. The Assyrians, who controlled the upper valley of the Tigris, were close to any number of metal deposits and had access to many potential military recruits. Further, it was a cardinal principle of Assyrian foreign policy to drive west, to gain control of the upper Euphrates and the Khabur River, as well as the grasslands of the al-Jazirah. In achieving these goals, the Assyrians would have a stranglehold on key trade routes entering Babylonia.

D. The Assyrians enjoyed a succession of truly able monarchs, stretching back into the Bronze Age.

   1. The first of these that we know anything about is Ashur-uballit I (1365–1330 B.C.), who shook off the power of the Mitanni.
   2. Ashur-uballit was followed by a succession of kings who expanded Assyrian power across northern Mesopotamia, overthrew the Mitanni, and threatened both Egypt and the Hittite Empire.
   3. The Assyrian emperor Tukulti-Ninurta I (1244-1208 B.C.) marched down the Tigris and briefly captured Babylon from the Kassite king.

III. During the ensuing two centuries of disruption, the Assyrian kings forged an army that would launch out to conquer the Near East.

A. In 911 B.C., Adad-nirari II (911–891 B.C.) launched a new series of wars in two directions: west, to bring the region between the Euphrates and the Mediterranean under Assyrian control, and east, toward Babylon. Throughout the 9th century B.C., Assyrian kings conducted massive raids in these areas to impose vassalage and exact tribute.

B. The self-image of Assyrian kings was one of great power. These rulers were often depicted on lion hunts, conducting campaigns, and subduing cities. The inscription for Ashur-nasirpal II (883–859 B.C.), for example, tells us of his brutal punishment of a rebellious city.

IV. By the end of the 9th century B.C., the Assyrians began to encounter far more difficult coalitions that they were unable to defeat easily.

A. In 853 B.C. at the Battle of Qarqar, for instance, King Shalmaneser III (858–824 B.C.) was checked by a coalition of 10 Syrian princes.

B. When the Assyrian general Pul seized the throne in 745 B.C. under the dynastic name Tiglath-Pileser III (745–727 B.C.), the administration of the dynasty was reorganized, and the Assyrians began to conquer and rule methodically, rather than simply plundering their neighbors.

C. Tiglath-Pileser III and his heirs incorporated many of the neighboring kingdoms as provinces. The Neo-Hittite kingdoms were annexed between 745–717 B.C., as were the Aramaean kingdoms in Syria.

D. The Assyrians also forced many of the states in the Near East to develop economically in order to pay tribute to their conquerors.

E. Further, the Assyrians constructed highways and established military garrisons. In regions where a client king was kept in place, he was usually supervised by an Assyrian inspector.

F. The result of this organization was that Tiglath-Pileser was able to carry out some spectacular campaigns.

    1. He annexed much of southeastern Asia Minor and northern Syria, securing access to the ports of the Mediterranean.

    2. He committed the Assyrian monarchy for the next century to penetration into Asia Minor. In so doing, he saddled his successors, Sargon II (721–705 B.C.) and Sennacherib (705–

681 B.C.), with long wars against the Phrygians and the Cimmerians.

V. At the same time, Tiglath-Pileser, by his expansion, left to Sargon II the problem of dealing with Egypt and Babylon.

   A. The Egyptian pharaohs encouraged revolts among the Phoenicians, Aramaeans, and Hebrews, then failed to provide aid. This brought the Assyrian armies into the Hebrew kingdoms and resulted in the destruction of Israel around 722 B.C. and the deportation of the Israelite tribes.

   B. The Babylonians repeatedly resisted Assyrian efforts to rule them. The grandson of Tiglath-Pileser, Sennacherib, twice moved into Babylon to put down major rebellions. In the second rebellion, Babylon was sacked (689 B.C.), and its cult statues were removed to the Assyrian capital.

   C. Sennacherib's son, Esarhaddon (681–669 B.C.), realized that Babylon was the natural economic and intellectual center of Mesopotamia and commissioned the rebuilding of the city.

   D. Esarhaddon also carried out his father's policy of reckoning with Egypt. He conducted the first successful invasion of Egypt for which we have records. The Assyrian army crossed the Sinai, entered the Delta, crushed the Kushite army, and occupied Memphis in 671 B.C.

   E. Unfortunately for Esarhaddon, the Assyrians failed to hold Egypt. Shortly after his death, his son, Ashurbanipal II (669–631 B.C.), faced a rebellion in Egypt, and the Assyrians were forced to give up this territory after 663 B.C.

   F. The reign of Ashurbanipal II marked both the epitome and the collapse of the Assyrian state.
      1. During his reign, Ashurbanipal II sponsored extensive economic and public activities.
      2. He faced, however, the same problem of winning the loyalty of the conquered populations than had plagued Assyrian monarchs since 911 B.C. As effective as the Assyrian administrative apparatus and military were, the empire was rocked by repeated rebellions.

   G. The failure of the Assyrians to reconcile the Babylonians to their rule, along with the organization of the Iranian peoples to the east (the Medes and Persians), probably resulted in the Assyrians' downfall.

1. Two years after the death of Ashurbanipal, the Chaldaean client king ruling in Babylon, Nabopolassar (627–605 B.C.), rebelled, declaring himself king of Babylon.
2. The reorganized Babylonian army, in alliance with the Medes from the east, took on the Assyrian Empire, capturing Nineveh in 612 B.C. after a three-year siege.

VI. For all the destruction of the Assyrian Empire and the evil reputation of the Assyrians, they had achieved a great deal. They had proved that the Near East could be united, breaking down provincial and local barriers by their policies of deportation and their application of central administration.

   A. We can draw a parallel between Sumer, Babylon, and Assyria, on the one hand, and Crete, Greece, and Rome, on the other.
   B. Sumer and Crete created the civilizations; Babylon and Greece brought those civilizations to their intellectual heights; and Assyria and Rome extended the political and legal boundaries of those civilizations.
   C. However, the Assyrians never had the genius of Rome in securing the loyalty and the energies of their conquered people. Nonetheless, the Assyrian imperial experiment was all-important to the last great people of the ancient Near East, the Persians.

Further Reading:

J. M. Russell, *Sennacherib's Palace without Rival at Nineveh.*

H. W. F. Saggs, *The Might That Was Assyria.*

Questions to Consider:

1. What resources did Assyria possess that enabled Neo-Assyrian kings to forge an imperial order in the Early Iron Age, circa 911–612 B.C.? How did Assyrian kings foster trade and prosperity in their empire?
2. How did Assyrian imperial policies force foes to organize and arm themselves? Why did Assyrian kings from Tiglath-Pileser III to Ashurbanipal II face repeated rebellions? Why did the Babylonians refuse to accept Assyrian rule?

Lecture Eleven—Transcript
Imperial Assyria

In this lecture, I plan to discuss the emergence of the Assyrian Empire and the Assyrians still have a remarkable reputation for ferocity. They gain this largely from the Old Testament accounts about the great, what we call, Neo-Assyrian emperors of the 9th and 7th centuries B.C. They also are not particularly well treated in the Egyptian accounts because of the great Assyrian invasion of the Nile Valley in 671 to 669 B.C., when there was a great deal of destruction wrought in the conquest of lower Egypt. Nonetheless, the Assyrians really need to be considered as one of the most important people to emerge out of the end of the Bronze Age, the beginning of the Iron Age.

They were descendants of Akkadian-speaking peoples who went back into the Bronze Age, and there is a recognizable kingdom of Assyria, or Ashur as they would prefer to call it—Assyria is the Greek designation of the land—probably as early as around 2000 or 2100 B.C., but it is only in the period starting from, let us say, around 911 B.C. when the Assyrians launch out into a series of campaigns that ends up uniting the entire Near East, including both the Nile Valley and the Tigris Euphrates Valley, into a single political order. What is becoming increasingly evident from recent scholarship and excavation is that the Assyrians set down many of the foundations upon which the Persians built their far more successful and larger empire. Very often, the Persians are credited with many administrative advances, which really go back to Assyrian models. The Assyrians are, in some ways, some of the most successful imperialists to come out of the ancient Near East. They also field an army in terms of its organization discipline, its use of what military historians would call a combination of arms—that is, different elements in the army, infantry, cavalry, chariots, heavy infantry, as opposed to light infantry, an army that really is not matched until the Roman legions. Even so, there is some truth in the reputation the Assyrians enjoy as being ferocious and pitiless conquerors and we'll discuss some of that in this lecture.

So, what I wanted to look at first is the background of Assyria and to answer the key question, why was it that the Assyrians, who emerged in the early Iron Age as the people who would unite the Near East and play a role as an Imperial people for close to 300 years, comparable to the role that was played by the Egyptians at the end of the late Bronze Age? And, what is even more significant in this question, why was it that the Egyptians or the

Babylonians—that is, the people of those river valley civilizations who had evolved the earliest civilizations and who had survived the Bronze Age collapse with most of their institutions intact—why did they not emerge to unite the Near East? Why was it Assyria in the valley of the northern Tigris and hitherto a rather minor state emerge as the most successful state in the Iron Age until the Persians in the 6th century B.C.?

This is an important question to answer. For one, it depended on the peculiar situation that the Egyptians and Babylonians found themselves in by the opening of the Iron Age. In the case of Egypt, I noted that by 1040, the Egyptians had lost their Asiatic Empire and, increasingly, Egyptian power rested in the hands of border people, notably Libyans, people from just west of Egypt, who essentially took over not only the military, but eventually the political reins of power in Egypt. Dynasties XXII through XXIV, dynasties of the early Iron Age centered in the Delta, were essentially Libyan warlords. Egypt, in effect, was ruled by a military foreign elite. Therefore, these Libyan pharaohs were far less concerned about extending the horizons of Egypt and far more concerned about maintaining their position in the Nile Valley. They also faced the rather disappointing fact that Egypt did not have iron deposits or easy access to iron deposits, and iron was increasingly becoming the metal choice for the manufacture of weapons and arms, certainly after 900 B.C., and for the Egyptians this meant a matter of importing those weapons and that equipment. So, Egypt was not in a position to play the role that she had done back in the late Bronze Age.

The same was true for Babylon. In the case of Babylon, it too was complicated in a division between a military, ultimately, foreign elite, that had moved in at the end of the Bronze Age and the general native population. You have the same tensions in Babylonia that you have in Egypt. In this case, the newcomers were the Chaldaeans, perhaps familiar to some readers of the Old Testament, and the Chaldaeans were kinsmen of the Aramaeans, a Semitic people from off the western Arabian Desert who had moved down the Euphrates and had seized control in Babylon and actually provided much of the military force. They were experts in camels. They often were used in tribal regiments. They retained their tribal identity, settling among the cities and villages of Babylonia and throughout the Iron Age, there was always a tension between people in the indigenous populations of the cities, in Babylon and Nippur, the ancient Sumerian cities, which all spoke Akkadian now, and the newcomers, the Chaldaeans, who were essential as the military elite in Babylonia. So, both in the case of

Egypt and Babylonia, neither society was in a position to generate that sort of political revival. Babylon, too, as being a land in a Delta area, did not have access to iron deposits.

Well, that moves us to Assyria and the Assyrians who controlled the upper valley of the Tigris, where conveniently located to all sorts of metal deposits, in part, to the east in the Zagros Mountains of Iran, immediately to their north, in the highlands that fade into Armenia and, furthermore, the Assyrian kings going back into the Bronze Age, always aspired to control both the upper Tigris and the upper Euphrates. It was a cardinal principle of Assyrian foreign policy to drive west, to gain control of the upper Euphrates, and also, that important tributary to the Euphrates, the Khabur River, and to bring under control the grasslands of the al-Jazirah and then to push over the Euphrates to the Mediterranean shore. That was the policy of Assyrian emperors in the early Iron Age and it's a policy that goes back deep into the Bronze Age. In so doing, the Assyrians would have a stranglehold on the key trade routes entering Babylonia. This is one reason for the animosity between the Babylonians and the Assyrians—that is, the Assyrians emerge in the Iron Age in a position where they can actually dictate the political and economic destinies of Babylon. That was always resented by the Babylonians who considered the Assyrians, at best, country bumpkins and imitators, whereas the city of Babylon was the greatest city of the Near East; it was a great cosmopolitan center since the time of Hammurabi. The Babylonians did not take well to Assyrian rule and repeatedly rebelled during the period of Assyrian rule and, eventually, would bring down the Assyrian Empire in alliance with several other peoples.

The Assyrians had the access to the iron, they had the control of the trade routes, and above all, they also had access to excellent potential soldiers. Assyria, in its widest sense—that is, not only the upper Tigris, but including the grasslands of the al-Jazirah, parts of the upper Euphrates—had many pastoralists, it had many shepherds, mountaineer people, excellent material for recruiting soldiers. The Syrian kings, from a very early day, also encouraged the immigration and settlement of Aramaeans within their domains. These Aramaeans were often brought in as immigrants; they were brought in sometimes as tribal regiments—that is, they were from a society where all men were versed in the use of arms. Many of the Aramaeans were eventually assimilated into the general Assyrian population. Some of them advanced very high in royal service, and what is now becoming clear from Assyrian records is that there wasn't any kind of racial or ethnic prejudice on absorbing new peoples into the Assyrian population. Assyria, in many ways, was a political designation rather than an ethnic designation. If you spoke literary Akkadia and you were loyal to the Assyrian king and you fought in the army, or you were loyal in royal service, then you were an Assyrian. Furthermore, the Assyrians enjoyed a succession of truly able monarchs. These monarchs stretched back into the Bronze Age.

The first monarch we know anything about is a fellow named Ashur-uballit I, who came to the throne around 1365 B.C., shook off the power of the Mitanni, largely because the Hittites had done most of the fighting for him, but he took the title Lord of the Universe, which is one of the old titles of Sargon of Akkad, and he really sets the tone in the late Bronze Age, already of Assyrian emperors seeing themselves as the heirs of the great Mesopotamian imperial tradition, stretching back to earliest times, back to 2400 B.C. with the old Akkadian empire. He's followed by a succession of different kings and these kings are able to expand Assyrian power across northern Mesopotamia, overthrow the power of the Mitanni—those mysterious chariot warriors of the late Bronze Age—and threaten both Egypt and the Hittite empire. In 1257 B.C., the pharaoh of Egypt, Rameses II, and the great king of Hatti, Hattušiliš III, signed an alliance with each other, largely out of fear of Assyrian aggression to the eastern Euphrates. It was the Assyrian King Tukulti-Ninurta I, who ruled from 1244–1208 B.C. that actually marched down the Tigris and briefly captured Babylon from the Kassite king. He announced this as one of the great victories and, essentially, fulfilled what all Assyrian monarchs thereafter would wish to do—that is, the unification of all Mesopotamia around the northern capital of Ashur, which is the capital of Assyria, not at Babylon. Tukulti-Ninurta I had to give up this conquest, could not hold on to Babylon, and after his death, the Assyrians experienced the same difficulties all the states did in the late Bronze Age, and that is the disruptions arising from the migrations of new peoples, the arrival of Aramaeans, we believe, the ancestors of the Iranians, the Medes, and the Persians were moving into western Iran already. There was the whole reconfiguration of Asia Minor with the collapse of the Hittite Empire. The sea peoples assaulted the Levantine shores, nearly brought Egypt to her knees. Assyria, too, was subject to a number of attacks.

It was during these centuries, these two dark centuries of Assyrian history, where the Assyrian kings forged the discipline and the tactics of that great army that launched out in 911 B.C. to conquer the Near East. It is at this time that the Assyrians learned the iron technology that now becomes common in the Near East and, fortunately for the Assyrian kings, they had iron to spare. The inventories at Ashur, the old religious capital, and Nineveh, which is the royal administrative center of the high Assyrian empire, both are filled with reports of the amount of iron that is stockpiled. The Assyrians also had excellent grasslands for raising horses, they could field both chariots and a new form of fighting, cavalry. So, the Assyrians came out of the Iron Age with the tradition of fighting tough border wars, and also well armed and well trained for their role as an imperial army. They're also led by a pragmatic set of kings who were more than willing to adapt the institutions of their victims and their allies if it would further Assyrian aims. They also had a sense of assimilating conquered people into the Assyrian Empire, using their abilities to augment the power of the Assyrian monarchy. We see this change already in 911 when the king Adad-nirari II launches a new series of aggressive wars and these are aimed in two directions—one is west, to bring the region between the Euphrates and the Mediterranean under Assyrian control. This is an area that is inhabited by various Neo-Hittite kingdoms and the Aramaean kingdoms of Syria, the Phoenician cities of the coast, and ultimately, the Hebrew kingdoms in the far south.

They also push in the direction of Babylon. Throughout the 9th century B.C., Assyrian kings repeatedly operate in these areas to bring these regions under control, to impose control of vassalage on these states, as well as to exact tribute. In many instances, the campaigns are often conducted as massive raids to sweep up livestock and skilled people who were then deported to the Assyrian kingdom and put to work for the Assyrian king. One feature that runs through the entire of Assyrian imperial history is, on the one hand, the Assyrian kings are seen by their victims as extremely destructive—on the other hand, within the Assyrian kingdom proper, which eventually becomes the Assyrian Empire, the kings promote industry, trade, and agricultural experimentation. Actually, they're the people who may have brought cotton into the Near East according to one account; various types of fruit trees are actually imported from the distant reaches of the empire into Mesopotamia. So, they are very conscious of securing revenues, of promoting prosperity in Assyria, and they're more than willing to take subject peoples and relocate them into the empire for that purpose. We often call this a deportation policy, and it's a feature that's generally hated by many of the subject peoples.

There's another aspect that comes out of these early Assyrian campaigns, which is also repeated in the later imperial age, starting with Tiglath-Pileser

III who really organizes an effective empire in the mid-8th century B.C. Already in the 9th century B.C., we can see that the royal self-image—we don't know what the Assyrian population thought—but the royal self-image was one of projecting great power, commissioning the magnificent reliefs that are now on display in many European museums, which amplified the remote and abstract power of the Assyrian king who is usually depicted in lion hunts. The Assyrian kings are actually responsible for wiping out the lions in the Near East. They did massive lion hunts. They're also depicted in very detailed relief works showing campaigns of capturing cities, subduing rebellious cities, or conquering new victims. In this regard, this was the official image and the Assyrians projected this image, and the reliefs and images are accompanied by cuneiform inscriptions, which are, essentially, a comic strip narration of the events going on. Again, this is a matter of official policy, but it does echo, somewhat, the images that come through the Old Testament and the Egyptian sources and, that is, Assyrian kings deliberately went out of their way to punish any defiance by acts of frightfulness, terrorism, and no one believed in the rules of the Geneva Conventions of War in the ancient world.

The Persians and Romans could be just as brutal as the Assyrians, but there is a certain chilling aspect of the Assyrian inscriptions on the reliefs that shows that these kings particularly used this as policy. I read just one excerpt from the annals of Ashurbanipal II in the early 9th century B.C. that sets the tone for what goes on. He tells us how he punishes a rebellious city.

> I built a pillar over against his city gate [that is the gate of the rebellious king] and I flayed all the chiefs who had revolted. And I covered the pillar with their skin. Some I walled up within the pillar. Some I impaled upon the pillar. And I cut the limbs of the officers, of the royal officers, who had rebelled. Many captives from them I burned with fire and many I took as living captives. From some I cut off their noses, their ears, and their fingers [You get the sense that the king's sort of experimenting here; it's a day out on campaign]. And in many I put out the eyes. I made one pillar of the living, and another of heads, and I bound their heads to tree trunks around the city. Their young men and maidens I burned in fire.

Again, this is official policy; it's intended to frighten various populations into subjection and it is a cardinal principle of Assyrian policy and probably accounts for the constant defiant rebellions that rocked the empire.

This led to some important consequences. By the end of the 9th century B.C., the Assyrians start running into far more difficult coalitions, which they cannot beat very easily, and the first sign of this is in 853 B.C. at the Battle of Qarqar, where King Shalmaneser III runs into a coalition of 10 Syrian princes, including, incidentally, King Ahab of Israel and he is checked. He claims in his inscriptions that he rained hailstorm down on the opposing armies, the way the storm god Adad does on the earth. But, fundamentally, Assyrian power was checked for over a generation.

The Assyrians face some considerable difficulty in fielding army as reports of civil war, draft evasion, and it's only when a general by the name of Pul seizes power in 745 B.C., takes the dynastic name Tiglath-Pileser III and establishes a new dynasty, where the Assyrian kings reorganize their administration and start to conquer and rule methodically, rather than just plundering their neighbors—that is, forges real imperial state for the next 150 years. Tiglath-Pileser III and his heirs vastly expand the royal bureaucracy. They incorporate many of the neighboring kingdoms as provinces. They put Assyrian governors in charge; the Neo-Hittite kingdoms, essentially, are all annexed between 745 and 717 B.C. They disappear. Kingdoms in Syria are annexed, brought directly into the Assyrian Empire. The population is subject to a census; the men are conscripted in the army or for labor services. The Assyrians impose a regularly collected tribute in silver. They force many of the states in the Near East to develop economically to pay this tribute in silver collected at regular intervals. This is bullion—it's not in coin money—and the Assyrians impose a standard weights and measure across the Near East and, actually, the Phoenicians and Aramaeans, as the commercial peoples of the Near East, prosper under Assyrian rule from this Assyrian imperial order and standardized laws, as well as weights and measures.

They also put in highways, military garrisons in those areas where a client king is kept in place; he's usually supervised by an Assyrian inspector backed up with the garrison. The Assyrians intend to rule their empire with a very tight rein drawing upon the administrative experiments of Imperial Egypt, of Babylon, and of the Hittite Empire. They increase the size of their royal army and its specializations ever more. Now, the result is that Tiglath-Pileser III really carries out some spectacular campaigns. He annexes much of southeastern Asia Minor and northern Syria. He secures access to the ports of the Mediterranean and commits the Assyrian monarchy for the next century to penetration into Asia Minor. And, in so doing, saddles his successors, notably Sargon II, who takes the name of the old Akkadian emperor deliberately, and his son Sennacherib, with long wars on the northern frontiers against two new peoples—the Phrygians from Asia Minor and the Cimmerians, a nomadic people coming across the Caucuses into Armenia, pressing on the northern borders of Assyria. Throughout much of the 7th century B.C., the Assyrian kings become committed to defending these new provinces along the northern frontier. This is a just a perpetual problem that all Assyrian kings face, especially Sargon II, Sennacherib, but even later kings such as Ashurbanipal II have to always deal with this northern frontier.

At the same time, Tiglath-Pileser III, by his expansion, leaves to his successor Sargon II the problem of dealing with Egypt and Babylon—the two great river valley civilizations, which we would expect would be the foci of a new imperial order in the Iron Age. Egypt turns out to be the broken reed of the Old Testament. The Egyptian pharaohs—who are largely Libyan pharaohs until Dynasty XXV, when Kushites from the south move in—but the Egyptian pharaohs always encourage revolts among Phoenicians, Aramaeans, and Hebrews, and then fail to provide aid. This brings the Assyrian armies into the Hebrew kingdoms. This is why Israel is crushed sometime around 722 B.C. and Sargon II deports those Israelite tribes.

Furthermore, the Babylonians, just as the Egyptians, resent this upstart power. The Babylonians repeatedly resist Assyrians efforts and it is the grandson of Tiglath-Pileser III, Sennacherib, who is remembered from the Old Testament as one of the most frightful kings of the Assyrian monarchy, he's the one who shows up in 701 B.C. and puts Jerusalem under siege and extorts an enormous ransom and, then, his army moves off to invade Egypt. But, the story is the angel of the Lord comes up and smites the Assyrian host. The Egyptians actually tell a story that the field mice went in and chewed up all the bow strings so that the Assyrians couldn't invade Egypt. More likely is that his army suffered logistical problems and malaria and withdrew before invading Egypt. But in any case, this is the same man, and Sennacherib has Egypt on the menu. He never succeeds in getting Egypt, but he does crush Babylon. Two times he moves into Babylon to put down major rebellions and the last one is a very long rebellion in which many cities are destroyed. Babylon is sacked and cursed in 689 B.C.; it's actually abandoned. The gods of Sumer and Akkad and Babylon are removed to the Assyrian capital and Babylon is essentially erased from the map.

Well, that doesn't last very long. Sennacherib's son Esarhaddon, who comes to the throne in 681 B.C., immediately realizes that Babylon is the natural economic, intellectual center of Mesopotamia and he actually commissions the rebuilding of the city shortly after his accession. So, Babylon is restored under an Assyrian-supervised client king. Esarhaddon also carries out his dad's policy of reckoning with Egypt. He conducts the first successful invasion of Egypt of which we don't have any information. We really don't know how the Hyksos did it and it's an impressive operation involving the Phoenician fleet. The Assyrian army crosses Sinai, enters the Delta, crushes the Kushite army—it's largely Kushites brought up from the Sudan—occupies Memphis and secures control of the Nile Valley. And, for the first time, Egypt is incorporated into a larger Imperial Order. It is a military achievement of the first order. Unfortunately for Esarhaddon, the Assyrians fail to hold Egypt. Shortly after Esarhaddon's death, his son, the last great imperial ruler of Assyria—his name is Ashurbanipal II—he comes to the throne, he faces a rebellion in Egypt almost immediately. The Assyrians after 663 B.C. essentially have to give up Egypt.

Ashurbanipal II's reign marks, in some ways, both the epitome and the collapse of the Assyrian state. It is during his reign that the great library was constructed at Nineveh, the newer capital—the administrative center of the empire. And, all the ancient literary texts of Babylon were copied, including the epic of *Gilgamesh*. Many of our best Akkadian copies of the literary and religious and intellectual text come from the library of Ashurbanipal. That library was destroyed in 612; the tablets were actually baked and, therefore, they survived in tact when the city was excavated in the 19th century. Furthermore, Ashurbanipal II sponsored all the types of economic and public activities I mentioned earlier and can be credited with important patronage of art, the relief work, the sculpture; one can study this Assyrian imperial art as a composite of various provincial arts, now put to the service of the Assyrian king.

But Ashurbanipal II, just as his father, his grandfather, and his great-grandfather, going all the way back to the first Assyrian monarchs of the Iron Age in 911 B.C., Adad-nirari II faced the same problem of winning the loyalty of the conquered populations. As effective as the Assyrian empire was in its administrative apparatus, as excellent as the Assyrian army was on the battlefield and in siege, nonetheless, the empire was rocked by repeated rebellions. These were rebellions that were not easily isolated and would generally drag on for years. Above all, it was Babylon. The failure of the Assyrians to reconcile the Babylonians to their rule is probably what did them in. The second group that did them in was the Iranian peoples to the east, the Medes and the Persians, newcomers who were on the Eastern

Frontier and subject to repeated Assyrian aggression and were forced to organize.

Two years after the death of Ashurbanipal II in 627 B.C., while his sons fought a civil war, the Chaldaean client king ruling in Babylon—and he is essentially the prince of a Chaldaean military regiment, Nabopolassar, the father of Nebuchadrezzar, or Nebuchadnezzar as he's known in the Old Testament—rebelled, declared himself king of Babylon. At this point, Assyrian rule was so unpopular that even the Babylonian population was willing to accept a Chaldaean warlord as their king and this reorganized the Babylonian army in alliance with the Medes—this new Iranian population to the east who were expert in cavalry—they took on the Assyrian Empire in an alliance, and in 612 B.C., the army of the Medes and the Babylonians put Nineveh under siege. They capture the city in 612, after a three-year siege, and what actually happened is the Tigris overflowed its banks during the spring flooding in the third year of the siege and undermined part of the wall. Assyria is captured and the city is obliterated.

Well, to some extent, the Babylonians were giving payback to the Assyrians by leveling Nineveh to the ground. But, also, the Babylonian king Nabopolassar intended to make sure that in the world following Assyria, there would never be a question again of an upstart city in Mesopotamia aspiring to play the role of Babylon. That division between what is now southern Iraq and northern Iraq, that tension has always been there and is already seen very clearly at the end of the 7th century. The Neo-Babylonian Empire that comes to succeed Assyria and take over, at least, the lands of the Fertile Crescent, makes sure that there is never an urban rival to emerge again in the Northern Regions of Mesopotamia. The Medes prosper, perhaps the most; they arrive now as a new imperial people.

Yet, for all the destruction of the Assyrian Empire, for all the evil reputation often associated with the Assyrians, they had achieved a great deal. They had proved that the Near East could be united. They had broken down provincial and local barriers by their policies of deportation and by their application of a single central administrative system. In many ways, they made the tasks of the Persian kings easier and some historians go so far as to say the Assyrians were an easy act to follow, especially with the Persian kings. The Assyrians did play that important role, but there is a proviso that I should add. That is, in looking at the civilizations of Mesopotamia, a parallel is often drawn—Sumer, Babylon, Assyria, to Crete, Greece, and Rome. Sumer and Crete created the civilization, Babylon and Greece brought that civilization to its intellectual heights, and Assyria and Rome were the third component in these civilizations, which extended the realms and the boundaries, the political and legal boundaries of those civilizations. I always think that the first two work out pretty well as an equation, but in the third parallel, that is Assyria to Rome, the Assyrians, for all their achievements that are being elucidated, fall far short from Rome. They never had the genius of Rome in securing the loyalty and the energies of their conquered people and to achieve what Rome did in her imperial civilization. Even so, the Assyrian Imperial experiment was all-important for the last great peoples of the ancient Near East, the Persians, who will be the subject of our final lecture.

Lecture Twelve
The Persian Empire

Scope: Four imperial orders, which emerged from the Neo-Assyrian Empire, shared rule over the Near East for two generations: Egypt under the Saite Dynasty XXVI, a resurgent Babylon under Chaldaean kings, the kings of Lydia in western Asia, and the Medes of western Iran. Between 550 and 525 B.C., these kingdoms fell to the Achaemenid kings of Persia, Cyrus the Great (559–530 B.C.) and Cambyses (530–522 B.C.). Darius I (521–486 B.C.), who seized the throne in a major rebellion, organized the Persian Empire based on Assyrian administration, drawing upon Mesopotamian political and cultural traditions. The Persian Empire was divided into satrapies administered by Persian or Median aristocrats bound by honor and service to the great king. The empire, spanning 3,000 miles from the Aegean shores to the Indus valley, was linked by a royal highway and defended by the first army to depend on cavalry. The Achaemenid kings adroitly adapted local institutions and co-opted native elites to win approval from subject peoples, such as the Hebrews, or admiration from their foes, the Greeks. In 500 B.C., King Darius reigned over a mighty empire, the climax and epitome of 30 centuries, but within the year, he was drawn into wars on his distant western frontiers against the Greeks, who had evolved along quite different lines since the Late Bronze Age. The ensuing Persian Wars altered the course of Western civilization.

Outline

I. In this lecture, we conclude our study of the great civilizations of the ancient Near East with the Persian Empire.

   A. We shall use the reign of King Darius the Great (521–486 B.C.) as a stopping point because it represents the climax of developments going back some 30 centuries.

   B. Darius ruled over a vast empire incorporating all three of the early river-valley civilizations.

C. The kings of Persia were regarded as the noblest of all kings of the Near East and are well known to us from Greek historical authors, notably Herodotus (c. 490–425 B.C.).

D. We shall have three goals for this lecture: First, we'll look at the Near East in the immediate aftermath of the destruction of the Assyrian Empire in 612 B.C. Then, we'll explore the question of why the Persians emerged in the political order after Assyria as the eventual "winners" in the Near East. Finally, we'll close with some remarks on the impact of these Near Eastern civilizations on the Western tradition.

II. After the fall of Assyria, four states emerged, including both Egypt and Babylon, which constituted themselves as great imperial orders.

A. Dynasty XXVI in Egypt, which came after the fall of Assyria, was founded by an Assyrian rogue governor, Psamtik I (Greek: Psammetichus I; 664-610 B.C.). This dynasty ruled with the cooperation of the Libyan military elite and succeeded in reuniting the Nile valley.

    1. The pharaohs of Dynasty XXVI launched a deliberate archaizing cultural program; that is, they restored ancient temples and shrines and sponsored arts inspired by models from the Old Kingdom. The Greeks entered Egypt under this dynasty in great numbers, arriving as mercenaries and merchants and establishing a commercial colony at Naucratis in the lower Delta.

    2. The pharaohs of Dynasty XXVI were loathe to become involved in the politics of the Near East. They were content to rule their traditional realm, which they did successfully down to 568 B.C. In that year, the dynasty was overthrown by a general named Amasis (568–525 B.C.). Shortly after his death, the Persians invaded and took over the Nile valley. Egypt thus played a relatively limited role in the wider Near East after the fall of Assyria.

B. The Neo-Babylonian, or Chaldaean, Empire was forged by Nabopolassar and his successors after 627 B.C., when the Chaldaeans destroyed the Assyrian Empire.

    1. Nabopolassar and his son, Nebuchadrezzar, campaigned extensively across the Fertile Crescent, reestablishing the old empire of Sargon, from the Red Sea to the Persian Gulf.

2. Just as their counterparts in Egypt had done, the Neo-Babylonians embarked on an archaizing program, while remaining content to rule over the traditional core areas of Mesopotamian civilization.

3. The Neo-Babylonians are best remembered for the victory of Nebuchadrezzar over the Hebrews of Judah and the deportation of the Jews from Jerusalem to Babylon in 586 B.C.

4. Nebuchadrezzar is also remembered for the construction of the second of the Seven Wonders of the Ancient World, the Hanging Gardens of Babylon.

5. Eventually, the Neo-Babylonian dynasty was also overthrown by Cyrus the Great of Persia. In 539 B.C., Babylon was put under siege and captured by the Persians. Babylon was later revered by the Persian aristocracy as its cultural capital.

C. The third realm that came out of the old Assyrian Empire was in Asia Minor, the kingdom of the Lydians. The Lydians were a new people who had emerged in western Anatolia at the city of Sardes in the Hermus valley.

1. The Lydian kingdom consolidated Asia Minor by the middle of the 7th century B.C. after a series of migrations disrupted political structures in Anatolia. These were the migrations of the Cimmerians, a nomadic people who had constantly plagued the northern border of the Assyrian Empire.

2. Just as Egypt and Babylon had done, the Lydian kingdom eventually fell to the Persians. The last king of the Lydian dynasty who ruled at Sardes was Croesus (561–546 B.C.), legendary in the Greek tradition for his wealth and his philhellenism.

D. Finally, the Medes ruled in northwestern Iran and had their capital at Ecbatana (today Hamadan). The Persians and the Medes were related Iranian peoples, but the Medes took the lead in political organization because they had born the brunt of Assyrian attacks in the 8th and 7th centuries B.C.

1. Under Cyaxares (653–585 B.C.), the Medes united the various tribes of Iran and fielded effective cavalry armies.

2. The second king of the Medes, Astyges (585–550 B.C.), proved unpopular with his nobility and was overthrown by his vassal king and kinsman, Cyrus of Persia.

III. At the time, this political change in Iran was probably considered nothing more than a change of dynasty; however, Cyrus became one of the great conquerors of the Near East and was remembered as a wise king.

A. In 546 B.C., Cyrus swiftly overthrew the Lydian kingdom and, about five years later, turned on Babylon; thus, he incorporated the Fertile Crescent and Anatolia into his realm. He died fighting the Scythians along his northeastern frontier.

B. His son, Cambyses (530–522 B.C.), fell heir to Cyrus's project of conquering Egypt. He invaded Egypt in 525 B.C. with the assistance of the Phoenician fleet and took out the Nile valley. The Persians were usually regarded as generous and tolerant conquerors, but this was not the case in Egypt.

C. Cambyses died under mysterious circumstances in Egypt in 522 B.C., and his death sparked a rebellion across the nascent Persian Empire. Several candidates vied for the throne of the empire, but the one who triumphed was Darius I (521–486 B.C.).

1. Darius reorganized the Persian Empire, drawing upon all the institutions that we have studied in this course.

2. He created 30 satrapies across the empire, each ruled by a satrap (governor). The satraps were chosen from among Persian noble families who had backed Cyrus in the rebellion of 522–521 B.C.

3. The Persian kings also understood the importance of separating the administration of a satrapy from its military and financial arms. Under this system, the empire was well run for 150 years.

4. Below the imperial administration, the Persians worked through local elites. This policy was the genius of the Persians: They managed to win over the Hebrews; they granted authority to the ancient Lydian aristocracy in Asia Minor; and they worked through the elites of Babylon.

D. By 500 B.C., the Persian Empire was the mightiest and most civilized organization to emerge in the Near East and was the heir to 30 centuries of remarkable developments.

    1. Yet in 499 B.C., Darius and his generals would be drawn into a rebellion by remote Greek subjects on the fringes of the empire. This event brought the Persians, first, into western Asia Minor, then, to Greece and would climax in the great invasion of King Xerxes (486–465 B.C.) in 480–479 B.C.

    2. In that conflict, the king of Persia would ultimately be defeated by an unlikely coalition, the Greek city-states of Athens and Sparta and their allies.

IV. The civilizations of the Near East laid many of the cultural, intellectual, and institutional foundations of later Greek civilization.

    A. Yet for all of their debt to the Near East, the Greeks represented a different civilization. The Greeks defined themselves by their method of government—they developed the institution of the *polis*, in which they governed themselves with laws passed by the citizens.

    B. A closing passage from Demosthenes defining the rule of law encapsulates the difference between the Greek civilization to come and the Near Eastern civilizations we have studied.

Further Reading:

J. M. Cook, *The Persian Empire.*

M. A. Dandamaev and V. G. Lukonin, *The Culture and Social Institutions of Ancient Iran.* Translated by P. L. Kohl and D. J. Dadson.

Questions to Consider:

1. What were the strengths and weaknesses of the four kingdoms that succeeded to the Assyrian imperial order?

2. Why did Cyrus the Great conquer the Near East so rapidly? How much did he owe to his military and political genius? How formidable were his foes? Why did Herodotus admire Cyrus and the Persian nobility?

Lecture Twelve—Transcript
The Persian Empire

In this lecture, I wish to conclude our study of the great civilizations of the ancient Near East with the Persian Empire. The Persian Empire acts as a good point to stop this lecture series; especially, let us take the year 500 B.C., in the reign of King Darius I, who ruled from 521 to 486 B.C. We can use that as our stopping point because, in many ways, Darius's reign represents the climax of developments going back some 30 centuries to the first cities we saw in lower Mesopotamia in the Uruk period. He ruled over a vast empire, some 3,000 miles in length, stretching from the Aegean to the Indus. It incorporated all three of the early river valley civilizations—that is, the Indus, the Tigris-Euphrates, and the Nile. Darius ruled over a very well run empire, perhaps the best ordered empire until the Roman age. He may have ruled over as many as 40,000,000 subjects. It's really difficult to know what the size of the population was, but it is clearly a brilliant imperial achievement.

Furthermore, of the great kings of Persia, or the great king as they just would be called in the Greek tradition or king sometimes, were regarded, in many ways, as the noblest of all kings of the Near East and they are particularly well known to us because of the Greek historical authors. Unlike the Assyrian kings—their immediate predecessors and the Assyrian are only essentially known from their official annals and their relief work, which were all for public consumptions—the Persian kings, who could be almost as remote and distant to us as the Assyrian kings, caught the imagination of Greek authors. Particularly, starting with the author Herodotus, the historian writing in the 5th century B.C. who took it upon himself to travel through the Persian Empire and, really, he devotes the third book of his history describing Persian institutions and the Persian monarchy. There are some really interesting wild and wooly tales in there and I'm sure Herodotus told more than his fair share of whoppers. Some would call Herodotus not so much the father of history, but the father of lies; I think that's uncharitable and uncalled for, but nonetheless, Herodotus does convey to us a very vivid image of who these monarchs were. Particularly, Cyrus, who created the Persian Empire and his successors, Cambyses, Darius, and above all, Xerxes, who invaded Greece and was defeated at the Battle of Salamis in 480 B.C. Without those Greek historical authors, the Persians would be, perhaps, as remote and distant as many of the Near Eastern monarchs that we've studied in this course.

On the other hand, they also deserve a great deal of credit for their success in running this empire and there's a reason why they caught the imagination of the Greeks. So, what I wish to do in this lecture is essentially accomplish three goals to conclude this series. First, is to look at the Near East in the immediate aftermath of the destruction of the Assyrian Empire in 612 B.C. The Assyrian Empire experienced a violent death in 612 B.C. There is no question that it was defeated and destroyed. Then, to look at why the Persians emerged in the political order after Assyria, as the eventual winners. The Assyrian Empire essentially broke up into four kingdoms, all of which, in part, traced their origins back to the Assyrian Imperial state. And yet, it was the Persians and especially the royal family of Persia, often known as the Achaemenid family—that is, they're descended from this hero or this King Achaemenes, who is the founder of this dynasty; we're using the Greek formation of this patronymic, the id is a Greek ending that designates descendants of—the Achaemenid Empire, therefore, ruled by the family that are the descendants of Achaemenes. Why was it that these Achaemenid Kings came to not only restore the imperial state, but to expand it far greater to any size that previous conquerors of the Near East could have imagined. We'll look at that section second. Then, we'll close with some remarks on the importance of this course and the impact of these Near Eastern civilizations on the Western tradition. So, it's essentially these three issues we need to deal with—the aftermath, the Persian achievement, and then, summing up the course.

Let's first look at the immediate aftermath with the fall of Assyria. Four states emerged and these included both Egypt and Babylon that constituted themselves as great imperial orders. The Egyptian pharaohs who came to rule in the aftermath of Assyria were founded by an Assyrian rogue governor—a man known in his Greek rendition, Psammetichus in Greek; that's the Greek rendition of the name, Psamtik in Egyptian. He established his own dynasty, Dynasty XVI; he centered his capital in the Delta at the city of Saite, so it's very often known as the Saite Dynasty. This Dynasty ruled with the cooperation of the Libyan military elite and was very successful in reuniting the Nile Valley, and the pharaohs of Dynasty XXVI actually launched deliberate archaizing cultural programs. That is, they restored the ancient temples and shrines and they sponsored arts, which were inspired on the models of the Old Kingdoms. There's many an undocumented Egyptian art object that can be dated either to the Old Kingdom or Dynasty XXVI, and it can't be really anything in between.

This is the world of Egypt that the Greeks visit. The Greeks enter Egypt under this Dynasty in great numbers. They arrive as mercenaries and then, later, as merchants. They're allowed to establish a commercial colony at Naucratis in the lower delta area, which is the Greek commercial center, and Herodotus travels to Egypt, then part of the Persian Empire. But, the society, they are seen is this very late Egyptian society in which there is a deliberate, studied veneration of the past and an invoking of the ancient traditions of Egypt. The pharaohs of Dynasty XXVI are very loath to get involved in the vortex of the politics of the Near East. They're content to rule their traditional realm and not to become involved in wars that would bring in a foreign conqueror, as had been the case of the earlier pharaohs who had provoked the Assyrian invasion of the 7th century B.C. The Egyptian pharaohs of Dynasty XXVI rule very successfully. The dynasty is overthrown by a general named Amasis, in 568 B.C., who rules essentially as a strong man pharaoh down to his death, and shortly after his death, the Persians will invade and take over the Nile Valley. But, Egypt plays a relatively limited role in the wider Near East and is content to articulate and to revere her traditions, rather than embark on any great imperial adventures.

The Neo-Babylonian Empire, or as it's sometimes called, the Chaldaean Empire, was forged by the Chaldaean General Nabopolassar and his successors who had also originally been—the Chaldaeans were originally, essentially, a vassal family of the Assyrian emperor and it was in 627 B.C., when the Babylonians rebelled under the leadership of the Chaldaean military elite and eventually destroyed the Assyrian Empire, that Nabopolassar and his son, the more famous Nebuchadrezzar in his Akkadian name, or Nebuchadnezzar as he's known in the Old Testament, both proved to be great warriors. They campaigned extensively across the ancient Fertile Crescent and reestablished that, essentially, Sargonite Empire in his territorial sense. They essentially ruled from the limits of the Red Sea to the Persian Gulf and they ruled with the traditional sobriquets of the Akkadian emperors and, again, there was a certain amount of archaizing in the cultural activities in Babylon—an invoking of the ancient past, the copying down of the ancient Babylonian epics, the reediting of the tradition. Just as their Egyptian contemporaries, this empire was essentially satisfied to rule the traditional core areas of Mesopotamian civilization. They are best remembered for Nebuchadrezzar's victory over the Hebrews of Judah, and the deportation of Jews from Jerusalem to Babylon, probably occurring sometime after 587 or 586 B.C. That was a decisive moment in the formation of Judaism, as I lectured earlier in this series.

Nebuchadrezzar is also remembered for the second ancient wonder—you know, the seven wonders of the ancient world—and that was the building of the Hanging Gardens of Babylon, which reputedly was constructed to appease his Medeian, that is, his Iranian, wife who really found it very depressing living in the Alluvial plains of Babylon. As a man who grew up in the northeast of the United States and now a long resident in New Orleans, I can appreciate this lady's problem—you're essentially living in a saucer; there's no horizon, no sunset as you understand it. So, what Nebuchadrezzar did was build this magnificent set of gardens, reputedly 75 feet high and about 400 feet square, enormous mud brick construction decorated with all sorts of exotic plants and animals, so that his wife could at least get some sense of the hills of Medea. Just to give you a sense of size though, this was an impressive structure by mud brick constructions. It's probably more ambitious than any ziggurat ever composed in Mesopotamia, but it still doesn't cover half the area that the Great Pyramid of Khufu covers. The Great Pyramid of Khufu covers 13 acres; it's 481 feet high and it's 786 feet square at its base, and it was built 2,000 years earlier of masonry architecture, just to get some sense of the perspective of the Egyptian achievements in architecture here. Nebuchadrezzar's family, however, never really won the support of the Babylonian ruling elite and, eventually, the Neo-Babylonian or Chaldaean Dynasty was also overthrown by the Persians, by Cyrus the Great in 539 B.C., when the city was put under siege and was captured by the Persians, in part, we believe, with the cooperation of the priesthood of Marduk. This is because Babylon does not suffer a sack under the Persian kings and, actually, Babylon is revered by the Persian aristocracy very much as their cultural capital. The Persian kings will draw a great deal on the Babylonian institutions and cultural achievements for the creation of their own imperial society.

The third realm that came out of the old Assyrian empire was in Asia Minor. This was the kingdom of the Lydians, a new people who emerged in western Anatolia at the city of Sardes in the Hermes Valley, or as it's known today, as the Gediz Chai in Western Turkey. The Lydian Kingdom consolidated Asia Minor by the middle of the 7th century B.C., after a series of migrations disrupted political structures in Anatolia. These were the migrations of the Cimmerians, these nomadic people who would constantly plague the northern border of the Assyrian Empire, and also overthrew the Phrygian kingdom in central Asia Minor and allowed the Lydian Kings to emerge as the premiere power. The Lydian kings consolidated most of the old western political legacy of the Hittite kings and they, too, were one of the great states to emerge in the aftermath of the Assyrian empire and they, just as Egypt and Babylon, eventually fell to the Persians.

The last king of the Lydian Dynasty that ruled at Sardes was known as Croesus. We still think of, "as wealthy as Croesus." He was legendary in the Greek tradition for his wealth and his philhellenism—that is, he patronized various Greek shrines and he actually consulted the oracle of Delphi when he contemplated going to war against King Cyrus of Persia. The question was, what will happen if I go to war against King Cyrus? The *pythia*, the seer, answered at the oracle, "Oh great king, if you cross the Halys River"—which was the boundary between the Lydian and Persian Empire, at that point—"a great empire will be destroyed." Sure enough, Croesus went to war and a great empire was destroyed, his own. He later complained to the oracle and the oracle pointed out, well you never said it was going to be your empire. So, consult oracles at your own risk. Also, Cyrus cheated. In the battle, he actually mounted his frontline with camel forces, the Lydian Calvary charged, couldn't stand the smell of the camels, and reared back, and the Persians mopped them off the battlefield. It's all told in Herodotus in one of his delightful tales of the conquests of King Cyrus of Persia.

Finally, the fourth people, the Medes ruling in the northwestern Iran today, had their capital at the ancient city of Ecbatana, which is today Hamadan in Iran, the great caravan center. The Medes were cousins to the Persians; the Persians and Medes were related Iranian peoples and it was the Medes who took the lead in political organization because they had borne the brunt of Assyrian attacks in the 8th and 7th centuries B.C., and it was their King Cyaxares who allied Nabopolassar of Babylon to take out the Assyrian Empire. The Medes united the various tribes of Iran and fielded the first effective Calvary armies in the world. We believe that the Medes and Persians are the first great imperial armies who shock power, whose decisive arm in battle depended on Calvary, which is now the preferred arm and considered superior, in many ways, to the chariot armies of the old Bronze Age and the early Iron Age. The second king of the Medes, his name is Astyges, apparently proved very unpopular with his nobility, and in 550 B.C., he was overthrown by his vassal king and relative, King Cyrus of Persia.

The Median kingdom quickly falls to the Persian King Cyrus. Now, this political change within Iran was, at the time, probably considered nothing more than change of dynasty, occurring in 550 B.C. At the time, there were the powerful kingdoms of Lydia, the Neo-Babylonian Empire, and Dynasty

XXVI in Egypt. To most observers, it was simply a case of one Iranian dynasty being replaced by another. But, Cyrus turned out to be one of the great conquerors of the Near East and, as I said, he captured the Greek imagination and there's not only the account of Herodotus, but later, many romances about Cyrus and the equivalent of the historical novels that persist well into the Roman Empire, where he is epitomized as the greatest of the Near Eastern conquerors, a wise and judicious king. Cyrus turned out to be the warrior king who overthrew the Lydian kingdom swiftly in a war dated around 546 B.C. and now dramatically demonstrated by the excavation going on at Sardes by the American team in western Turkey today. He then turned on Babylon and in 539 B.C.—that is, about five years later— captured the Babylonian monarchy and so incorporated the entire Fertile Crescent and all of Anatolia into his realms. He died fighting along the northeastern frontier, in what is now called Transoxiana, against various Scythian—that is, Iranian nomadic peoples. But, he had essentially created a great empire from the Hindu Kush to Aegean and Mediterranean shores.

His son Cambyses came to the throne in about 530 or 529 B.C. and he fell heir to Cyrus' project of conquering Egypt. Cambyses invades Egypt in 525 B.C. This is the second documented invasion we have that is a great mass of details. The Persian Army, just as the Assyrian Army, enlists the assistance of the fleet of the Phoenicians, crosses the Sinai, and the Persian Army takes out the Nile Valley. This conquest was in contrast to other Persian victories. I mentioned that the Persians were usually regarded as very generous and tolerant conquerors, quite in contrast to the Assyrians. There are cases of deportation. There are cases where cities were sacked and examples were made out of some of the population, but those were the exceptions, not the rule. We don't have the equivalent of the kinds of annals I read in the last lecture of the Persian kings delighting in mutilating and torturing their defeated captives.

In the case of Egypt, the resistance was particularly difficult; the Egyptians fought with great determination, particularly the military elites in the Delta, and the conquest was notoriously hard. There are reports coming through Herodotus in the Greek sources, that King Cambyses went a little crazy in the process—that the animal worship of the Egyptians offended him. In the earliest conceptions of the gods, the Egyptians usually associated their gods with animals and some of the most exquisite representation of Egyptian art, particularly coming from the Middle Kingdom, is the depiction of gods in animal form. I think, particularly, this included depictions of Horus as a great cobra-type serpent, Anubis the jackal-headed god, the crocodile god, all of the creatures, and above all, the bull Apis, which is the god Osiris. The report is in Memphis that Cambyses went out of his way to kill the bull Apis, which is the sacred symbol of Osiris, and in later accounts, the claim was that he actually held a barbecue with the Persian army. That's probably not true, but it's the top of the stories that circulated. He violated tombs, destroyed the mummies of pharaohs, all of this in an effort to break resistance, and died under mysterious circumstances in Egypt in 522 B.C. The Egyptians have no doubt why it was; it was because the gods sent a curse on him and a fever for his impious behavior and throughout the entire of the Persian period—that is, down to the conquest of Egypt by Alexander the Great—the Egyptians were the one subject people within the Persian Empire that never really reconciled to the Persians and who really disliked the Persians.

The Greeks, who fought the Persians on many occasions, admired the Persians to no end. The Egyptian sources are hostile to the Persian administration. In part, that's because the Persian king could not play the role of pharaoh. He could not reside in Egypt, in Memphis, and that was an enormous disadvantage for any foreign king. The Assyrian king faced the same problem. The second reason is the Egyptian civilization was so homogeneous and so ancient that the Egyptians never took to foreign rule and, so, throughout the Persian period, Egypt is rocked with repeated rebellions. The Nile Valley is very heavily garrisoned by the Persian kings and the administration in Egypt is something of an exception from the rest of the Persian Empire. Whereas in our other major literary accounts—that is, the Hebrew accounts and the Greek accounts—the Persians come across as the noblest of conquerors, the noblest of imperial people, and the Greek find in the Persians, that marvelous quality of Greek literature of praising the Persians and all of their noble characteristics, especially in Cyrus the Great. Herodotus points out that Cyrus, as all Persians, is taught to ride well, shoot straight with bow and arrow, and always tell the truth—you know, would that the Greeks be as good as the Persians. There are many stories in Herodotus' account dealing with the Persian Wars between the Greeks and the Persians, where the Persians come off as, in many ways, by far nobler than many of the Greeks and this is a tradition that continues in the Greek historical tradition down to the 4th century B.C.

Cambyses, as I said, died under mysterious circumstances in 522 B.C. and that death, in Egypt, sparked a rebellion across the nascent Persian Empire and in that rebellion between 522 and 521 B.C., several candidates emerge as possible representatives to the throne. The one who triumphed was a man named Darius, Darius I, who secured the backing of the leading Medes and Persians, the leading nobility, and put down the rebellions and went on to reorganize the empire. In Herodotus's opinion, Cyrus was the conqueror. Cyrus was essentially the man who won the empire, but Darius was the man who was the administrator, the shopkeeper, *quaestor*—the word in Greek is *epimeletes*—the guy who organized the empire. Darius, as a man who had some claim to the throne, he was of a cadet line and he married the daughter of Cyrus Atossa, who is the mom of King Xerxes, who carries out the great invasion of Greece. Darius went on to reorganize the Persian Empire, drawing upon all the institutions that we have studied in this course, going back to the Sargonid Empire and the New Kingdom of Egypt. He created thirty satrapies, great super provinces across the Persian Empire, and in each of these provinces, satrapies, he appointed a satrap. It's a term that we still use today in English and that satrap came from that charmed group of Persian or Median families—that is, the two principle Iranian peoples who ran the Persian Empire—and these were families that had backed Cyrus back in the rebellion of 522–521 B.C. They came from the same leading families. They were responsible, directly to the king, for the administration of their satrap and, furthermore, they were checked up by what are often called, in the Greek sources, either the eye or the ear of the king, who was an inspector who came from the Persian capital in Persepolis in southern Iran today, or the region that is called Fars—southwestern Iran, the old Persian heartland. He would show up just to make sure that everything was running properly.

The Persian great kings also knew that it was important to separate the administration satrapy from its military and financial aspects. And so, the military forces in the satrapy and the financial officer in the satrapy were separately answerable to the king. Persian administration was based on a long tradition of developing writing offices, administration, correspondence to the provinces, and then dividing up the responsibilities in the province so that no one official could challenge or undermine royal policy. It worked very well for the first 150 years of the empire. The empire is extremely well run, particularly so long as the great king reserved the right to rotate those senior officials in the satrapy and it didn't become hereditary. Late in the empire, they tend to become hereditary and then you start running into problems.

Furthermore, below that Persian administration, the Persians very cleverly, as many imperial conquerors in the past, worked through local elites. This is the genius of the Persians. They manage to win over the Hebrews. They allowed the reconstruction of the temple Jerusalem, they put the priestly elites in charge, and they allow the Hebrews their traditional religion, rites, and customs. They put in charge the ancient Lydian aristocracy in Asia Minor. They definitely work through the elites of Babylon. So, across the Persian Empire, especially in the areas of the western sections—that is, the non-Iranian sections and, again, Egypt is something of an exception—the Persians gain high marks in their use of local institutions for imperial needs. And this accounts for the favorable image and it accounts for the stability of the Persian Empire for the next, almost, 250 years. That is really a testimony to the genius of Darius in organizing this empire. When Alexander the Great overthrows the Persian Empire, for the Persian part of his empire, he essentially just carries over the old Achaemenid administration. He doesn't need to innovate them; it's already there. Alexander's problem is not running Persia; it's dealing with his Greek allies. Finally, the Persian kings also built a great royal word, a pony express system; they improved the communications across the Near East and they carried out many of the same kinds of cultural policies we saw with the Assyrian emperors and then repeated by the Egyptian pharaohs of Dynasty XXVI and the Neo-Babylonian kings, and that was to endow temples and shrines, to sponsor cultural activities.

So, in 500 B.C., the Persian Empire is by far the mightiest and most civilized structure that has emerged in the Near East and is the heir to 30 centuries of remarkable developments and achievements. Darius could well congratulate himself on the success of forging this empire. Yet, in 499 B.C., the next year, his generals and Darius himself would be drawn into a rebellion on the remote fringe of his empire in western Asia Minor to put down these recalcitrant Greek subjects, who didn't know any better and rebelled from what was really a very responsible and tolerant Persian rule. That even drew the Persians first into Asia Minor to put down these Greek rebels on the shores of western Asia Minor and, ultimately, in Greece, and would climax in the great invasion of King Xerxes in 480 and 479 B.C. in which the great king of Persia would be defeated by the most unlikeliest of coalitions, the Greek city-states of Athens and Sparta, and their allies in these great battles in which the Persian Empire is not only checked, but the Greeks manage to establish and to uphold their peculiar institutions of the city-state.

It's with that thought that I'd like to close—the opening of that great Persian war, which acts as fitting point to close this course and to act as a window into other courses offered in The Teaching Company series, notably the courses on ancient Greece. There are number of them in which these issues can be followed up. But, what I'd like to stop with is my thoughts on the achievement of the Near East. That is, these civilizations, in many ways, laid a lot of the cultural and intellectual and, even, institutional foundations of later Greek civilization. We saw that in the lectures on Greece, and on Crete, and the Bronze Age. Many of these institutions would be transmitted by the Persians and the subject peoples of the Persians to Greece, during the Persian period. The Greeks themselves would come to embrace many of these achievements in the aftermath of the conquest of Persia by Alexander the Great. Yet, the Greeks, for all of their debt to the Near East, represented a different civilization. The most significant difference between the Greeks and the peoples of the Near East was their conceit that they, as Greeks, were different because of the way they governed themselves; that they depended on the rule of law. Also, that they evolved the institutions of a city-state, a polis, in which they governed themselves by laws passed by the citizens. I think it's very well to capture that difference, the type of world that Darius and then Xerxes marched against, with the closing passage from Demosthenes from one of his private orations. This encapsulates the difference between the Greek civilization to come and the Near Eastern civilization I've just summed up.

This is Demosthenes speaking before an Athenian jury:

> The whole life of men, Athenians, whether they dwell in a large state or a small one [and he uses the word *polis*] is governed by nature [*physis*] and by the laws [*nomoi* and the Greek is very specific; it's the laws of men, not divine law *themis*, not the type of law that would be invoked in the code of Hammurabi or even in the Old Testament]. Of these, nature is something irregular and incalculable and peculiar to each individual. But the laws are something universal, definite, and the same for all. Now, nature, if it be evil, often chooses wrong and that is why you find men of an evil nature committing errors. But the laws desire what is just and honorable and salutary. They seek for it and when they find it, they set it forth as general commandment, equal and identical for all. [Sound familiar?] The law is that which all men ought to obey for many reasons, but above all, because every law is the invention and the gift of the gods [well, we've heard this before] a tenet of wise men [fairly familiar] and a corrective of errors, voluntary and involuntary, and a general covenant of the whole state in accordance with which all men in that state ought to regulate their

lives. [That is a new concept.] For there are two objects, men of Athens, for which all laws are framed: to deter any man from doing what is wrong and by punishing the transgressor to make the rest better men.

This is a new departure in intellectual thinking. It is the conceit that will separate the Greeks from their Near Eastern contemporaries, and it's a fitting point to close this course, where we have summed the great traditions of the Near East who are, in effect, the ancestors of the western tradition, and we now open a door to the new chapter, the Greeks, who are the parents of the western tradition.

Maps

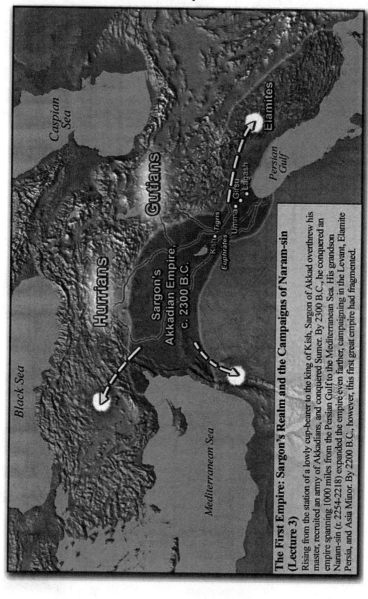

The First Empire: Sargon's Realm and the Campaigns of Naram-sin (Lecture 3)

Rising from the station of a lowly cup-bearer to the king of Kish, Sargon of Akkad overthrew his master, recruited an army of Akkadians, and conquered Sumer. By 2300 B.C., he conquered an empire spanning 1000 miles from the Persian Gulf to the Mediterranean Sea. His grandson Naram-sin (r. 2254-2218) expanded the empire even farther, campaigning in the Levant, Elamite Persia, and Asia Minor. By 2200 B.C., however, this first great empire had fragmented.

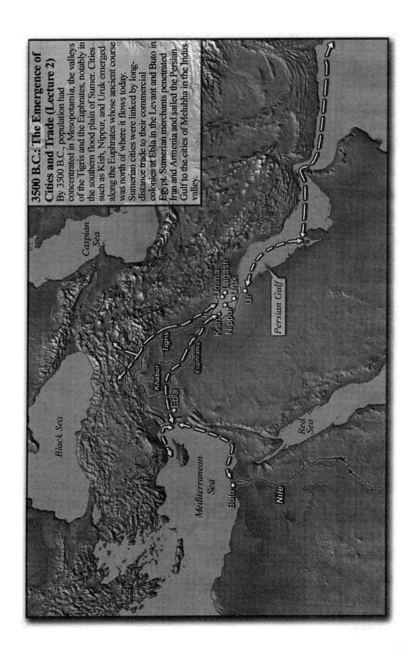

3500 B.C.: The Emergence of Cities and Trade (Lecture 2)

By 3500 B.C., population had concentrated in Mesopotamia, the valleys of the Tigris and the Euphrates, notably in the southern flood plain of Sumer. Cities such as Kish, Nippur, and Uruk emerged along the Euphrates whose ancient course was north of where it flows today. Sumerian cities were linked by long-distance trade to their commercial colonies at Ebla in the Levant and Buto in Egypt. Sumerian merchants penetrated Iran and Armenia and sailed the Persian Gulf to the cities of Meluhha in the Indus valley.

Caspian Sea

Black Sea

Mediterranean Sea

Red Sea

Nile

Buto

Ebla

Khabur

Tigris

Euphrates

Kish
Nippur
Umma
Lagash
Uruk
Ur

Persian Gulf

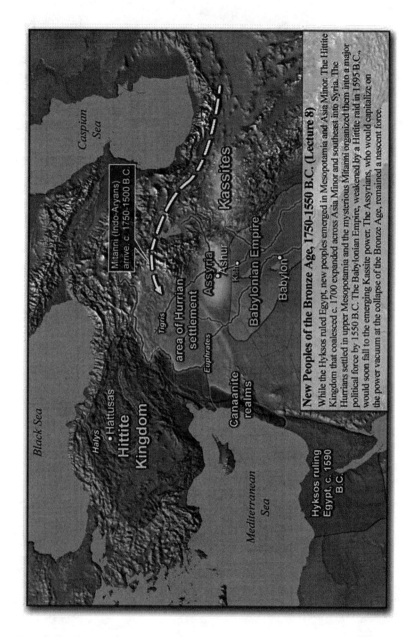

New Peoples of the Bronze Age, 1750-1550 B.C. (Lecture 8)

While the Hyksos ruled Egypt, new peoples emerged in Mesopotamia and Asia Minor. The Hittite Kingdom that coalesced c. 1700 expanded across Asia Minor and southeast into Syria. The Hurrians settled in upper Mesopotamia and the mysterious Mitanni organized them into a major political force by 1550 B.C. The Babylonian Empire, weakened by a Hittite raid in 1595 B.C., would soon fall to the emerging Kassite power. The Assyrians, who would capitalize on the power vacuum at the collapse of the Bronze Age, remained a nascent force.

Caspian Sea

Black Sea

Mitanni (Indo-Aryans) arrive, c. 1750-1500 B.C.

Kassites

Babylonian Empire

Ashur

Kish

Babylon

Assyria

area of Hurrian settlement

Tigris

Euphrates

Halys

•Hattusas

Hittite Kingdom

Canaanite realms

Mediterranean Sea

Hyksos ruling Egypt, c. 1590 B.C.

Egyptian Expansion, 2700-1500 B.C.: From the Old to the New Kingdom (Lectures 5-7)

In 3100 B.C., Narmer united Lower Egypt (the Delta north of Memphis) and Upper Egypt (between Memphis and the First Cataract) into a single kingdom. The pharaohs of the Old Kingdom erected the great pyramids. The pharaohs of the Middle Kingdom extended Egyptian power to the Third Cataract. The pharaohs of Dynasty XVIII expelled the Hyksos by 1544 B.C. and forged the New Kingdom, conquering an empire from the Upper Euphrates to Kush in central Sudan.

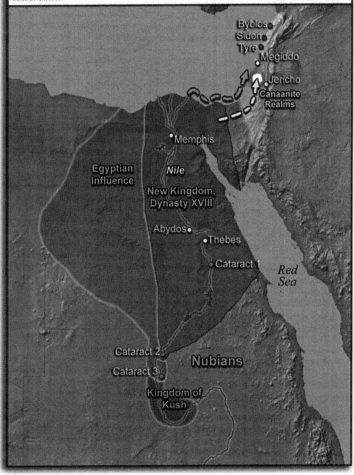

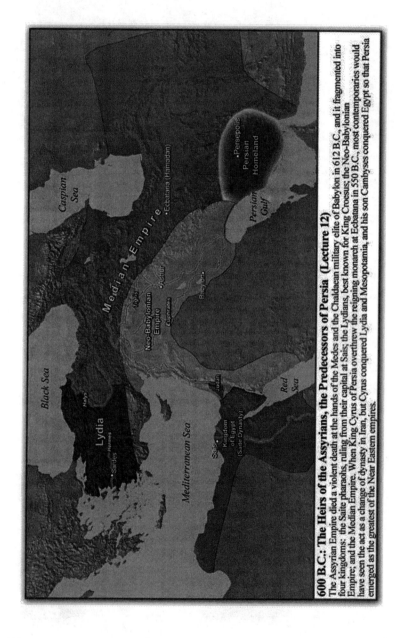

600 B.C.: The Heirs of the Assyrians, the Predecessors of Persia (Lecture 12)

The Assyrian Empire died a violent death at the hands of the Medes and the Chaldaean military elite of Babylon in 612 B.C., and it fragmented into four kingdoms: the Saite pharaohs, ruling from their capital at Sais; the Lydians, best known for King Croesus; the Neo-Babylonian Empire; and the Median Empire. When King Cyrus of Persia overthrew the reigning monarch at Ecbatana in 550 B.C., most contemporaries would have seen the act as a change of dynasty in Iran, but Cyrus conquered Lydia and Mesopotamia, and his son Cambyses conquered Egypt so that Persia emerged as the greatest of the Near Eastern empires.

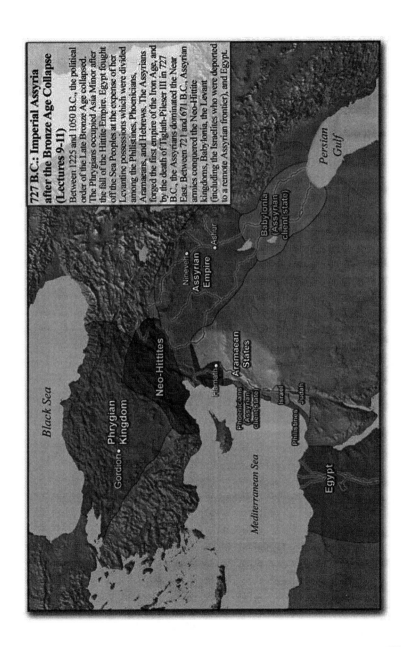

727 B.C.: Imperial Assyria after the Bronze Age Collapse (Lectures 9-11)

Between 1225 and 1050 B.C., the political order of the Late Bronze Age collapsed. The Phrygians occupied Asia Minor after the fall of the Hittite Empire. Egypt fought off the Sea Peoples at the expense of her Levantine possessions which were divided among the Philistines, Phoenicians, Aramaeans, and Hebrews. The Assyrians forged the first empire of the Iron Age, and by the death of Tiglath-Pileser III in 727 B.C., the Assyrians dominated the Near East. Between 721 and 671 B.C., Assyrian armies conquered the Neo-Hittite kingdoms, Babylonia, the Levant (including the Israelites who were deported to a remote Assyrian frontier), and Egypt.

Black Sea

Phrygian Kingdom

Gordion

Neo-Hittites

Hamath

Aramaean States

Phoenicians (Assyrian client state)

Israel

Philistines

Judah

Mediterranean Sea

Egypt

Nineveh

Assyrian Empire

Ashur

Babylonia (Assyrian client state)

Persian Gulf

189

Timeline

11,000–6000 B.C. .... Incipient agriculture and stock-raising in eastern Asia Minor.

7000–5000 B.C. .... Neolithic Age; emergence of villages at Çatal Hüyük, Jarmo, and Jericho.

c. 4500–3500 B.C. .... al-Ubaid Period in Mesopotamia; growth of villages and shift of population to southern Mesopotamia.

c. 3500–3100 B.C. .... Emergence of cities and literacy in Sumer (Uruk Period); Bronze Age (3500–1000 B.C.); Gerzean culture in the Nile valley: genesis of Egyptian civilization.

3100 B.C. .... Proto-Literate Period (3100–2800 B.C.) in Sumer; Narmer (Menes), first pharaoh, unifies Lower and Upper Egypt; Archaic (Early Dynastic) Age of Egypt, Dynasties I–II (3100–2700 B.C.); Invention of Egyptian hieroglyphics.

2800 B.C. .... Early Dynastic Period (2800–2300 B.C.); warring city-states in Sumer.

c. 2700–2650 B.C. .... Gilgamesh, *ensi* of Uruk; Dynasty III rules in Egypt.

c. 2650 B.C. .... Pharaoh Zoser constructs Step Pyramid at Sakkara.

2600 B.C. .... Emergence of the cities of Meluhha (Indus valley, 2600–1700 B.C.)

c. 2550–2500 B.C. .... Pharaohs Khafre and Menkaura construct the second and third pyramids at Gizeh.

c. 2450 B.C.	Eannatum, *ensi* of Lagash, defeats rival Umma.
2334–2279 B.C.	Reign of Sargon I: creation of Akkadian Empire.
2300–2100 B.C.	Migration of Hittite-speaking peoples into Asia Minor.
2275–2185 B.C.	Reign of Pharaoh Pepi II, Dynasty VI; First Intermediate Period (c. 2200–2050 B.C.).
2254–2218 B.C.	Reign of Akkadian emperor Naram-sin.
2200–2100 B.C.	Collapse of Akkadian Empire.
2200–1800 B.C.	Migration of Hurrians into northern Mesopotamia and Syria.
2112–2095 B.C.	Reign of Ur-nammu; creation of the Neo-Sumerian Empire (Ur Dynasty III).
2094–2047 B.C.	Reign of Shulgi, king of Ur; administrative consolidation.
2060–2010 B.C.	Pharaoh Mentuhotep II, Dynasty XI, reunifies Egypt from Thebes; birth of the Middle Kingdom (Dynasties XI–XV, 2050–1674 B.C.).
1991 B.C.	Pharaoh Amenemhet I seizes the throne at Thebes; foundation of Dynasty XII (1991–1786 B.C.).
1934–1924 B.C.	Reign of Lipith-Ishtar, Amorite king at Isin, who issues law code.
1878–1843 B.C.	Reign of Pharaoh Senworset III; Egyptian conquest of Nubia; Zenith of Middle Kingdom; flourishing of Egyptian letters and arts.
1799–1790 B.C.	Reign of Amenemhet IV; decline of Middle Kingdom.

1792–1750 B.C. .... Reign of King Hammurabi; creation of Babylonian Empire.

1674–1544 B.C. .... Hyksos rule over Egypt from Avaris in the Delta.

1650–1620 B.C. .... King Hattušiliš I of the Hittites founds Hattušas as capital.

1620–1590 B.C. .... Reign of Hittite king Mursiliš I; conquests in northern Syria.

1595 B.C. .... King Mursiliš I of the Hittites sacks Babylon; decline of Hittite power in Asia Minor (1590–1350 B.C.).

1570–1550 B.C. .... Pharaoh Khamose founds Dynasty XVIII at Thebes ;foundation of New Kingdom (Dynasties XVIII–XX, 1570–1075 B.C.); Egyptian resurgence against Hyksos rule.

c. 1570 B.C. .... Eruption of volcano of Thera (Santorini).

1550–1544 B.C. .... Reign of Pharaoh Ahmose; expulsion of the Hyksos from Egypt.

1544–1520 B.C. .... Reign of Amenhotep I; first Egyptian attacks into the Levant.

1540 B.C. .... Kassites conquer and rule Babylon (1540–1157 B.C.).

1489–1479 B.C. .... Reign of Queen Hatshepsut; consolidation of Egypt.

1482 B.C. .... At Battle of Megiddo, Prince Thutmose III crushes Canaanite coalition.

1479–1426 B.C. .... Reign of Pharaoh Thutmose III; creation of Egyptian Empire.

1400 B.C.	Mycenaean Greeks (Achaeans) sack Cnossos and settle Crete; Mycenaean thalassocracy (1400–1225 B.C.).
1365–1330 B.C.	Reign of Ashur-uballit I, king of Assyria.
1352–1335 B.C.	Reign of heretic pharaoh Akhenaton (Amenhotep IV).
1344–1322 B.C.	Reign of Hittite emperor Šuppiluliumaš I.
1335–1325 B.C.	Reign of Tutankhamun; restoration of gods and return of court to Thebes.
1322–1293 B.C.	Pharaoh Horemheb initiates Egyptian military recovery.
1321–1295 B.C.	Reign of Hittite emperor Mursiliš II.
1295–1272 B.C.	Reign of Hittite emperor Muwatallis.
1293 B.C.	Rameses I founds Dynasty XIX (1293–1175 B.C.).
1279–1212 B.C.	Reign of Pharaoh Rameses II; restoration of Egyptian rule in Asia.
1275 B.C.	Battle of Kadesh between Rameses II and Muwatallis.
1267–1237 B.C.	Reign of Hittite emperor Hattušiliš III; reform of Hittite cults and construction of sanctuary of Yazilikaya.
1257 B.C.	Treaty between Pharaoh Rameses II and Emperor Hattušiliš III.
1244–1208 B.C.	Reign of King Tukulti-Ninurta I of Assyria.
1237–1209 B.C.	Reign of Hittite emperor Tudhaliyas IV.
c. 1210 B.C.	Israel named in the memorial stele of Pharaoh Merneptah.

1209–1190 B.C............................Reign of Hittite emperor Šuppiluliumaš II; rebellions and civil wars in Hittite Empire.

1182–1150 B.C............................Attacks of Sea Peoples on Egyptian Delta and Asian provinces.

1100–1000 B.C............................Perfection and spread of iron technology: Early Iron Age (1100–500 B.C.); migration of Phrygians into Asia Minor.

1000–800 B.C...............................Invention of alphabet by Phoenicians; migration of Aramaeans into Syria and Mesopotamia.

950–900 B.C.................................Emergence of Phrygian kingdom at Gordion in Asia Minor.

911–891 B.C.................................Reign of Adad-nirari II of Assyria; foundation of the Neo-Assyrian Empire (911–612 B.C.).

884–873 B.C.................................Reign of King Omri of Israel.

873–852 B.C.................................Reign of King Ahab and Queen Jezebel of Israel.

858–824 B.C.................................Reign of King Shalmaneser III of Assyria.

853 B.C...Battle of Qarqar; setback for Shalmaneser III.

745–727 B.C.................................Reign of Tiglath-Pileser III; revival of Assyrian power.

727–698 B.C.................................Reign of King Hezekiah of Judah.

724–721 B.C.................................Assyrian conquest of Israel; deportation of the Ten Lost Tribes.

721–705 B.C.................................Reign of Sargon II; conquest of Neo-Hittite kingdoms.

705–681 B.C.	Reign of Sennacherib; conquest of Babylonia and Elam.
705–680 B.C.	Cimmerian invasion and migrations into Anatolia.
681–669 B.C.	Reign of King Esarhaddon of Assyria.
671–669 B.C.	Assyrian conquest of Egypt.
669–631 B.C.	Reign of Ashurbanipal II, king of Assyria; construction of the great library at Nineveh.
640–609 B.C.	Reign of King Josiah of Judah; cleansing of the Temple at Jerusalem.
627 B.C.	Nabopolassar rebels from Assyrian rule.
612 B.C.	Babylonians and Medes capture Nineveh; end of the Assyrian Empire.
605–556 B.C.	Reign of King Nebuchadrezzar II of Babylon.
587–586 B.C.	Siege and capture of Babylon by Nebuchadrezzar II.
586–539 B.C.	Babylonian Captivity of the Hebrews.
585–550 B.C.	Reign of Astyges, king of Media.
568–525 B.C.	Reign of Pharaoh Amasis.
561–546 B.C.	Reign of King Croesus of Lydia.
559 B.C.	Accession of Persian king Cyrus (559–530 B.C.).
550 B.C.	Cyrus hailed king of the Medes; unifies Iran.
546 B.C.	Cyrus defeats King Croesus of Lydia; Persian conquest of Asia Minor.
539 B.C.	Cyrus received in Babylon; Persian conquest of the Fertile Crescent; return

of Hebrew deportees to Jerusalem; birth of Judaism.

530 B.C. .... Accession of King Cambyses of Persia (530–522 B.C.).

525–522 B.C. .... Persian conquest of Egypt.

522–521 B.C. .... Great Revolt in the Persian Empire; accession of King Darius of Persia (521–486 B.C.).

499–494 B.C. .... Ionian Revolt; Persians crush bid for independence by Greeks of Asia.

490 B.C. .... Battle of Marathon; Athenians defeat first Persian invasion; birth of Herodotus, father of history (c. 490–425 B.C.).

480 B.C. .... King Xerxes of Persia invades Greece; battles of Thermopylae and Salamis.

479 B.C. .... Battle of Plataea: defeat of second Persian invasion.

Glossary

Abu Simbel: Nearly 300 miles southwest of modern Aswan in ancient Nubia, a monumental temple complex carved out of living rock by Rameses II (r. 1279–1212 B.C.) to commemorate his victories over the Hittites at Kadesh.

Achaeans (Classical Greek: *Akhaioi*): Denotes the Greeks of the Bronze Age; used as a synonym for **Mycenaeans**.

Achaemenid: Descendants of Achaemenes; refers to the royal family of Persia who ruled the Near East in 550–330 B.C.

Agglutinative language: Denotes a language in which the grammatical functions of words are indicated by suffixes and prefixes, rather than internal sound changes in the root words. Sumerian was such a language; thus, in its principles, it is comparable to the family of Ural-Altaic languages of Eurasia.

Akkad: Lies immediately north of Sumer, straddling the middle Tigris and Euphrates valley. The Akkadians were speakers of an East Semitic dialect who adopted the urban, literate civilization of Sumer.

Akkadian Empire (c. 2330–2200 B.C.): The first territorial empire of the Fertile Crescent, forged by Sargon I, king of Akkad.

Alaça Hüyük: Northeast of Hattušas in central Turkey, this was the seat of a palace in the Early Bronze Age (2600–2300 B.C.) with rich royal graves. It lies northeast of the later Hittite capital. In the Hittite imperial age, Alaça Hüyük was either the sacred city of Arinna or Zippalanda.

al-Jazirah: The grasslands of northwestern Mesopotamia and western Syria; traditional home to pastoralists engaged in stock-raising.

al-Ubaid Period (c. 4500–3500 B.C.): Denotes the period that witnessed the emergence of villages and irrigated farming in Mesopotamia; the name is from a site in southern Iraq.

Amurru (Old Testament: Amorites): The "Western peoples" in Akkadian texts; Semitic-speaking pastoralists who entered lower Mesopotamia in 2000–1800 B.C. and, ultimately, founded Babylon.

Anatolia: "Land of the rising Sun;" denotes the peninsula of Asia Minor or, more specifically, the central plateau that occupies half of the peninsula.

Aramaeans: West Semitic pastoralists who expanded across the Levant and Mesopotamia in c. 1100–900 B.C., promoting the use of the camel. Their language, Aramaic, written in a version of the Phoenician alphabet, displaced Akkadian as the *lingua franca* of the Near East by 500 B.C.

Archaic Period: (1) The Egyptian period of Dynasties I–II (c. 3100–2700 B.C.). (2) The period that witnessed the birth of Greek civilization (750–480 B.C.).

ba: In Egypt, the soul residing in the body placed in the tomb.

Baal: "Lord," the Canaanite title of address for the tutelary god of a city in the Levant. This god was often represented by an aniconic baetyl, or sacred stone, rather than by a cult statue.

Babylonian Captivity (586–539 B.C.): The period when the Hebrews lived as captives in Mesopotamia. King Nebuchadrezzar II (r. 605–556 B.C.) deported the Hebrew elite after his capture of Babylon; the Persian king Cyrus (r. 559–530 B.C.) permitted the Hebrews to return and to rebuild Jerusalem. The period witnessed the birth of Judaism.

Bible, editorial traditions: Refers to the Pentateuch or Torah of Moses; the first five books of the Bible (Genesis, Exodus, Leviticus, Numbers, and Deuteronomy) were put in final form c. 500–200 B.C. These books reveal four distinct editorial traditions designated by scholars as E (for *Elohim*), the earliest of the editor(s); J (for Jehovah; Latin for Yahweh); P, for the Priestly editor(s) writing after the return from Babylon; and D, the Deuteronomist editor(s). See **Deuteronomist historian**.

Book of the Dead: This Egyptian text of the New Kingdom contained spells and charms to enable the deceased to pass the trials in the underworld administered by the god Thoth. The text was initially carved on the sarcophagus; from 1550 B.C. on, texts were included in the casket. This tradition can be traced back to the earlier Pyramid Texts (c. 2600–2300 B.C.) and Coffin Texts (c. 2000 B.C.).

Bronze Age (c. 3500–1100 B.C.): Refers to the period when bronze was the most sophisticated metal alloy produced by technology.

Cataract: Refers to the five great falls that break the flow of the Nile valley. Egypt lies north of the first cataract.

Chaldaeans: West Semitic pastoralists who settled in Babylonia c. 1100–900 B.C. and became the military elite of Babylon. The Chaldaean general Nabopolassar (r. 627–605 B.C.) overthrew Assyrian rule and founded the Chaldaean, or Neo-Babylonian, Empire.

Cimmerians: Nomadic horsemen from southern Russia who crossed the Caucasus Mountains in the late 8th century B.C. and invaded Asia Minor and Mesopotamia. The Cimmerians shattered the kingdoms of Urartu and Phrygia and, thus, allowed for the rise of the Lydians as the major power in Asia Minor after 650 B.C.

Cnossos (Greek: Knossos): Near modern Herakleion, this city emerged as the principal palace for the royal family that ruled Minoan Crete in 2100–1400 B.C.

Deir el-Bahri: The great mortuary complex of Queen Hatshepsut.

determinatives: Subsidiary marks in cuneiform script that denote the grammatical or syntactical function of a symbol.

Deuteronomist historian: The editor(s) responsible for the narrative books on the histories of Israel and Judah composed in the spirit of Deuteronomy (Joshua, Judges, 1 and 2 Samuel, and 1 and 2 Kings).

dualism: The religious outlook that draws a sharp distinction between views of an evil physical world and a good spiritual world.

Early Dynastic Period (c. 2800–2330 B.C.): Designates the early historical period of warring city-states in Sumer, Akkad, and Elam.

Elam: In southwestern Iran, Elam was home to the Elamites, speakers of an undeciphered language who adopted cuneiform and Sumerian urban civilization.

en: "Overseer"; the Sumerian official who managed the properties and temple of the tutelary god of a city-state.

ensi or *ensi-gar*: "Lord"; the title of the earliest rulers in Sumer.

Enuma Elish: The Babylonian epic of creation, in which Marduk slays the monster Timat and creates the cosmos.

Fayum (classical Lake Moeris): A lake and depression, 80 miles south of Memphis and to the west of the Nile. The region, rich in fowl and fish, witnessed the earliest cultivation of crops in Egypt; pharaohs from the Middle Kingdom on regulated the lake and reclaimed its arable.

First Intermediate Period (c. 2200–2050 B.C.): This period witnessed the collapse of royal authority with the death of Pharaoh Pepi II (r. 2275–2195 B.C.). Mentuhotep II (r. 2060–2010 B.C.) ended this period of disorder by reuniting Egypt and inaugurating the Middle Kingdom.

Gerzean Period (c. 3500–3100 B.C.): This period saw the spread of towns and agriculture and the genesis of the cultural foundations of pharaonic Egypt.

Hattušas (modern Bogazkale): The political and ritual capital of the Hittites.

henotheism: A religious outlook accepting a single divine power manifested by multiple deities.

hieroglyphics: "Sacred script;" the earliest Egyptian writing system, adapted from pictograms on Naqada II ware (c. 3800–3200 B.C.). The application of these symbols to writing might have been inspired by the example of cuneiform used by Sumerian merchants settled in Buto in the Egyptian Delta.

Hittites: Descendants of Indo-European–speaking peoples who entered Asia Minor c. 2300–2100 B.C.; they unified Asia Minor into the first effective kingdom, then imperial order, in the Middle and Late Bronze Ages.

Hurrians: Speakers of an Asianic language written in cuneiform who settled in northern Syria and Mesopotamia c. 1800–1600 B.C.

Hyksos: "Foreigners;" Canaanite-speakers who conquered and ruled Egypt as Dynasty XVI (1674–1540 B.C.) from their fortress capital Avaris in the Delta.

ideogram: A symbol representing a concept in writing systems.

inflected language: Refers to a language in which grammatical function is denoted by sound changes within the root word. The Indo-European languages and Hamito-Semitic (or Afro-Asiatic) language families are so classified.

Iron Age: The period of ancient history when iron was the most sophisticated metal (c. 1100 B.C.–500 A.D.). The Early Iron Age (c. 1000–500 B.C.) witnessed the political and cultural reordering of the Near East and Greece.

ka: The twin soul of the body destined for the afterlife in Egyptian religion.

Kadesh (1275 B.C.): The great battle between Pharaoh Rameses II (1279–1212 B.C.) and the Hittite emperor Muwatallis (r. 1295–1272 B.C.). It was a strategic victory for Muwatallis and confirmed Hittite conquests in northern Syria.

karum: A consortium of merchants in Mesopotamia who established commercial settlements throughout the Near East.

Kassites: Indo-European speaking tribes of western Iran who conquered and ruled Babylonia in 1540–1157 B.C.

Knossos: See **Cnossos**.

Kush: Central Sudan between the third and fifth cataracts; the Egyptian designation for a succession of African kingdoms. The Kushites adapted Egyptian material culture and perfected the smelting of iron. Egypt was ruled by Kushite pharaohs in Dynasty XXV (712–656 B.C.).

Levant: The region of Syria, Lebanon, Israel, and Jordan.

lex talionis (Latin: "law of like punishment"): The legal principle for settling criminal disputes in early Mesopotamian law. The aggrieved party had the right to demand equal suffering on the part of the offending party.

Linear A: The syllabary employed in Minoan Crete (c. 1900–1400 B.C.); the language on Linear A tablets is as yet undeciphered.

Linear B: The syllabary adapted from Linear A and employed in Mycenaean Greece (c. 1600–1225 B.C.). Michael Ventris deciphered Linear B, proving that the language was an early form of Greek.

lugal: "Great man;" the title taken by a Sumerian *ensi* who claimed primacy over other city-states in the Early Dynastic Period. With Sargon I, the term designated king.

ma'at: "Justice;" the virtue associated with the Egyptian god Osiris and upheld as the prime virtue of pharaohs from the Middle Kingdom.

mastaba: The royal funerary complexes built in limestone by the pharaohs of Dynasties I–II.

Media: Northwestern Iran; home of the Medes, who organized the first effective Iranian kingdom under Cyaxares (r. 653–585 B.C.) in response to Assyrian aggression.

Megiddo (1482 or 1457 B.C.): The decisive battle and siege by which Thutmose III smashed the Canaanite kings and conquered the Levant. The battle inspired the apocalyptic Armageddon of the Bible.

Mesopotamia: "Land between the rivers;" denotes the arable between the Tigris and Euphrates Rivers that today is Iraq.

Middle Kingdom (c. 2050–1674 B.C.): Egypt under Dynasties XI–XV.

Minoan: Denotes the civilization of the Bronze Age on Crete (2800–1400 B.C.); the name is derived from the legendary king Minos.

Mitannians: Speakers of an Indo-Aryan language related to Sanskrit. Expert charioteers, they welded the Hurrian and Canaanite cities of northern Mesopotamia and Syria into an effective kingdom c. 1600–1320 B.C.

Mycenaean: Denotes the civilization of the Bronze Age in Greece (1600–1225 B.C.) and, after 1400 B.C., in the Aegean islands and Crete. The name is from Mycenae, the great palace that was the capital of Agamemnon in Greek legend. See **Achaeans**.

Narmer palette: A ceremonial stone emblem that depicts Narmer's conquest of Lower Egypt c. 3100 B.C.

Neolithic Age (c. 7000–5000 B.C.): "New Stone Age;" this period witnessed the domestication of plants and animals and the shift to settled life in villages in the Near East.

New Kingdom (1550–1075 B.C.): Denotes the imperial age of Egypt under Dynasties XVIII–XX.

Old Kingdom (c. 2700–2200 B.C.): This period witnessed the flowering of Egyptian civilization under Dynasties III–VI; often designated the Pyramid Age.

Persian Empire (550–330 B.C.): The last great Near Eastern empire, founded by Cyrus the Great (559–530 B.C.) and conquered by Alexander the Great (336–323 B.C.). See **Achaemenid**.

Pharaoh: Egyptian *per-aa*, meaning "great house;" the title of respect to the Egyptian monarch. The term came into general use in the New Kingdom.

Philistines: Refugees from Crete who were among the Sea Peoples who attacked Egypt in the Late Bronze Age. They settled the Levantine shore from Akko (Acre) to Gaza c. 1100–1000 B.C. and clashed with the Hebrews.

Phrygians: Indo-European speakers who migrated from the Balkans into central Asia Minor after the collapse of the Hittite Empire c. 1100–900 B.C. The Phrygians, from their capital Gordion, founded the first Anatolian kingdom of the Early Iron Age.

Proto-Literate Period (c. 3100–2800 B.C.): This period witnessed the spread of literacy and urban civilization in Sumer, Akkad, and Elam.

Punt: The Egyptian designation for Somalia. Queen Hatshepsut (r. 1489–1479 B.C.) sent a celebrated trade mission to Punt.

Qarqar (853 B.C.): A strategic victory by a coalition of Neo-Hittite, Aramaean, and Hebrew kings against the Assyrian king Shalmaneser III. The victory checked Assyrian expansion in the Levant for 75 years.

satrapy: One of the 30 provinces of the Persian Empire as organized by Darius I (521–486 B.C.). Ruled by a Persian or Median governor called a *satrap*.

Sea Peoples: Coalitions of invaders from the Aegean world and Libya who attacked the Egyptian Delta and the Levant with great fleets in 1182–1150 B.C. Sundry Sea Peoples were later settled as allies and mercenaries in the Levant by the pharaohs of Dynasties XX and XXI. See also **Philistines**.

Second Intermediate Period: The period of Hyksos rule in Egypt; see **Hyksos**.

syllabary: A writing system designating syllables rather than basic sounds of an alphabet.

syncretism: "Mixing with;" the religious outlook of identifying gods of one locale with their counterparts in another locale. Hence, in Egypt, the Sun god Ra of Lower Egypt was identified with Amon of Thebes in Upper Egypt.

talent: "Balance;" a Mesopotamian weight of a large sum subdivided into 60 *minae* and 3,000 shekels. The Assyrian kings promoted reckoning in the Near East by demanding tribute in silver paid by the talent.

talatat: Arabic for a fragment of smashed reliefs and inscriptions of the shrine of Aton constructed by Akhenaton (r. 1352–1335 B.C.). The thousands of fragments were reassembled and translated by Donald Redford, who reassessed the pharaoh's religious reforms.

Tel el-Amarna: The modern village near Akhetaton, ritual capital of Akhenaton, 300 miles north of Thebes. The administrative documents uncovered at the site are known as the *Amarna letters*; the naturalistic visual arts of the period are known as the *Amarna style*.

Ten Lost Tribes: Members of the upper classes and craftsmen of Israel who were deported by the Assyrians in 724–721 B.C. These Hebrews were assimilated into the Assyrian population. See also **Samaritans**.

thalassocracy: "Sea power;" term coined by the Athenian Thucydides (c. 465–400 B.C.) to designate the leading naval power in the Aegean.

Third Intermediate Period (1075–715 B.C.): This period witnessed the loss of Asian provinces and the rule of Egypt by the Libyan kings of Dynasties XXII–XXIV (945–715 B.C.).

Urartu (biblical Ararat): Centering around Lake Van, this city was the cultural basis for classical Armenia. The kings of Tuspha (Van) turned Urartu into a rival of the Neo-Assyrian Empire (911–612 B.C.). Urartian was an Asianic language, perhaps related to Hurrian, written in cuneiform.

Uruk Period (c. 3500–3100 B.C.): This period witnessed the emergence of true cities and literacy in Sumer.

wanax: "Lord;" the Achaean or Mycenaean title for king, c. 1600–1225 B.C.

waret (Greek: *epistrategos*): Royal administrator placed over one of the three districts of Egypt as reorganized by the pharaohs of Dynasty XII in the Middle Kingdom.

Yazilikaya (Turkish: "carved rock"): One mile northeast of Hattušas was an open-air Hittite royal sanctuary carved out of living rock. The reliefs have been linked to religious reforms sponsored by King Hattušiliš III (r. 1267–1237 B.C.) and Queen Pudahepa.

ziggurat: A multi-story Mesopotamian temple constructed of mud brick. In Genesis, the ziggurat was recalled as the Tower of Babel, "a gateway to Heaven."

Biographical Notes

Adad-nirari II (r. 911–891 B.C.): King of Assyria; founded a new line of Neo-Assyrian kings who forged the first imperial order in the Near East during the Iron Age.

Ahab (r. 873–852 B.C.): Omrid king of Israel; the first biblical figure named in contemporary Near Eastern records; a participant at the Battle of Qarqar and named in the stele of Mesha.

Ahmose (r. 1550–1544 B.C.): The second pharaoh of Dynasty XVIII; he expelled the Hyksos from the Delta and imposed his rule throughout Egypt.

Akhenaton (r. 1352–1335 B.C.): Pharaoh of Dynasty XVIII, who succeeded with the dynastic name Amenhotep IV. In the sixth year of his reign, he changed his name to Akhenaton and proclaimed the monotheistic solar cult of Aton as the only religion in Egypt.

Amasis (r. 568–525 B.C.): Pharaoh of Egypt and the commander of the Greek mercenaries who seized power and overthrew the legitimate Dynasty XXVI. **Amenemhet I** (Greek: Ammenemes; r. 1991–1962 B.C.): Founded Dynasty XII and initiated the recovery of royal power in Egypt.

Amenhotep III (r. 1391–1352): "The Magnificent;" ruled the Egyptian Empire at its zenith under Dynasty XVIII.

Ashurbanipal II (r. 669–631 B.C.): The last great Assyrian king, he built the great library of Nineveh and patronized arts and letters.

Ashur-uballit I (r. 1365–1330 B.C.): King of Assyria; asserted Assyrian independence in the wake of the defeat of the Mitannians by the Hittite king Šuppiluliumaš.

Astyges (r. 585–550 B.C.): King of Media, he alienated the ruling elite and was overthrown by his nephew Cyrus, king of the Persians.

Cambyses (r. 530–522 B.C.): Great king of Persia and son of Cyrus; he invaded and conquered Egypt.

Croesus (r. 561–546 B.C.): Philhellene king of Lydia noted for his wealth; he blundered into a war with King Cyrus of Persia that resulted in his defeat and the conquest of his kingdom by Cyrus.

Cyaxares (r. 653–585 B.C.): King of Media; he organized the Medes into the first effective cavalry army in history and allied with Nabopolassar of Babylon to destroy Assyrian power.

Cyrus (r. 559–530 B.C.): "The Great;" he ascended the Persian throne as a Median vassal, but in 550 B.C., he conquered Media and was proclaimed Great King. He conquered Lydia in 546 B.C. and Babylonia in 539 B.C.

Darius (r. 521–486 B.C.): Great king of Persia and scion of the Achaemenid family, Darius was proclaimed king during the Great Revolt of 522–521 B.C. **Eannatum** (c. 2450 B.C.): *Ensi* of Lagash who recorded his victory over the rival city Umma in the memorial Stele of Vultures.

Entemena (c. 2400 B.C.): *Ensi* of Lagash and nephew and successor of Eannatum; he humbled the power of Umma.

Esarhaddon (r. 681–669 B.C.): King of Assyria; he restored Babylon and waged tough frontier wars in Asia Minor against the Cimmerians.

Gilgamesh (Sumerian: Bilgames; c. 2700–2650 B.C.): *Ensi* of Uruk who inspired Sumerian and, later, Akkadian poets to celebrate his legendary combats and his quest for immortality.

Hammurabi (r. 1792–1750 B.C.): King of Babylon; he reunited Mesopotamia into the third territorial empire of the Bronze Age.

Hatshepsut (r. 1489–1479 B.C.): The first Egyptian queen to rule in her own right as pharaoh. She was the daughter of Thutmose II (r. 1500–1489 B.C.).

Hattušiliš I (r. 1650–1620 B.C.): Hittite king who consolidated control over the Hatti, founded Hattušas as his capital, and brought the petty dynasts of eastern Anatolia under his control.

Hattušiliš III (r. 1267–1237 B.C.): Hittite king who concluded a treaty with Rameses II in 1257 B.C. that confirmed Hittite rule in northern Syria.

Herodotus (c. 490–425 B.C.): "Father of history" and citizen of Halicarnassus, Herodotus wrote the first history, dealing with the clash between the Greeks and the Persians.

Hezekiah (r. 727–698 B.C.): King of Judah; he is remembered as a righteous king who cleansed the Temple of Jerusalem of idolatry, smashing the brazen serpent.

Horemheb (r. 1322–1293): Pharaoh of Egypt; served as commander of the chariots under Tutankhamun.

Josiah (r. 640–609 B.C.): King of Judah; hailed as the righteous king responsible for discovering Deuteronomy. He reformed the worship of Yahweh and ended worship of the Canaanite gods on the high places.

Khafre (Greek: Chephren; c. 2550–2525 B.C.): Pharaoh of Dynasty IV and successor of his brother, Khufu; he built the Sphinx and the second great pyramid at Gizeh.

Khamose (r. 1570–1550 B.C.): Prince of Thebes; he founded Dynasty XVIII, drove the Hyksos out of the Nile valley, and restored Egyptian military and political power.

Khufu (Greek: Cheops; c. 2600–2550 B.C.): Pharaoh of Dynasty IV and son of Snefru; he built the first and greatest of the pyramids at Gizeh.

Lipith-Ishtar (r. 1934–1924 B.C.): Amorite king of Isin; issued a law code in Sumerian, the second known code from Mesopotamia.

Manetho: Egyptian priest of Sebennytos; he wrote in Greek an account of Egyptian history in c. 280 B.C. and arranged the pharaohs into a scheme of dynasties.

Menkaura (Greek: Mycerinus; c. 2525–2480 B.C.): Pharaoh of Dynasty IV; he built the third and last of the great pyramids at Gizeh.

Mentuhotep II (r. 2060–2010 B.C.): Pharaoh of Dynasty XI; he ended civil wars and reunited Egypt, ushering in the Middle Kingdom.

Mentuhotep III (r. 2009–1998 B.C.): Last pharaoh of Dynasty XI and an active builder; he was overthrown by his minister Amenemhet, founder of Dynasty XII.

Merneptah (r. 1212–1200): Pharaoh of Dynasty XIX; he restored Egyptian rule in southern Syria and Palestine, and his memorial stele mentions Israel as a subject nation in Asia.

Mursiliš I (r. 1620–1590 B.C.): Hittite king; conquered northern Syria and sacked Babylon in 1595 B.C.

Mursiliš II (r. 1321–1295 B.C.): Hittite king and son of Šuppiluliumaš I; he extended Hittite hegemony over western Asia Minor, crushing the rival Luwvian state Arzawa.

Muwatallis (r. 1295–1272 B.C.): Hittite king and brother of Mursiliš II; he fought Pharaoh Rameses II at Kadesh in 1275 and consolidated Hittite rule in Syria.

Nabopolassar (r. 627–605 B.C.): King of Babylon; a Chaldaean mercenary commander who rebelled against the Assyrians. In alliance with the Median king Cyaxares, he captured Nineveh and founded the Neo-Babylonian Empire.

Naram-sin (r. 2254–2218 B.C.): Akkadian emperor and grandson of Sargon I, he campaigned deep into Anatolia and northwestern Iran. He probably sacked the city of Ebla in Syria, and he pursued a generous policy of patronizing Sumerian shrines.

Narmer (Greek: Menes; c. 3100 B.C.): Prince of Upper Egypt; he united Egypt and ruled as the first pharaoh.

Nebuchadrezzar II (r. 605–556 B.C.): Chaldaean king of Babylon; he conquered the Levant and, in 587–586 B.C., captured and sacked Jerusalem, ending the Davidic dynasty and deporting the Hebrews.

Omri (r. 884–873 B.C.): King of Israel; a mercenary captain who seized the throne of Israel in the aftermath of the end of the Davidic line. Omri and his heirs transformed Israel into an urban, bureaucratic kingdom, and he was remembered as a devotee of Yahweh.

Pepi II (r. 2275–2195 B.C.): The last pharaoh of Dynasty VI, he ruled ineffectively over Egypt as *nomarchs* asserted their regional authority.

Psamtik I (Greek: Psammetichus; r. 664–610 B.C.): Was appointed as Assyrian client king of Egypt, but he soon declared independence and founded Dynasty XXVI, ruling from the capital Sais in the Delta.

Rameses I (r. 1293–1291 B.C.): Pharaoh of Egypt; the minister of Horemheb, he succeeded legally and founded Dynasty XIX.

Rameses II (r. 1279–1212 B.C.): Pharaoh of Dynasty XIX, he fought the Hittites at the Battle of Kadesh in 1275 B.C.

Sargon I (2334–2279 B.C.): Sargon I seized the throne of Agade and united the Akkadians into a kingdom.

Sargon II (721–705 B.C.): King of Assyria, he was likely a usurper who overthrew the legitimate monarch, Shalmaneser V.

Sennacherib (r. 705–681 B.C.): King of Assyria and son of Sargon II, he constructed the great palace at Nineveh. He ruthlessly put down two Babylonian rebellions, in 703–700 and 694–689 B.C.

Senworset III (Greek: Sesostris; r. 1878–1843 B.C.): The greatest pharaoh of Dynasty XII; he extended Egyptian power into Nubia, reformed royal administration, and initiated the reclamation of the arable of the Fayum.

Shalmaneser III (r. 858–824 B.C.): King of Assyria; he campaigned against Babylon and the Neo-Hittite kingdoms, but Assyrian western expansion was checked by the Battle of Qarqar in 853 B.C.

Shulgi (r. 2094–2047 B.C.): King of Ur; he succeeded his father, Ur-nammu, as ruler of the Neo-Sumerian Empire.

Snefru or **Sneferu** (Greek: Soris; c. 2610–2600 B.C.):

Šuppiluliumaš I (r. 1344–1322 B.C.): Hittite king who humbled the Mitannian kingdom and exploited Egyptian weakness under Akhenaton to conquer northern Syria. He also forged the imperial bureaucracy and provincial administration.

Šuppiluliumaš II (r. 1209–1190 B.C.): Hittite king and second son of Hattušiliš III and Pudahepa; he completed the relief programs at Yazılıkaya.

Thutmose III (r. 1479–1426 B.C.): The greatest pharaoh of Dynasty XVIII, hailed as the "Napoleon of the Ancient Near East;" Thutmose III initiated Egyptian expansion into the Levant in the final years of his aging consort, Hatshepsut.

Tiglath-Pileser III (r. 745–727 B.C.): King of Assyria; originally the commander Pul, who seized the throne in a coup. He reorganized the Assyrian army and administration.

Tudhaliyas IV (r. 1237–1209 B.C.): Hittite king and son of Hattušiliš III, he sponsored religious reforms intended to create a sacral monarchy.

Tukulti-Ninurta I (r. 1244–1208 B.C.): King of Assyria; he threatened Hittite frontiers and briefly conquered and ruled Babylon.

Tutankhamun (r. 1335–1325 B.C.): Pharaoh of Dynasty XVIII; surmised to be the son of Akhenaton. He succeeded as a boy of 10 and, thus, was guided by his ministers to restore the old gods.

Ur-nammu (r. 2112–2095 B.C.): King of the Third Dynasty of Ur, he cleared Sumer of barbarian invaders and forged the Neo-Sumerian Empire. He issued the first known law code in Mesopotamia.

Utnaphistim: "I who found life;" the pious mortal of Shuruppak, rescued from the deluge by the god Ea in the Babylonian Epic of Gilgamesh. He and his wife dwelled in blessed Dilmum, where he was visited by Gilgamesh about the secret of immortality. See **Ziusudra**.

Xerxes (r. 486–465 B.C.): Son of Darius I and Atossa, daughter of Cyrus, Xerxes succeeded as Great King of Persia after the death of his father.

Zoser of Djoser (c. 2700 B.C.): Pharaoh of Dynasty III; he commissioned his architect, Imhotep, to design the first pyramid, the so-called Step Pyramid, at Sakkara.

Bibliography

Texts and Sources in Translation:

Breasted, J. H. *Ancient Records of Egypt*. 5 vols. Chicago: University of Chicago Press, 1906–1907. Classic translation of inscriptions and sources.

Budge, Sir E. A. Wallis. *The Book of the Dead: An English Translation of the Chapters, Hymns, etc., of the Theban Recension*. 2nd ed. London: Kegan Paul, 1909. Classic translation and commentary.

Dalley, S. *Myths from Mesopotamia: Creation, the Flood, Gilgamesh, and Others: A New Translation*. Oxford: Oxford University Press, 1989. Modern translations of the main cuneiform texts.

George, Andrew, trans. *The Epic of Gilgamesh*. New York: Penguin Books, 1999. Best modern translation of the various texts on Gilgamesh; essential for studying the evolution of the epic.

Herodotus. *The Histories*. 2nd ed. Translated by A. de Selincourt. New York: Penguin Books, 1972. Recommended translation of the "father of history," who is the main source for the Near East under Persian rule.

Hoffner, H. A., Jr., trans. *Hittite Myths*. Atlanta: Scholars Press, 1990. The only complete English translation of Hittite myths; includes discussion of Mesopotamian parallels.

Lichteim, Miriam. *Ancient Egyptian Literature: A Book of Readings*. 3 vols. Berkeley: University of California Press, 1973–1980. An impressive collection of sources in translation; indispensable.

Moran, W. L., trans. *The Amarna Letters*. Baltimore: John Hopkins University Press, 1987. Collection of administrative documents and diplomatic letters of the New Kingdom.

Pritchard, J. B. *The Ancient Near East: An Anthology of Texts and Pictures*. 2 vols. Princeton: Princeton University Press, 1958. Fundamental collection of translations of texts and illustrations of significant monuments.

Reeves, Nicholas. *The Complete Tutankhamun: The King, the Tomb, the Royal Treasure*. London: Thames and Hudson, 1990. The best introduction to the objects and inscriptions of the only intact royal tomb.

Sandars, N. K., trans. *Poems of Heaven and Hell from Ancient Mesopotamia*. Baltimore: Penguin Books, 1971. Readable prose translation with excellent glossary and notes.

Simpson, William K., ed. *The Literature of Ancient Egypt: An Anthology of Stories, Instructions, Stelae, Autobiographies, and Poetry.* 3rd ed. New Haven: Yale University Press, 2003. Translations of many important historical texts by one of the foremost American Egyptologists.

Textbooks and Introductions:

Burney, Charles. *From Village to Empire: An Introduction to Near Eastern Archaeology.* Oxford: Phaidon Books, 1977. Emphasizes the material culture and achievements of modern archaeology in documenting the birth of civilization.

The Cambridge Ancient History. Vols. 1–2, 3rd ed.; vols.. 3–4, 2nd ed. Cambridge: Cambridge University Press, 1970–1991. Definitive, detailed studies of all relevant civilizations by leading scholars; extensive bibliographies, chronologies, and maps.

Dunstan, William E. *The Ancient Near East.* New York: Harcourt, Brace College Publishers, 1998. Recommended introduction.

Frankfort, Henri, et al., eds. *The Intellectual Adventure of Ancient Man: An Essay on Speculative Thought in the Ancient Near East.* Rev. ed. Chicago: University of Chicago Press, 1977. Thoughtful essays on religion and society in Mesopotamia and Egypt; also a provocative concluding essay on Hebrew and early Greek thought.

Hallo, William W., and William Simpson. *The Ancient Near East: A History.* New York: Harcourt Brace Jovanovich, 1971. Detailed political and institutional accounts with an emphasis on Mesopotamia and Egypt.

Lloyd, Seton. *The Art of the Ancient Near East.* London: Thames and Hudson, 1961. Best introduction to the arts of all civilizations.

Pope, Maurice. *The Story of the Decipherment: From Egyptian Hieroglyphic to Linear B.* London: Thames and Hudson, 1975. Introduction to the reading of the earliest writing systems.

Atlases:

Haywood, John. *Historical Atlas of the Ancient World, 4,000,000 to 500 B.C.* New York: Metro Books, 2001. Recommended atlas.

Roaf, Michael. *Cultural Atlas of Mesopotamia and the Ancient Near East.* New York: Facts on File, 1990. Lavish atlas with excellent photographs, reconstructions, and plans of sites and monuments.

Origins of Civilization:

Cohen, Mark N. *The Food Crisis in Prehistory: Overpopulation and the Origin of Agriculture.* New Haven: Yale University Press, 1989. Controversial thesis for the birth of agriculture and the domestication of animals.

Diamond, J. *Guns, Germs, and Steel: The Fates of Human Societies.* New York: W.W. Norton & Co., 1997. An intriguing, if overstated, examination of the impact of disease, food supply, and climate in human development.

Henry, Donald G. *From Foraging to Agriculture: The Levant at the End the Ice Age.* Philadelphia: University of Pennsylvania Press, 1989. Recommended study for the role of Levantine crops and animals.

Mellaart, James. *The Neolithic of the Near East.* London: Thames and Hudson, 1975. A readable account of the birth of agriculture.

Mesopotamia:

Adams, R., and H. R. Nissen. *The Uruk Countryside.* Chicago: Chicago University Press, 1972. Model study of archaeological and survey information for the growth of early cities.

Algaze, Guillermo. *The Uruk World System: The Dynamics of Expansion of Early Mesopotamian Civilization.* Chicago: University of Chicago Press, 1993. Provocative study on the growth of Sumerian cities; recommended.

Beaulieu, Paul-Alain. *The Reign of Nabondius, King of Babylon, 556–530 B.C.* New Haven: Yale University Press, 1989. Fundamental on Babylon in the Chaldaean period.

Dalley, S. *Mari and Karana: Two Old Babylonian Cities.* London: Longman, 1984. The newest study on these two important cities of the Middle Bronze Age.

Hinz, Walther. *The Lost World of Elam: Re-creation of a Vanished Civilization.* Translated by J. Barnes. New York: New York University Press, 1973. Best introduction to the little-known civilization of southwestern Iran.

Hooke, S. H. *Babylonian and Assyrian Religion.* Norman: University of Oklahoma Press, 1963. Thoughtful discussion of the role of myth and ritual.

Jacobsen, Thorkild. *The Treasures of Darkness: A History of Mesopotamian Religion*. New Haven: Yale University Press, 1970. A classic, literate study.

Kramer, Samuel Noah. *History Begins at Sumer*. Garden City, NY: Doubleday Books, 1969. Introduction to Sumerian achievements.

———. *Sumerian Mythology*. Rev. ed. New York: Harper Torchbacks, 1961. Recommended texts and discussion of distinct myths and worship of Sumerians.

Lloyd, Seton. *The Archaeology of Mesopotamia: From the Old Stone Age to the Persian Period*. Rev. ed. New York: Thames and Hudson, 1984. Recommended survey of the main sites and excavations.

———. *Foundations in the Dust: The Story of Mesopotamian Exploration*. Rev. ed. London: Thames and Hudson, 1980. Recommended account of the discoveries of the first modern archaeologists in the 19th century.

Neugebauer, O. *The Exact Sciences in Antiquity*. 2nd ed. New York: Dover Books, 1969. Best introduction to mathematics and science in Mesopotamia.

Nissen, H. R. *Archaic Bookkeeping: Early Writing and Techniques of Economic Administration in the Near East*. Translated by P. Larsen. Chicago: University of Chicago Press, 1988. Explores the role of literacy in economic and political developments.

———. *The Early History of the Ancient Near East, 9000–3000 B.C.* Translated by E. Lutzeier and K. Northcott. Chicago: Chicago University Press, 1988. Excellent discussion of the emergence of villages and cities.

Olmstead, A. T. *History of Assyria*. New York: Scribner's, 1923. Narrative political and military account based on royal inscriptions.

Oppenheim, A. L. *Ancient Mesopotamia: Portrait of a Dead Civilization*. Rev. ed. Chicago: University of Chicago Press, 1977. Classic study on daily life and society.

Postgate, J. N. *Early Mesopotamia: Society and Economy at the Dawn of History*. London: Routledge, 1992. Recommended study on economic growth in early Sumer.

Roux, Georges. *Ancient Iraq*. 2nd ed. New York: Penguin Books, 1980. Best introduction, with excellent notes, bibliography, and maps.

Russell, J. M. *Sennacherib's Palace without Rival at Nineveh*. Chicago: Chicago University Press, 1991. Excellent study of royal reliefs as art and propaganda.

Saggs, H. W. F. *Civilization before Greece and Rome*. New Haven: Yale University Press, 1991. Recommended discussion of economic and technological achievements, writing, and social institutions; emphasis on Mesopotamia.

————. *The Greatness That Was Babylon*. New York: Mentor Books, 1962. Readable study of society and cultural achievements of Hammurabi's Babylon.

————. *The Might That Was Assyria*. London: Sidgwick and Jackson, 1984. Best modern introduction; reassesses Assyrian imperial institutions.

Stein, Gil, and Mitchell S. Rothman, eds. *Chiefdoms and Early States in the Near East: The Organizational Dynamics of Complexity*. Madison, WI: Prehistoric Press, 1994. Crucial studies by American anthropologists on the transmission of Mesopotamian civilization to Anatolia.

Tigay, Jeffrey H. *Evolution of the Gilgamesh Epic*. Philadelphia: University of Pennsylvania Press, 1982. Recommended for the literary life of Babylon and Assyria.

Woolley, Sir Leonard. *Ur of the Chaldees: A Revised and Updated Edition of Sir Leonard Woolley's Excavations at Ur*. Revised by P. R. S. Moorey. Ithaca, NY: Cornell University Press, 1982. Exciting account of the discovery of the royal tombs at Ur by a pioneer archaeologist.

Egypt:

Aldred, Cyril. *Akhenaten: King of Egypt*. Rev. ed. London: Thames and Hudson, 1984. The classic study superceded by Redford's work.

————. *Egyptian Art: In the Days of the Pharaohs, 3100–320 B.C.* London: Thames and Hudson, 1980. Classic and well-illustrated study.

Arnett, William S. *The Predynastic Origin of Egyptian Hieroglyphics*. Washington, DC: University Press of America, 1982. Seminal study in the origins of Egyptian writing.

Arnold, Dieter. *Building in Egypt: Pharaonic Stone Masonry*. Oxford: Oxford University Press, 1991. Recommended study for the construction of pyramids, Egyptian mathematics, and principles of Egyptian architecture.

Bryan, B. M. *The Reign of Thutmose IV*. Baltimore: Johns Hopkins University Press, 1991. Important study on the origins of solar monotheism.

Emery, W. B. *Archaic Egypt*. Baltimore: Penguin Books, 1961. Recommended study for the origins of Egyptian civilization and the creation of the kingdom.

Katan, N. J., and M. Mintz. *Hieroglyphics: The Writing of Ancient Egypt.* Rev. ed. London: British Museum Publication, 1985. Recommended introduction.

Kitchen, K. A. *Pharaoh Triumphant: The Life and Times of Ramesses II.* Warminster: Aris and Phillips, 1982. Readable account of the pharaoh and the institutions of the Egyptian Empire.

Mendelsohn, Kurt. *Riddle of the Pyramids*. New York: Greenwood Press, 1986. Standard study with statistics on pyramids of the Old Kingdom.

O'Connor, David, and Eric Cline. *Amenhotep III: Perspectives on His Reign*. Ann Arbor: University of Michigan Press, 1988. Important essays on administration and life in the New Kingdom.

Redford, Donald B. *Akhenaton: Heretic Pharaoh*. Princeton: Princeton University Press, 1984. Brilliant study of the religious reforms of Akhenaton with reconstruction of texts. Supersedes all other studies on the pharaoh.

———. *Egypt, Canaan, and Israel in Ancient Times*. Princeton: Princeton University Press, 1992. Most important study of the history of Egypt and the Hebrews in the past 50 years by a leading Egyptologist.

Smith, William S., and W. Simpson. *The Art of Ancient Egypt*. Rev. ed. New Haven: Yale University Press, 1998; Recommended introduction, with an excellent bibliography.

Winlock, H. E. *The Rise and Fall of the Middle Kingdom in Thebes*. New York: Macmillan Company, 1947. Classic study of the period.

Early India:

Allchin, R., and B. Allchin. *The Rise of Civilization in India and Pakistan*. Cambridge: Cambridge University Press, 1982. Emphasis on the long Neolithic traditions leading to the rise of the first cities of India.

Kenoyer, J. M. *Ancient Cities of the Indus Valley Civilization*. Oxford: Oxford University Press, 1998. Recommended introduction; excellent maps and illustrations.

Parpolva, Asko. *Deciphering the Indus Script*. Cambridge: Cambridge University Press, 1994. The most current study on the Indus valley script.

Wheeler, Sir Mortimer. *The Indus Civilization*. Cambridge: Cambridge University Press, 1962. Classic account of discovery and interpretation.

Asia Minor and the Levant in the Bronze Age:

Akurgala, Ekrem. *The Art of the Hittites*. Translated by C. McNab. London: Thames and Hudson, 1962. Excellent study by the foremost Turkish archaeologist.

Alexander, Robert L. *The Sculpture and Sculptors of Yazilikaya*. Newark, NJ: University of Delaware Press, 1986. Important study on the religious reforms of Hattušiliš III.

Bermant, Chaim, and Michael Weitzman. *Ebla: A Revelation in Archaeology*. New York: Times Books, 1979. Popular but well-argued introduction to this important Syrian city of the Early Bronze Age.

Bittel, Kurt. *Hattusha: The Capital of the Hittites*. New York: Oxford University Press, 1970. The indispensable study on the Hittite ritual capital.

Bryce, Trevor. *The Kingdom of the Hittites*. Oxford: Oxford University Press, 1998. The best modern account of political and military history.

———. *Life and Society in the Hittite World*. Oxford: Oxford University Press, 2002. The companion study on society and economy.

Gordon, Cyrus. *The Common Background of Greek and Hebrew Civilizations*. New York: W.W. Norton & Co., 1965. Eccentric and unconvincing argument for common Greek and Hebrew cultural origins in the Canaanite world of the Middle Bronze Age.

———. *Ugarit and Minoan Crete: The Bearing of Their Texts on Western History*. New York: W.W. Norton & Co., 1967. Unsupported argument for Minoan civilization as part of the Canaanite civilization of the Early and Middle Bronze Ages. Useful translation of Ugarite texts and myths.

Gurney, O. R. *The Hittites*. 2nd ed. Baltimore: Penguin Books, 1990. Classic introduction.

Lloyd, Seton. *Early Anatolia: The Archaeology of Asia Minor before the Greeks*. Harmondsworth: Penguin Books, 1956. Well-written survey of the earliest civilizations in Asia Minor, by a leading British archaeologist.

———. *Early Highland Peoples of Anatolia*. London: Thames and Hudson, 1967. Well-illustrated introduction to the first civilizations.

MacQueen, J. G. *The Hittites and Their Contemporaries in Asia Minor*. Rev. ed. London: Thames and Hudson, 1986. Revisionist political geography and account now vitiated by the new discoveries clarifying Hittite boundaries.

Matthiae, Paolo. *Ebla: An Empire Rediscovered.* Translated by C. Holme. London: Hodder and Stoughton, 1980. Well-written popular account of the excavations and site by the excavator.

Mellaart, James. *The Archaeology of Ancient Turkey.* London: Bodley Head, 1978. The best introduction, by a leading archaeologist.

Pettinato, G. *Ebla: A New Look at History.* Translated by G. F. Richardson. Baltimore: Johns Hopkins University Press, 1991. Interpretation of the Eblaite historical texts by the philologist of the excavation.

Wilhelm, G. *The Hurrians.* Translated by J. Barnes. Warminster: Aris and Phillips, 1989. Recommended introduction; excellent illustrations.

Minoan Crete and Mycenaean Greece:

Blegen, Carl W. *Troy and the Trojans.* London: Praeger Books, 1963. Well-written account by the American excavator; excellent illustrations and plans.

Boardman, John. *The Preclassical: From Crete to Archaic Greece.* Harmondsworth: Penguin, 1967. Provocative and concise introduction to the evolution of Greek visual arts.

Chadwick, John. *The Mycenaean World.* Cambridge: Cambridge University Press, 1976. Recommended introduction.

Evans, Sir Arthur. *The Palace of Minos.* 4 vols. Oxford: Ashmolean Museum, 1921–1935. The definitive excavation report by one of the giants in archaeology.

Finley, M. I. *Early Greece: The Bronze and Archaic Ages.* New York: W.W. Norton & Co., 1970. Recommended introduction.

Mellink, M. *Troy and the Trojan War.* Bryn Mawr: Bryn Mawr University Press, 1986. Best current scholarly opinion on the historical basis of the Trojan War.

Palmer, L. *Mycenaeans and Minoans* London: Faber and Faber, 1969. Seminal revisionist thesis on the development of Aegean civilization in the Bronze Age.

Willets, R. F. *The Civilization of Ancient Crete.* Berkeley: California University Press, 1978. Recommended study of the archaeology and historical geography of Minoan Crete.

Collapse of the Bronze Age:

Drews, Robert. *The End of the Bronze Age: Changes in Warfare and the Catastrophe ca. 1200 B.C.* Princeton: Princeton University Press, 1993. Seminal study, stressing the role of warfare and fiscal crisis in the fall of the great empires.

Redford, D. *Egypt, Canaan and Israel in Ancient Times.* Princeton: Princeton University Press, 1992. Recommended chapters on the Sea Peoples and changing conditions at the end of the Bronze Age.

Rhys, Carpenter. *Discontinuity in Greek Civilization.* New York: W.W. Norton & Co., 1968. Provocative study arguing for climatic change in the collapse of the Bronze Age.

Sandars, N. *The Sea Peoples: Warriors of the Ancient Mediterranean, 1250–1150 B.C.* London: Thames and Hudson, 1978. Recommended study on migrations in the Late Bronze Age.

Asia Minor and the Levant in the Iron Age:

Aubert, M. E. *The Phoenicians and the West: Politics, Colonies, and Trade.* Translated by M. Turton. Cambridge: Cambridge University Press, 1993. Best modern account on the Phoenician impact in the Early Iron Age.

Burney, Charles, and David M. Lang. *Peoples of the Hill: Ancient Ararat and Caucasus.* New York: Praeger Books, 1971. Excellent chapters on Urartu and the origins of Armenian civilization.

Dothan, T., and M. Dothan. *People of the Sea: The Search for the Philistines.* New York: Macmillian, 1992. Recommended study on the current state of the evidence.

Hanfmann, G. M. A. *From Croesus to Constantine: The Cities of Western Asia Minor and Their Arts in Greek and Roman Times.* Ann Arbor: University of Michigan Press, 1975. Survey of the evolution of city life in Asia Minor; excellent on the Lydian kingdom.

———. *Sardis from Prehistoric to Roman Times: Results of the Archaeological Exploration of Sardis, 1958–1975.* Cambridge, MA: Harvard University Press, 1983. Definitive study on the Lydian capital.

Moscati, Sabatino. *The World of the Phoenicians.* Translation by A. Hamilton. London: Weidenfeld and Nicolson, 1968. Recommended introduction by the foremost authority on the Phoenicians.

Piotrovsky, B. P. *The Ancient Civilization of Urartu.* Translated by J. Hogarth. London: Cowles, 1969. Scholarly account on Urartu.

Young, Rodney. *The Gordion Excavations: Final Reports.* Philadelphia: University of Pennsylvania Press, 1981. The definitive account on the Phrygian capital and civilization.

Hebrews:

Anderson, B. W. *Understanding the Old Testament.* 4th ed. Englewood Cliffs, NJ: Prentice-Hall, 1986. Recommended introduction.

Blenkinsopp, J. *The Pentateuch: An Introduction to the First Five Books of the Bible.* New York: Anchor Books, 1992. Scholarly and readable study on the composition of the first five books.

Clements, R. E., ed. *The World of Ancient Israel: Sociological, Anthropological and Political Perspectives.* Cambridge: Cambridge University Press, 1989. Controversial essay applying anthropological models to Hebrew society as presented in Scripture.

Cross, F. M. *Canaanite Myth and Hebrew Epic.* Cambridge, MA: Harvard University Press, 1973. Brilliant analysis of the relationship of older myths of the Levant to the Hebrew tradition by a leading biblical scholar.

Finkelstein, I., and N. A. Silberman. *The Bible Unearthed: Archaeology's New Vision of Ancient Israel and the Origin of Its Sacred Texts.* New York: The Free Press, 2001. Indispensable; supersedes previous studies on the relationship of archaeological evidence and biblical texts; excellent critical bibliography.

Freidman, R. E. *Who Wrote the Bible?* New York: Simon and Schuster, 1987. Recommended popular introduction to the literary traditions.

Mazar, A. *Archaeology of the Land of the Bible, 10,000–586 B C.E.* New York: Anchor Books, 1990. Convenient discussion of the main sites, but the conclusions must be revised in light of Finkelstein and Silberman.

Pritchard, J. B. *Ancient Near Eastern Texts Relating to the Old Testament.* Princeton: Princeton University Press, 1969. Important parallel Near Eastern texts for understanding early Hebrew society.

Redford, Donald B. *Egypt, Canaan, and Israel in Ancient Times.* Princeton: Princeton University Press, 1992. Brilliant analysis of Hebrew origins and relations with Egypt.

Sandmel, Samuel. *The Hebrew Scriptures: An Introduction to Their Literature and Religious Ideas*. Oxford: Oxford University Press, 1978. Excellent for the spiritual and literary traditions.

Persian Empire:

Boyce, Mary. *A Historian of Zoroastrianism*. 3 vols. Leiden: E. Brill, 1975–1991. The current definitive account.

Burn, A. R. *Persia and the Greeks: Defense of the West, 546–478 B.C.* New York: Minerva Books, 1962. Recommended narrative account of Greek-Persian relations.

The Cambridge History of Iran. Vols. 1–3. Cambridge: Cambridge University Press, 1968–1983. Excellent narrative accounts and studies of all aspects of Iranian civilization down to the Sassanid Age.

Cook, J. M. *The Persian Empire*. New York: Schocken Books, 1983. Recommended introduction.

Dandamaev, M. A., and V. G. Lukonin. *The Culture and Social Institutions of Ancient Iran*. Translated by P. L. Kohl and D. J. Dadson. Cambridge: Cambridge University Press, 1989. Excellent on social and economic history, by two leading Soviet historians.

Frye, Richard N. *The Heritage of Persia*. Cleveland: World Press, 1965. Provocative introduction, stressing cultural continuity from the Achaemenid through the Buyid periods.

Ghirsham, R. *Iran from the Earliest Times to the Islamic Conquest*. Harmondsworth: Penguin, 1954. Readable narrative account.

Olmstead, A. T. *History of the Persian Empire: Achaemenid Period*. Chicago: Chicago University Press, 1948. Still the best narrative of political history based on mastery of the Greek literary sources.

Roux, Georges. *Ancient Iraq*. 2nd ed. New York: Penguin Books, 1980. Excellent chapters on Mesopotamia under Persian rule.

Roaf, Michael. *Sculptures and Sculptors of Persepolis*. London: British Institute for Persian Studies, 1983. Main study for the ritual capital.

Notes

Notes

Notes

Notes

Notes

Notes